$\mathscr{H}$IGH $\mathscr{C}$RIMES

Dear Elizabeth,

thank you for standing up
and TAKING ACTION!

COURAGE!

Alan Grayson, FMC

HIGH CRIMES

THE IMPEACHMENT OF DONALD TRUMP

FORMER CONGRESSMAN ALAN GRAYSON

Waterside Publishing

Printed in the United States of America

First Printing, 2019

ISBN-13: 978-1-941768-67-9 print edition
ISBN-13: 978-1-941768-95-2 eBook edition

 Waterside Publishing

2055 Oxford Ave
Cardiff, CA 92007
www.waterside.com

"The severity of [Trump's] misconduct demands that elected officials in both parties set aside political considerations and do their constitutional duty. That means the House should initiate impeachment proceedings against the President of the United States."

– Sen. Elizabeth Warren (D-MA)[i]

"You can reach in a bag and pull so many things out that are impeachable of this President. I support impeaching this President."

– Rep. Alexandria Ocasio-Cortez (D-NY)[ii]

"Impeach the m*th*rf*ck*r!"

– Rep. Rashida Tlaib (D-MI)[iii]

$\mathcal{T}$ABLE OF CONTENTS

$\mathcal{I}$NTRODUCTION

"What's past is prologue."
     – William Shakespeare, <u>The Tempest,</u> Act 2, Scene 1 (1610).

I don't think that Donald Trump should be impeached for throwing paper towels at the devastated victims of Hurricane Maria in Puerto Rico, and telling them to "have a good time."[iv]

I don't think that Donald Trump should be impeached because the bereaved widow of a dead U.S. soldier says that Trump told her that her husband "knew what he signed up for."[v]

I don't think that Donald Trump should be impeached because he has confessed that he'd like to date his daughter.[vi]

In sum, I don't think that Donald Trump should be impeached because he is a putz – quite possibly, the worst putz ever to hold any public office in the United States. He is our Idi Amin, our own Idiot Amin, minus the cannibalism. At least as far as we know. (But is there any doubt that if Mar-a-Lago did offer human flesh on the menu, Trump would tout it as the best, the very best human flesh ever available anywhere, absolutely *primo* human flesh, better than even what was for sale during the Siege of Leningrad?)

BUT. I do believe that Donald Trump should be impeached — for the numerous high crimes and misdemeanors that he has committed. Donald Trump should be impeached because, as Doonesbury once said of Richard Nixon, Trump is "Guilty, Guilty, Guilty!"[vii]

Yes, yes, I understand that it's tempting to say that Trump should be impeached because it seems as though an Evil Clown from a Stephen King novel has wandered into the White House. It's tempting to say that Trump should be impeached because, as President, he is the WOAT (Worst of All Time).

You don't have to take my word for this. The American Political Science Association (APSA) is a nonpartisan organization of political scientists. After Donald Trump's first year in office, a survey of the members of APSA named Donald J. Trump the Worst President of All Time. President Andrew Johnson, who was impeached and almost removed from office, ranked fifth-worst. President Richard Nixon, who resigned after the U.S. House Judiciary Committee voted for impeachment, ranked 12th worst. President Bill Clinton, who was impeached by the House and then (like Andrew Johnson) won the conviction vote in the Senate and remained in office, was ranked 13th best.[viii]

So, yes, I understand the impulse to say that Trump should be impeached because he is a terrible, horrible, no good, very bad President. But when it comes to the impeachment of Donald Trump, we can, and we should, be more specific than that. Donald Trump is impeachable because the Constitution of the United States says that he is, for the reasons stated therein. The U.S. Constitution says that the impeachable offenses are: (1) treason, (2) bribery, (3) "high crimes," and (4) "misdemeanors."[ix]

So then, specifically, what is an impeachable offense? This is where things might start to get a little blurry, except for the fact that Donald Trump deserves impeachment under any plausible definition of an impeachable offense.

Admittedly, there is some debate on the subject. There is, for instance, the "Anything is an Impeachable Offense, Even Spitting" School of Thought:

> *"The grounds for impeachment are…a matter for the House of Commons to decide."*
>
> – U.K. Parliament website.

> *"What, then is an impeachable offense? The only honest answer is that an impeachable offense is whatever a majority of the House of Representatives considers [it] to be at a given moment in history; conviction results from whatever offense or offenses two-thirds of the other body [the U.S. Senate] considers to be sufficiently serious to require removal of the accused from office."*
>
> – House Minority Leader & Future President
> Gerald Ford, 116 Cong. Rec. at 3113-14.

"In Senate the principal subject considered was the report of the Committee on the Rules on Impeachments. Mr. Giles gave us his theory of impeachments under our present Constitution. According to him, impeachment is nothing more than an enquiry, by the two Houses of Congress, whether the office of any public man might not be better filled by another. This is undoubtedly the source and object of Mr. Chase's impeachment, and on the same principle any officer may easily be removed at any time."

– Memoirs of John Quincy Adams 323 (of Dec. 1804).[x]

[Paraphrasing a political opponent:] *"A removal by impeachment was nothing more than a declaration by Congress to this effect: You hold dangerous opinions, and if you are suffered to carry them into effect you will work the destruction of the nation. We want your offices, for the purpose of giving them to men who will fill them better."*

– Memoirs of John Quincy Adams, again.[xi]

"[A]ll the Senate had to determine was the question whether the accused was a fit person to continue to hold the office to which he had been appointed...."

– Alexander Pope Humphrey, "The Impeachment of Samuel Chase," The Virginia Law Register, Vol. 5, No. 5 (Sept., 1899), pp. 281, 285 (describing the views of the proponents of the impeachment and removal of Justice Chase).[xii]

The House and Senate may expel a member for conduct *"inconsistent with the trust and duty of a member,"* even if such conduct is *"not a statutable offense nor was it committed in his official character, nor was it committed during the session of Congress, nor at the seat of government."*

– In re Chapman, 166 U.S. 661, 669-70 (1897) (the U.S. Supreme Court, per Fuller, C.J.), referring to the expulsion of Sen. William Blount.[xiii]

Applying the "Anything is an Impeachable Offense" School of Thought, is there any doubt, any doubt whatever, that the Office of the Chief Executive presently "might…be better filled by another"? Let's be honest: there are monkeys who would be better as President than Donald Trump is. And also less likely to befoul the Oval Office.

But here's the thing: even if you adopt the *exact opposite* perspective, the view that a public official commits an impeachable offense only when he mis-uses his authority on a grand scale, to undermine the functioning of government, Donald Trump still should be impeached, convicted, and removed from office. *Écoutez*:

> *"The subjects of [impeachment are] the abuse or violation of some public trust…, injuries done immediately to the society itself."*
> – Alexander Hamilton, The Federalist Papers: No. 65 (1788).

> *"Congress has repeatedly defined "other high Crimes and misdemeanors" to be serious violations of the public trust, not necessarily indictable offenses under criminal laws."*
> – The U.S. House Judiciary Committee, in the impeachment of Judge Walter Nixon.[xiv]

> *High crimes and misdemeanors "consist[] of the violation of some Federal law of a nature so grave as to be classed with treason and bribery."[xv]*
> – Justice Benjamin Curtis, Associate Justice of the Supreme Court, speaking in defense of President Andrew Johnson at Johnson's impeachment trial.

> *"We know the nature of impeachment. We have been talking about it awhile now. It is chiefly designed for the President and his high ministers to somehow be called into account. It is designed to 'bridle' the Executive if he engages in excesses. It is designed as a method of national inquest into the conduct of public men. The framers confined in the Congress the power, if need be, to remove the President in order to strike a delicate balance between a President swollen with power and grown tyrannical and preservation of the independence of the Executive."*
> – Rep. Barbara Jordan (D-TX), voting to impeach President Richard Nixon.[xvi]

"Would it put at risk the liberties of the people to retain the President in office?"
     – White House Counsel Charles Ruff, defending President
     Clinton at his impeachment trial in the U.S. Senate.[xvii]

"We [in Congress] define an impeachable crime or misdemeanor to be one in its nature or consequence subversive of some fundamental or essential principle of government or highly prejudicial to the public interest; and this may consist of a violation of the Constitution, of law, of an official oath, or of duty, by an act committed or omitted; or without violating a positive law, by the abuse of discretionary power from improper motives or for any improper purpose."
     – Benjamin Butler, quoted in George H. Hayes,
     II, *The Senate of the United States* 858 (1938).

"If our duty is to do it, we will do it. If it's not, we won't. Impeachment is not a punishment. It is not a political act to say we think it's a good idea to get rid of the President. Impeachment is a defense of the Constitution, a defense of liberty."
     – Rep. Jerry Nadler, TIME magazine.[xviii]

If you adopt the narrowest plausible view of what is an impeachable offense – an offense of misusing the authority of public office on a grand scale, to undermine the functioning of government — then Donald Trump *still* ought to be impeached, convicted, and removed from office, as the 200+ pages below amply demonstrate.

Now I must concede that we have a President who will *admit* to nothing: "no collusion, no obstruction." If Trump started to speak in Farsi, he would insist thereafter that there was "no confusion." If he accidentally dropped a nuclear weapon on Philadelphia, he would maintain that there was "no destruction." "No confusion, no destruction."

It doesn't matter. In fact, we've had *a lot* of truly awful public officials who have, nevertheless, insisted that they were as pure as the driven snow. (Or, in Trump's case, as pure as the orange glow.) It doesn't matter, it hasn't mattered, and it shouldn't matter. It doesn't take a confession to find some-one guilty of high crimes and misdemeanors. As you will see.

We will, below, demonstrate that our own Angry Creamsicle is the *capo di tutti i capi* ("boss of all the bosses") when it comes to impeachable offenses. He is Benedict Donald. Historically, impeachable offenses fall into these nine categories:

- Divided loyalty
- Corruption
- Obstruction of justice
- Other abuse of power
- Campaign misconduct
- Sexual misconduct
- Tax evasion
- Conflicts of interest, and
- Conduct unbecoming a public official.

Particularly "bad *hombres,*" as Donald Trump would call them, have been guilty of *two* types of impeachable offenses on this list. In Trump's case, you can find impeachable acts for *all nine.* Donald Trump literally is guilty of *every* impeachable offense.

But first, consider that Donald Trump should be impeached, convicted and removed from office even if you accept the *realpolitik* perspective offered by Alexis de Tocqueville and others. They suggest that it doesn't matter what you *think* is an impeachable offense, because impeachment really isn't about legal standards at all, but rather about the separations of powers, and the exercise of power by the legislature. And that cynical point of view gives rise to cynical and dour warnings about impeachment:

> *"By preventing political tribunals from inflicting judicial punishments the Americans seem to have eluded the worst consequences of legislative tyranny, rather than tyranny itself; and I am not sure that political jurisdiction, as it is constituted in the United States, is not the most formidable weapon which has ever been placed in the rude grasp of a*

popular majority. When the American republics begin to degenerate it will be easy to verify the truth of this observation, by remarking whether the number of political impeachments augments."
    – Alexis de Tocqueville, I <u>Democracy in America</u> ch. 7 (1831).[xix]

"As is usually the case in impeachment crises, the most decisive issues seldom appear above the surface. In our democracy, even removal charges must be sugar-coated, or the political repercussions might be embarrassing to those instrumental in forcing the issue .... [At his impeachment trial, t]he governor wasted little time in discussing that nebulous thing called the law of impeachment."
    – Historian Cortez A.M. Ewing, on the impeachment of Texas
        Gov. James E. Ferguson (D-TX),
    "The Impeachment of James E. Ferguson," *Political Science Quarterly*, Vol. 48, No. 2, 184, 205 (June 1933).[xx]

"In the United States the impeachment process has rarely been employed, largely because it is so cumbersome. It can occupy Congress for a lengthy period of time, fill thousands of pages of testimony, and involve conflicting and troublesome political pressures."
    – "Impeachment," <u>Encyclopedia Britannica</u>[xxi]

"[I]mpeachment is a farce which will not be tried again."
    – President Thomas Jefferson, writing to Senator
    William Giles following the failure of the Senate
    to convict Justice Samuel Chase (1807).[xxii]

"Quis custodiet ipsos custodes?" [Who judges the judges?]
    – Juvenal, Satire VI, lines 347-48.

Well, Thomas Jefferson, who was right about so many things, was wrong about this one. As detailed below, the U.S. House of Representatives has impeached 16 individuals since Jefferson said it would never happen again. Ten of them were then convicted, or they resigned. (As a matter of fact, when I was in Congress, I voted to impeach two of them, and I was two for two.)

Our two centuries of experience since the failed Senate trial of Justice Samuel Chase have provided quite definite guidance as to what is an impeachable offense, and Donald Trump has committed more of them than he could count on his fingers or his toes, or whatever other means he uses for his calculations. The hammer of official misconduct has hit the anvil of corrective action often enough, after two centuries and more, for us to know what that sounds like. History has *not* limited impeachment to occasions when dictatorship looms, whether or not you believe that Donald Trump is the one looming it, or causing it to loom, or whatever it is that a person does in relation to a looming. And no disrespect, de Tocqueville, but the noticeable uptick in impeachments in the past three decades does not presage a legislative dictatorship and sound the death-knell for the republic. Because when a public official commits high crimes and misdemeanors (or, in Trump's case, revels in them), *what else are you going to do* – ignore them? Look the other way? Close your eyes, and hope that they disappear?

For those of us old enough to experience object permanence, that just doesn't work anymore.

Impeachment, like you and me, was not born yesterday. It follows some basic rules established in the U.S. Constitution, 230 years ago, but beyond that, each new impeachment proceeding adds a ring to the tree. We've had Presidents, Vice Presidents, federal judges, Governors and others impeached and convicted during those two-plus centuries. We've had Senators and Representatives expelled from Congress, too. Actually, we have quite a lot of experience in what has justified non-violent defenestration of a public official before his term in office expires – and what has not. And that experience is a good way – a very good way — to show why Donald Trump should be impeached and removed from office.

History provides us a set of scales for impeachment. We're not going to weigh the deceased's heart against the Feather of Truth, as the god Anubis did in the Egyptian *Book of the Dead.* Instead, we'll pile the High Crimes and Misdemeanors of Donald Trump on the left side, the High Crimes and Misdemeanors of other impeached and convicted officials on the right, and we'll see which way the scales tilt. How does Donald Trump stack up against the other miscreants who have soiled American history? When you measure this Scalawag-in-Chief against all the other scalawags, does his scala wag the most? Is Trump's political stench – *eau de Trump,* his branded cologne — as putrid as theirs? (Trump once tried to sell a Trump cologne, in a phal-lus-shaped bottle. The *Chicago Tribune* reported that it smelled like a "strip club."[xxiii]) In sum, is this President unprecedented?

(If you'd rather just read about Trump's high crimes and misdemeanors and not everyone else's, I'm cool with that. The Trump sections are marked, and easy to find. The payoff, at the end, is seven air-tight – even skin-tight – articles of impeachment against Donald J. Trump. This book is yours now; do as you wish. Also, no one will ever know.)

I confess that this notion – to listen to what history tells you — is not an original idea. Lawyers and judges call it *stare decisis,* Latin for "to stand by things decided."[xxiv] Psychologists call it "commitment bias," the tendency to be consistent what we have already done, because inconsistency is not a desirable trait.[xxv]

I'm not suggesting that precedent is a straitjacket. I am suggesting that it's a fair test. Donald Trump has committed High Crimes and Misdemeanors that are as bad as, or worse than, those of other officials who have committed High Crimes and Misdemeanors, and therefore, he should be impeached and removed from office. Q.E.D.

And I'll go one step further. If you take an oath of office to uphold the Constitution – as I did, as every Member of Congress has done – then that's how you should see it, too. In this one regard, I agree with journalist Glenn Greenwald:

> *"If you really believe that Donald Trump committed serious crimes, it's the Constitutional duty of the Democrats in the House to impeach Donald Trump, and then present the arguments and the evidence that he should be removed from office."*
>
> – Glenn Greenwald, "Democracy Now"
interview (Apr. 19, 2019, 14:10-14:15).

$\mathcal{P}$ART I –
<u>TREASON & BRIBERY</u>

$\mathcal{C}$HAPTER I:
DIVIDED LOYALTY

So let's begin. Article II, Section 4 of the U.S. Constitution says: "The President, Vice President and all civil Officers of the United States, shall be removed from Office on Impeachment for, and Conviction of, Treason, Bribery, or other high Crimes and Misdemeanors." The House of Representatives impeaches, and the Senate convicts and thereby removes officials from office.

Let's start with treason. American history provides us with only one case of expulsion from office because of disloyalty to the United States (leaving aside Civil War episodes — they are fundamentally different, which is why we have performed an appendectomy, and put them in an appendix.). The Constitution narrowly defines the term "treason," but the question is whether the Impeachment Clause (treason, bribery, high crimes, misdemeanors) subsumes a more fundamental – and impeachable – issue, that of divided loyalty.

(Warning: if history is boring to you, if it's just not your cup of covfefe, then skip to the Trump section below.)

None of us is likely to live long enough ever to see any federal official found guilty of "treason" as the Constitution uses that term (in a federal judiciary clause separate from the Impeachment Clause), as follows: "Treason against the United States, shall consist only in levying War against them, or in adhering to their Enemies, giving them Aid and Comfort. No Person shall be convicted of Treason unless on the Testimony of two Witnesses to the same overt Act, or on Confession in open Court."[xxvi]

According to Founder George Mason at the Constitutional Convention, the Constitution's definition of treason applies to treason in the context of impeachment.[xxvii] There is no indication in the text itself that the Founders had two different meanings in mind, especially since the Constitutional definition uses the term "only" in the judicial definition of treason.

It looks like there might be some "play" in the treason term "adhering to their Enemies, giving them Aid and Comfort." This clause is analyzed at great length in the U.S. Supreme Court decision *United States v. Cramer*, however, concluding:

> *the crime of treason consists of two elements: adherence to the enemy; and rendering him aid and comfort. A citizen intellectually or emotionally may favor the enemy and harbor sympathies or convictions disloyal to this country's policy or interest, but so long as he commits no act of aid and comfort to the enemy, there is no treason. On the other hand, a citizen may take actions, which do aid and comfort the enemy—making a speech critical of the government or opposing its measures, profiteering, striking in defense plants or essential work, and the hundred other things which impair our cohesion and diminish our strength but if there is no adherence to the enemy in this, if there is no intent to betray, there is no treason.*[xxviii]

A fair reading of this decision is that the term "Enemies" in the formulation "Enemies, giving them Aid and Comfort" refers only to military enemies in wartime. There hasn't been a formal declaration of war by the United States in 77 years. The current "authorizations for the use of military force" (AUMF) likely establish Al-Qaeda and (more controversially) ISIS as "Enemies" for whom giving aid and comfort might qualify as treason, but not anyone else (unless unilateral cyberwarfare qualifies one as an Enemy, and who knows what the Founders would have thought about that?).

Early in our history, Vice President Aaron Burr (you know, Alexander Hamilton's co-star) was criminally tried for egregious misconduct that certainly sounds like treason, and he was acquitted, because the Constitutional definition is so narrow. According to an August 1804 letter by William Merry, an English diplomat, Burr proposed to Merry that Burr and England team up to split off the territory of the United States west of the Appalachians ("endeavoring to effect a separation of the Western part of the United States from that which lies between the Atlantic and the mountains"), leaving Burr in charge of "the Western part." Burr finished his term as Vice President in March 1805, before his scheme came to light (although not before Burr killed Alexander Hamilton in a duel; Burr faced charges for that while he was still Vice President). Even though the English declined Burr's generous offer, Burr nevertheless went on trial for treason in 1807, in a trial overseen by U.S. Supreme Court Chief Justice John Marshall. Chief Justice Marshall ruled that the "overt Act" requirement in the Constitution applied at Burr's trial, and since the scheme had aborted, the evidence came up short. Marshall also ruled that under the Article III definition, "levying War" against the United States meant only "a body of men be[ing] actually assembled for the purpose of effecting by force a treasonable object," like splitting the country or overthrowing the government.[xxix] Hence Burr was found "not guilty."[xxx]

The Burr trial illustrates how difficult it would be to conclude that anyone has committed the impeachable office of "Treason" *per se,* as defined in the Constitution. However, the "lesser included offense" of divided loyalty is enough to justify removal from office, as the case of Senator William Blount establishes.

William Blount

U.S. Senator. Charges: Conspiracy, Divided Loyalty. Expelled July 7, 1797.

William Blount

Senator William Blount was expelled from the U.S. Senate for conspiring with a foreign power. He was impeached as well, but his expulsion made a Senate conviction following impeachment moot.

Blount was a land speculator who amassed 2.5 million acres – 4000 square miles – of property in the new State of Tennessee. Tennessee was admitted to the United States in 1796, and Blount became one of its U.S. Senators.

The Mississippi River was Tennessee's outlet to the sea. The French had initially claimed the Mississippi River territories, starting with exploration by Marquette and Jolliet in 1673. At the end of the French and Indian War in 1763, France ceded its Mississippi River territories to Spain, in the Treaty of Paris. So it was – the Mississippi River territories belonged to Spain — through the Revolutionary War. This made the Spanish (formerly French) territories Tennessee's neighbor to the west when the Revolutionary War ended, with another Treaty of Paris, in 1783. Tennessee claimed the land to the eastern shore of the Mississippi River, putting Spain on the western shore and also downstream from Tennessee.

Six years later, in 1789, the French Revolution began. Blount *correctly* anticipated that the revolution would lead France to try to recoup its former Mississippi River territories from Spain. (This actually happened in 1800, after Blount's scheme was over, and after he had been expelled from the U.S. Senate. France took back its Mississippi River territories in the secret Third Treaty of San Ildefonso between Napoleon and the Spanish King in 1800,[xxxi] followed by the Louisiana Purchase of those territories three years later, in 1803. But again, this took place after Blount's scheme was *kaput*.)

During the War of the Pyrenees from 1793 to 1795, Revolutionary France proved itself to be much stronger militarily than royal Spain. France inflicted 21,000 casualties on Spain, at the cost of only 6500 French troops. [xxxii] At the end of the War of the Pyrenees, France took what later became the Dominican Republic from Spain, as war booty. (Haiti, the other half of the Caribbean island of Hispaniola, had been in rebellion against France starting four years earlier, in 1791.) After the War of the Pyrenees was over, Spain decided to ally itself with France, and Spain left the "First Coalition" against France. The transfer of the war prize of Eastern Hispaniola from Spain to

France suggested to Blount and other observers that Spain's Mississippi River territories might soon follow Eastern Hispaniola into French hands.[xxxiii]

The reason why this concerned Blount is that American settlers had established *de facto* open navigation for themselves along the Mississippi River under *laissez faire* Spanish rule, giving Tennessee settlers an outlet to the sea. Blount believed that if the French controlled the Mississippi River, France would tax this trade (a tariff), or shut it down entirely (an embargo). A French move limiting Tennessee's outlet to the sea would crush the value of Blount's Tennessee property, largely paid for with borrowed money, and could have forced him into bankruptcy.

In 1796, the very year that Blount was elevated to the U.S. Senate by the good people of Tennessee, he conceived and started to execute a plan to have Great Britain (which had been at war with the United States just 13 years earlier) seize the Mississippi River territories from Spain, with the assistance of Native American tribes and American settlers in Tennessee. If this plan had been successful, then Great Britain essentially would have surrounded the United States on land, since it also controlled Canada. Hence after Blount's scheme was exposed, most Americans at the time viewed it as completely contrary to U.S. strategic interests. Blount's scheme also went hard up against Washington's injunction, that year, that the United States must avoid "foreign entanglements."[xxxiv]

Blount tried to enlist the support of the Cherokee Tribe for his plot. His scheme came to light through a letter dated April 21, 1797, that he wrote to James Carey, whom the U.S. Government had hired as an "interpreter" to facilitate trade at Cherokee Nation trading posts. Blount wrote as follows:

"Among other things that I wished to have seen you about [if I hadn't had to go to Philadelphia to serve in the Senate] was the business of Captain Chisholm mentioned to the British Minister last Winter, in Philadelphia. I believe, but am not quite sure, that the plan then talked of will be attempted this Fall, and, if it is attempted, it will be in a much larger way than then talked of; and if the Indians act their part, I have no doubt but it will succeed. A man of consequence has gone to England about the business, and if he makes the arrangements as he expects, I shall myself have a hand in the business, and probably shall be at the head of the business on the part of the British.... [Y]ou must take care ... not to let the plan be discovered by ... any other person in the interest of the United

States or Spain.... [A] discovery of the plan would prevent the success, and much injure all the parties concerned. "[xxxv]

And sure enough, a discovery of the plan prevented its success, and much injured all the parties concerned. On July 3, 1797, President John Adams sent a confidential message to the U.S. House and Senate, describing the plot and including Blount's letter to Carey from two months earlier. In one of the most dramatic confrontations in the history of the U.S. Senate, Vice President Thomas Jefferson, presiding over the Senate, read it to Blount's face, and asked him whether he had written it. Blount said that he wasn't sure; he would need to check his records. (Oh, come on!) That ridiculous response was good enough to get Blount "sequestered" (suspended) from the Senate indefinitely, five days later on July 8, 1797, by a vote of 25 to 1.

This incident was reported at the time as Blount working with the hated British to foment divisions within the United States, and driving it into war with Spain. George Washington wrote that Blount "should be held in detestation by all good men."[xxxvi] There also was a great deal of resentment toward Blount for enlisting the help of Native American tribes, who had been constantly at war with encroaching American settlers. After an investigation, the U.S. House, on January 29, 1798, voted to impeach Blount for Blount's stated intention to cooperate with Great Britain on a military expedition against the Spanish possessions of Louisiana and Florida, and attempting to engage the Creek and Cherokee Indians in the expedition, thereby corrupting relations between the United States and the Indians.[xxxvii]

Blount was charged with five articles of impeachment. They reflected substantial thought about what "high crimes and misdemeanors" Blount had committed. The first article noted that the United States and Spain were at peace with each other, but Blount had conspired to conduct a hostile military expedition against Spain to conquer Spain's territories for Great Britain, "intending to disturb the peace and tranquillity [sic] of the United States, and to violate and infringe the neutrality thereof." The second article charged Blount with violating the friendship treaty between the United States and Spain, notably the section requiring the two countries to "restrain by force all hostilities on the part of the Indian nations." The third article noted that Benjamin Hawkins had been appointed the principal agent for Indian affairs in the area, and that Blount had undermined his authority. The fourth article observed that James Carey had been appointed by the United States Government to work at Cherokee trading posts for the purpose of "liberal trade," and that Blount had "seduce[d]" Carey to assist in Blount's criminal conspiracies. The final article charged Blount with trying to "diminish and impair the confidence of the said Cherokee Nation in the Government of the United States, and to create and foment discontents and disaffection among the said Indians toward the Government of the United States."[xxxviii]

Note that none of these articles charged Blount with treason, as defined in the Constitution. If they had, the charges wouldn't have stuck. Blount hadn't plotted to attack the United States itself, Britain was not (at that moment) an "Enemy," and with Blount having acted surreptitiously, there weren't two witnesses to any one "overt act." In fact, none of these articles charged Blount what General-Congressman-Governor Benjamin Butler later outlined as impeachable offenses, *i.e.,* "a violation of the Constitution, of law, of an official oath, or of duty, by an act committed or omitted; or without violating a positive law, by the abuse of discretionary power from improper motives or for any improper purpose."[xxxix] (By "positive law," Butler meant a law that required Blount to do something, or refrain from doing it.) Instead, the focus of the Blount articles of impeachment passed by the U.S. House of Representatives was on Blount attempting to *act against the interests of the United States*, working in league with an unfriendly foreign power, and thwarting or perverting the efforts of government agents.

IMPEACHMENT INSIGHT—

AS IN THE *BLOUNT* CASE, IMPEACHMENT OR EXPULSION NEED NOT BE BASED ON THE IMPEACHED PERSON HAVING VIOLATED A SPECIFIC LEGAL OR OFFICIAL DUTY.

When the House's impeachment vote against Blount arrived at the U.S. Senate, the Senate appears to have viewed it as an attempt to scramble an omelet. The Senate already had "sequestered" Blount, with a nearly unanimous vote. Blount remained "sequestered," and never returned to his seat in the U.S. Senate. Article I, Section 5 of the U.S. Constitution states that "Each House may…with the concurrence of two thirds, expel a member." That's essentially what happened to Blount. In contrast, the Impeachment Clause, Article II, Section 4 of the Constitution, states that: "*The President, Vice President and all civil officers of the United States*, shall be removed from office on impeachment for, and conviction of, treason, bribery, or other high crimes and misdemeanors." The Impeachment Clause doesn't say anything about impeachment of Senators or Members of Congress. On January 11, 1799, the U.S. Senate voted to dismiss the Blount impeachment, for lack of jurisdiction.[xl] It appears that the Senate concluded that the proper resolution of the charges against Blount was what it had already done — expulsion under Article I, Section 5, rather than impeachment and conviction under Article II, Section 4[xli] (although the Senate itself has said that its reasoning when it dismissed the Blount impeachment was unclear).[xlii]

In any case, the Blount case makes it clear that merely *attempting* to collude with a foreign power in a manner against the interests of the United States is sufficient to justify removal from office. What Blount had done, specifically, was to:

- Talk to the British Ambassador about the scheme;
- Write a letter directed to an Indian tribe, asking for help;
- Send John Chisholm, the "man of consequence" in Blount's letter, to England to recruit support (Chisholm proved to be less consequential than expected; he ended up in debtor's prison in England); and
- Work with Nicholas Romayne in Philadelphia to try to sell western lands to English investors.

The fact that Blount's scheme basically went nowhere didn't matter; what mattered was that he was a U.S. Senator attempting to work with a hostile foreign country in a manner widely perceived to be against the interests of the United States. And so he was removed from office.

[Blount apparently fancied himself quite an expert on impeachment, having been the first person impeached by the U.S. Government. Blount sought to use that to his advantage in a separate incident, in which he had tried to interfere in settlement of a boundary dispute between the United States Government and the Cherokee Nation. (The man simply couldn't stay out of trouble.) A commissioner appointed to settle the Cherokee boundary dispute wrote about Blount's interference, and Blount then sued him for libel. A Tennessee judge dismissed Blount's case. In December 1798 – while Blount's own impeachment was pending before the U.S. Senate – Blount persuaded the Tennessee House to impeach the judge who had dismissed Blount's libel case. Nine days later, however, the Tennessee Senate acquitted the judge — even though Blount had gotten himself named Speaker of the Tennessee Senate a few weeks earlier, presumably to press his case against the judge to a successful conclusion.][xliii]

The case of Senator William Blount provides a vivid antecedent, from the earliest days of the American Adventure, as to what qualifies as divided loyalty justifying the removal of a public official.

Donald Trump

Discussion of Donald Trump's divided loyalty often starts with the divided loyalty of his son, Donald Trump, Jr. Before the infamous Trump Tower meeting on June 9, 2016, during the Presidential campaign, Donald Trump, Jr. was informed: "This is obviously very high level and sensitive information but is part of Russia['s] and its government's support for Mr. Trump." Donald Trump, Jr., replied: "If it's what you say I love it ... ." When this e-mail exchange became public, Congressman Seth Moulton (D-MA) said: "If this isn't treasonous, I'm not sure what is."[xliv]

As we now know, this incident is part of a much larger pattern of cooperation between Donald Trump and his minions on one hand and Russia, Russian oligarchs and Russian interests on the other — both before and during the Trump Presidency. The examples are numerous:

Donald Trump

Trump Fun Fact: In a 1988 article in Spy magazine, Graydon Carter accurately described Donald Trump as a "short-fingered vulgarian." Impeachment Charges: Treason, Espionage, Divided Loyalty.

- Starting in 1987, Trump sought to develop property in Moscow.[xlv] Moscow-born Felix Sater, a main proponent of the project, started working with Trump in 2006.[xlvi] The Mueller Report picks up the story in 2013, and notes that *during the Presidential campaign, Trump personally signed a letter of intent for Trump Tower Moscow.* [xlvii] Sater suggested giving a $50 million penthouse in Trump Tower Moscow to Russian President Vladimir Putin for free.[xlviii] The offer was conveyed to Putin through Putin's staff. (Sater said that this was to entice buyers, but it could have just as easily been to smooth development of the project, or attract Kremlin financing – *or encourage Russian interference in Trump's favor in the Presidential election.*) As this was happening, Trump falsely denied having – or even having had – *any* business interests in Russia.

- Deutsche Bank lent Donald Trump $2 billion, and continued lending to him even after he defaulted on the loans, sued Deutsche Bank, and blamed Deutsche Bank for the 2008 world financial crisis.[xlix] In 2017, Deutsche Bank was hit with $630 million in fines for laundering $10 billion for Russian oligarchs.[l] It simply isn't known yet whether Deutsche Bank's odd servitude to Trump was motivated by

Deutsche Bank's Russian clients, for instance through their guaranteeing Trump's loans. (This is why investigators investigate.)

- In 2004, Trump bought a Palm Beach estate for $41 million, and in 2008, he sold it to a Russian oligarch (Dmitry Rybolovlev) for $95 million.[li] Between 2003 and 2017, buyers from the former USSR bought 86 Trump properties, and paid $109 million – *in cash.* All-cash purchases are an indication of money laundering.[lii]

- In 2008, at a real estate conference in New York, Donald Trump, Jr., said that "Russians make up a pretty disproportionate cross-section of a lot of our assets.... We see a lot of money pouring in from Russia."[liii]

- Against this backdrop, Trump hired Paul Manafort as his Presidential Campaign Chairman from June 2016 to August 2016. Manafort had worked for years to advance pro-Russian interests in the Ukraine, and reputedly had been paid tens of millions of dollars to do so.[liv] Manafort provided confidential polling and voter targeting information and strategy to a Russian intermediary, which seems to have served no purpose other than to help Russia target its social media interference in the Presidential campaign. Manafort also worked with a Russian spy on a pro-Russia "peace" plan for the Ukraine.[lv] Trump campaign operatives Carter Page, Rick Gates and George Papadopoulos also had close links to Russia.[lvi]

- On June 9, 2016, Donald Trump, Jr., Paul Manafort and Trump's son-in-law Jared Kushner met at Trump Tower with Russian lobbyists who offered dirt on Hillary Clinton. As noted, Donald Trump, Jr., said, by e-mail, "if it's what you say, I love it." Neither Donald Trump, Jr., nor anyone else at the meeting reported the meeting to the authorities.[lvii] During the campaign, there were 251 contacts between Trump's campaign/business teams and operatives linked to Russia.[lviii]

- On July 27, 2016, at the last news conference of his campaign, Trump said, "Russia, if you're listening, I hope you're able to find the 30,000 emails that are missing," evidently referring to Hillary Clinton's deleted e-mails. *Five hours later,* Russian hackers attacked Hillary Clinton's personal office email servers, for the first time.

Russia did, in fact, hack the Democratic National Committee's e-mails, and released them through WikiLeaks.[lix] Russian operatives gave the Trump campaign a preview of the Russian plan to distribute the stolen e-mails. According to Trump lawyer Michael Cohen, Trump knew personally, in advance, about their distribution through WikiLeaks, from Roger Stone.[lx]

- Both during his campaign and as President, Trump has denied and denigrated the conclusion of all United States intelligence agencies that this cyberattack was conducted by the Russian government, suggesting instead that perhaps the perpetrator was "somebody sitting on their [sic] bed that weighs 400 lbs."[lxi] Trump also said that he had "no reason not to believe" President Putin when Putin denied responsibility.[lxii] (In the ensuing uproar, Trump amended this to say that he had "no reason to believe" Putin. Darn those double negatives. Maybe Trump meant to say that he had no reason not to disbelieve Putin, or not-Putin.)

- The Russian Government funded and organized a deceptive social media campaign for Trump and against Hillary Clinton during the Presidential campaign. The campaign actively concealed its identity.[lxiii] Foreign expenditures on American elections are illegal. Shortly after the presidential election, all 17 U.S. intelligence agencies reported that, in effect, "there were two campaigns to elect Trump – one operating out of Trump Tower and the other out of the Kremlin."[lxiv]

- At the Republican National Convention, the Republican Party platform was changed to make it more "Russia-friendly." (The Mueller Report found no evidence that this was a direct result of Russian aid to the Trump campaign, though, notwithstanding Russian Ambassador Kislyak's meeting with Sen. Jeff Sessions at the convention that week, which led to Sessions' recusal as Attorney General.)[lxv]

- On Dec. 1, 2016, Flynn and Kushner met with Russian Ambassador Kislyak at Trump Tower, and tried to set up a "back channel" at the Russian Embassy that would have allowed them to communicate with the Kremlin without being monitored by U.S. law enforcement and intelligence agencies.[lxvi]

- When he took office, Trump appointed Michael Flynn as his National Security Advisor. Flynn immediately tried to end U.S. sanctions against Russia unilaterally.[lxvii] Before taking office as National Security Advisor, Flynn had been paid $45,000 to attend a dinner in Moscow, where he sat next to Russian President Vladimir Putin. Flynn was an unregistered foreign agent. When the FBI investigated Flynn for this, Trump did dismiss Flynn as National Security Advisor, but Trump then asked FBI Director James Comey to drop the investigation of Flynn. When the investigation continued, Trump fired Comey.

- Trump appointed Rex Tillerson as Secretary of State, the agency (together with the Treasury Department) involved in enforcing sanctions against Russia. Tillerson has known Russian President Vladimir Putin since the 1990s. He reportedly has spent more time with Putin than any American other than Henry Kissinger. Putin awarded Tillerson the "Russian Order of Friendship." In 2006, Tillerson became the CEO of Exxon, the largest private oil company in the world, on the strength of his Russia relationships. In 2011, Tillerson and Exxon struck an enormous deal with Rosneft to develop Siberian oil resources. Rosneft is owned by the Russian Government. Exxon thus had an enormous direct interest in seeing sanctions against Russia relaxed.[lxviii] Tillerson owned more than $200 million in Exxon stock and stock options.[lxix]

- Trump appointed Wilbur Ross as Secretary of Commerce. Ross owns a shipping company that has contracts with Sibur, a Russian company under U.S. sanctions.[lxx]

- In his application for security clearance, Kushner omitted numerous meetings with Russians. He had to amend his application at least four times. Trump's national security staff opposed giving Kushner access to classified information. Trump eventually overruled national security staffers and ordered clearance for Kushner.[lxxi]

- On May 10, 2017, the day after Trump fired FBI Director Comey, he met with the Russian Foreign Minister and the Russian Ambassador in the White House Oval Office. He told them that he had "faced great pressure because of Russia," and the pressure had been 'taken off' by his firing Comey. [lxxii]

- Trump disclosed classified information to the Russian Foreign Minister and the Ambassador during the meeting in the Oval Office. [lxxiii] This was a clearcut violation of U.S. espionage law, unless one adopts the Nixonian formulation, "when the President does it, that means that it is not illegal."[lxxiv]

- At international events, Trump has met with Putin privately, for as long as two hours. After one meeting, he confiscated his own interpreter's notes, and ordered her not to discuss the meeting with anyone in his own Administration. [lxxv]

- Trump's Treasury Secretary, Steve Mnuchin, has lifted sanctions on companies controlled by Russian oligarch Oleg Deripaska. [lxxvi] Derispaska lent Trump Campaign Chair Paul Manafort $10 million. [lxxvii] House and Senate Democrats noted that Ukrainian-born Len Blavatnik had invested with Mnuchin in an entertainment business, Blavatnik was a major owner in Deripaska's company Rusal, and Blavatnik had given $3 million to Republican campaigns during the 2016 election. [lxxviii] Mnuchin released the Russian aluminum company from sanctions.

- Trump has refused to implement new sanctions against Russia. [lxxix]

- Trump has threatened to withdraw from NATO, whose *raison d'etre* is to prevent Russian aggression against Europe and the United States, [lxxx] and Trump called NATO "obsolete."[lxxxi] Trump also supports pro-Russian European leaders like Victor Orban in Hungary and Marine LePen in France (who took millions of dollars in Russian money in her last campaign). [lxxxii]

- Trump has reversed United States policy and ordered American troops to withdraw from Syrian territory. Syria is a Russian ally, and Russian's only foreign naval base is in Syria. [lxxxiii]

In response, Trump has said that he has been "far tougher" on Russia than any other President. [lxxxiv] (With all due respect, if this proves anything, it proves that whatever Trump says, you can assume that the exact opposite is true. Every day is Opposite Day during the Trump Administration.)

Although none of this would make Trump guilty of "Treason" under the Constitution, there are many other laws that may apply to Trump (and those acting on his behalf) that are relevant here: the espionage laws, the Russian sanctions laws, the law against soliciting campaign contributions from foreign nationals, and the law prohibiting conspiring against the United States, for instance.

What the foregoing demonstrates are: (a) reciprocated efforts between Trump, his family and his colleagues on one hand, and Russian agents and oligarchs on the other, with or without a criminal agreement to do so, (b) Trump, his family and his colleagues serving as Russian assets furthering Russian interests, wittingly or unwittingly, and (c) leverage or influence that Russia has had over Trump, his family and his colleagues.

(The Mueller Report only reinforces these conclusions. For instance, the Mueller Report states that there were no charges brought directly resulting from the Trump Tower meeting because although that meeting *did* appear to involve soliciting campaign "contributions" from foreign nationals, Mueller couldn't pin down what those "contributions" actually were worth.[lxxxv])

More fundamentally, Trump-Russia is clear and compelling evidence of Trump's *divided loyalty*. Russia-controlled and Russia-influenced persons and institutions have showered Trump with billions of dollars, and dangled a quarter-of-a-billion-dollar project (Trump Tower Moscow) before him even during his campaign. Russia hacked and released his Presidential campaign opponents' e-mails, and ran a secret and deceptive social media campaign in his favor. Trump has responded in kind, appointing multiple Russian sell-outs and cut-outs in his Cabinet and other high office, conveying classified information to the Russian Foreign Minister in the Oval Office, easing and delaying mandatory U.S. sanctions against Russia, and reversing fundamental U.S. foreign policy going back as far as decades. As columnist Max Boot wrote in the *Washington Post:* 'If Trump isn't actually a Russian agent, he is doing a pretty good imitation of one."[lxxxvi]

If anything, that's an understatement. Barring the possibility that the novel "The Manchurian Candidate"[lxxxvii] will somehow being transcribed into real life, one doubts than any will ever see a clearer case of divided loyalty. And divided loyalty is a basis for removal from office. It was for Senator Blount, even though his scheme to aid a hostile foreign power *failed.*

Trump and Russia *succeeded* in working together to elect Trump as POTUS. A parallel to Blount's failed scheme today would be if Trump attempted to plot with Russia to allow a Russian attack on Canada (so that Trump could build Trump Tower Punkeydoodles Corners in Ontario, or whatever/wherever), *and the plot failed*. Far worse than that, though, in our corner of the multiverse, Trump (and his family and his campaign) *asked for* ("Russia, if you're listening . . . .") and *received* illegal Russian aid not to take over the Government of Canada, but rather, the *Government of the United States.*

As the U.S. Supreme Court said in commenting on the Blount precedent, divided loyalties justify removal from office because they are "inconsistent with the trust and duty" of the office.[lxxxviii] Under the Impeachment Clause, divided loyalty is a "High Crime," a crime against the responsibilities of public office.

If Senator Blount was removed from office because of divided loyalty, then shouldn't Donald Trump be removed from office?

$\mathscr{C}$HAPTER II(A): BRIBERY

Bribery *Before Taking Office*

After "Treason," the Impeachment Clause specifies "Bribery" as an Impeachable offense. Up to this time, we have somehow managed to pass through 230 years of American history without a President being suspected of that (until now). Vice Presidents, though, not so much. We have had not one, not two, but three Vice Presidents who were accused of bribery and corruption, and who faced impeachment or would-be impeachment because of that.

John C. Calhoun

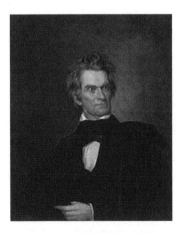

Secretary of War, Vice President. Charge: Bribery (before office) Exonerated by the House, Feb. 18, 1827

Vice President John C. Calhoun

John C. Calhoun served as the Secretary of War from December 1817 through March 1825, when he was elevated to the Vice Presidency under, first, John Quincy Adams, and then, Andrew Jackson. In December 1826, a Washington, D.C. newspaper reported the corruption allegation that Calhoun had taken the profits from a military contract while he had been Secretary of War. Hence Calhoun was accused of misconduct dating from a time before he took office as Vice President.

IMPEACHMENT INSIGHT—

AS IN THE *CALHOUN* CASE (AND ALSO *AGNEW* AND *ARCHBALD*), IMPEACHMENT CAN BE BASED ON MISCONDUCT WHILE HOLDING A PREVIOUS OFFICE.

Calhoun's response illustrates that some people are cut from a different cloth than others. Reacting in a manner that Vice President Agnew later said that he could "better quote than rival,"[lxxxix] Calhoun *requested an investigation to determine whether he should be impeached.* As he said to the House: *"An imperious sense of duty, and a sacred regard to the honor of the station which I occupy, compel me to approach your body in its high character of grand inquest of the nation.*

"Charges have been made against me of the most serious nature, and which, if true ought to degrade me from the high station in which I have been placed by the choice of my fellow-citizens, and to consign my name to perpetual infamy.

"In claiming the investigation of the House, I am sensible that, under our free and happy institutions, the conduct of public servants is a fair subject of the closest scrutiny and the freest remarks, and that a firm and faithful discharge of duty affords, ordinarily, ample protection against political attacks; but, when such attacks assume the character of impeachable offenses, and become, in some

degree, official, by being placed among the public records, an officer thus assailed, however base the instrument used, if conscious of innocence, can look for refuge only to the Hall of the immediate Representatives of the People. It is thus I find myself most unexpectedly placed.

"... I am accused of the sordid and infamous crime of participating in the profits of a contract formed with the Government, through the Department of War, while I was entrusted with the discharge of its duties, and that the accusation has been officially presented as the basis of an official act of the War Department, and consequently to be placed among its records, as a lasting stigma on my character.

"Conscious of my entire innocence in this and every other public act, and that I have ever been incapable, in the performance of duty, of being influenced by any other motive than a sacred regard to the public interest, and resolved, as far as human effort can extend, to leave an untarnished reputation to posterity, I challenge the freest investigation of the House, as the only means effectually to repel this premeditated attack to prostrate me, by destroying forever my character. "[xc]

And then Calhoun tweeted out, spasmodically, "No corrruption! No delusionn!" followed by confirmatory smoke signals. Just kidding.

The House responded to Calhoun's request by establishing a select committee, subpoenaing witnesses and documents, holding hearings, and preparing a comprehensive report. The report, dated February 13, 1827, exonerated Calhoun, which laid the matter to rest.[xci]

Calhoun did avoid "a lasting stigma on [his] character." During the following year, Andrew Jackson invited Calhoun to join his Presidential ticket, and they prevailed. No one has been elected Vice President under two different Presidents since then.[xcii]

Living, as we do, in a time of pervasive stonewalling, obstruction and cover-ups, Calhoun's example is barely comprehensible to many of us. Calhoun could have made a statute of limitations argument. He didn't. Calhoun could have argued (as Agnew did) that a sitting Vice President cannot be indicted. He didn't. Calhoun could have argued that he could not be impeached from the Vice Presidency for any acts preceding his term of office. He didn't; nor did the House of Representatives suggest that it lacked

21

the jurisdiction to impeach him for prior acts. He could have argued that a Secretary of War could legally participate in military contractor profits. He didn't. (Notable contrasts: Dick Cheney's $34 million payday when the former Secretary of Defense left military contractor Halliburton to become Vice President.[xciii] And, of course, the Trump Dump that sits five blocks east of the White House on Pennsylvania Avenue, a 10-story example of Donald Trump *"participating in the profits of a contract formed with the Government . . . while . . . entrusted with the discharge of its duties."* More on that below.)

Calhoun believed that the people of the United States didn't deserve to have a Vice President with a cloud like this hanging over him, so he invited an impeachment inquiry, instead of stonewalling, or trying to raise artificial, legalistic impediments to it.

How refreshing. And how foreign to our time.

Schuyler Colfax

Secretary of War, Vice President. Charge: Bribery (before office) Ran out the clock in the House on Feb. 24, 1863 (eight days before leaving office).

Vice President Schuyler Colfax

The next portrait in our rogue's gallery of Vice Presidents allegedly stuffing bribes into their waistcoats and spittoons is Schuyler Colfax, who probably could have concealed a few illicit gold coins in his beard. Colfax was elected Vice President under Ulysses S. Grant, in 1868. The Grant Administration was a petri dish of corruption,[xciv] which reached as high as the Vice Presidency. But in the case of Schuyler Colfax, the U.S. House of Representatives had to address the question of whether corruption *before* Colfax took office was impeachable. Acting in a manner *directly opposite* from the Calhoun case, it answered this question in the negative.

In 1872, the Credit Mobilier bribery scheme came to light. It started during 1867-68, when Rep. Oakes Ames (R-MA) had given shares in the transcontinental Union Pacific Railroad to thirty Senators and Congressmen at par value, a price far under actual value, in exchange for favorable federal treatment for the railroad. (Among other things, the government gave the railroad massive land grants.) Colfax, who was Speaker of the House in 1867-68, was among those investigated.

[The entire political class of that time was corrupted by the scandal. Senator Henry Wilson (R-MA) also was investigated, but in Wilson's case, he established that his wife had paid for the stock, and when concerns arose, he had reversed the transaction. Somehow, this was regarded as exonerating Wilson.[xcv] At the Republican National Convention on June 6, 1872, Wilson dethroned Colfax as Vice Presidential nominee, replacing him on the GOP ticket, evidently because Wilson appeared to be slightly less dirty. Soon-to-be President Garfield did a similar dance; despite having taken the Union Pacific Railroad shares at par, he was elected President in 1880.][xcvi]

Although the Credit Mobilier bribery had taken place toward the end of the Andrew Johnson Administration, it wasn't investigated until much later, toward the end of the Grant-Colfax Administration. On Dec. 2, 1872, after Henry Wilson had been elected to replace Colfax as Vice President, and with only four months left in Grant-Colfax Administration, the House began investigating the Credit Mobilier bribery charges. In essence, this was the House investigating the House, along with notable alumni like Colfax.

On Feb. 24, 1873, with *eight days* left in the Grant-Colfax Administration, the House Judiciary Committee issued its report on Colfax. It noted that the alleged bribing of Colfax had taken place before he had assumed the office of Vice President, discussed the fact that any crime committed before taking office can be prosecuted as a crime regardless of impeachment, and concluded as follows:

"[T]he remedial proceedings of impeachment should only be applied to high crimes and misdemeanors committed while in office, and which alone affect the officer in discharge of his duties as such, whatever may have been their effect upon him as a man, for impeachment touches the office only and qualifications for the office, and not the man himself."[xcvii]

However, what really seems to have been on the minds of the Members of the House Judiciary Committee is this:

"the sentence [for impeachment and conviction] may be only removal from an office whose term extends for a few days only, as in the case under consideration."[xcviii]

With eight days left in Colfax's term of office, there was no chance that the House could schedule a trial, present its evidence to the Senate, give Colfax his own opportunity to be heard, and conduct a Senate vote – all before the expiration of Colfax's term made the whole endeavor moot. The Judiciary Committee's conclusion regarding whether conduct before office is impeachable, while striking, is what the courts refer to as *obiter dictum* – "a gratuitous or voluntary representation … which a party is not bound to make."[xcix] As discussed elsewhere here, there are numerous cases of impeachment for misconduct preceding the currently held office – including the cases of the two other Vice Presidents, Calhoun and Agnew.

Spiro Agnew

Vice President. Charge: Bribery (before office). Requested impeachment in lieu of indictment; House deferred until criminal charges resolved. Pled guilty to tax evasion and resigned as part of plea agreement on Oct. 10, 1973.

Vice President Spiro Agnew

Vice President Spiro Agnew was Executive of Baltimore County from 1962 to 1966, then Governor of Maryland from 1966 to January 1969, then Vice President from January 1969 to 1973. In 1973, Federal investigators started investigating Agnew for bribery and kickbacks dating from his time as County Executive. It may have seemed like ancient history, until one contractor confessed that he had paid $10,000 in cash to Agnew in the White House, for prior services rendered.

Agnew, like Calhoun, asked for an impeachment investigation, but the Speaker of the House said no, deferring to the criminal investigation that was underway. Neither Agnew nor the Speaker even suggested that the fact that the bribery may have taken place before Agnew's term as Vice President could defeat Agnew's potential impeachment. The criminal investigation resulted in Agnew pleading guilty to one charge of tax evasion, and resigning. This rendered impeachment of Agnew moot.

Hence all three Vice Presidents who have faced impeachment proceedings for bribery and corruption were charged with misconduct that took place before they occupied that office – in the cases of Calhoun and Colfax, a Cabinet position, and in the case of Agnew, a state office. Likewise, federal judges and governors have been impeached and removed from office for misconduct that preceded their then-current positions. Clearly, impeachable conduct is not limited to the here-and-now.

Bribery *in Office*

American political history is remarkably generous in providing many examples of officials who engaged in impeachable bribery and corruption. Frankly, Donald Trump makes them all seem like amateurs, but first let's discuss Members of Congress. Leaving aside three Representatives who expelled from Congress for supporting the Confederacy (together with many of their Senate brethren), there have been only two other cases of expulsion from the U.S. House of Representatives. Both were expelled for bribery.

By way of background, as noted above, the U.S. Constitution provides that each body of Congress can expel one of its members by a two-thirds vote.[c] Since the time of Senator Blount, that is the procedure that has been used for removing Members of Congress, rather than impeachment (or, for that matter, 23 stab wounds, which is how the Roman Senate removed Julius Caesar from office).

Michael Myers

Congressman. Charge: Bribery. Expelled from the U.S. House of Representatives on October 2, 1980, by a vote of 376 to 30.

Michael Myers

Michael Myers – the Congressman, not the slasher horror film character — was expelled from the U.S. House of Representatives for bribery. Myers was caught in the FBI's Abscam "sting operation." Although he was expelled under the Expulsion Clause of the U.S. Constitution, not the Impeachment Clause, his misconduct obviously would have qualified as "Treason, Bribery or Other High Crimes and Misdemeanors."

Elected in 1976, Myers accepted a $50,000 bribe from FBI undercover agents posing as rich Arab sheiks seeking access to lawmakers. At that meeting, he contributed to the English language the memorable phrase, "money talks in this business, and bullshit walks."[ci]

The House Ethics Committee did not necessarily take issue with Myers's insight, but it did take issue with his ethics. In a very succinct, no-nonsense, five-page report, it recommended this House Resolution:

"*Resolved, That,* pursuant to Article I, Section 5, Clause 2 of the United States Constitution, Representative Michael J. Myers be, and hereby is[,] expelled from the House of Representatives."

The vote was 10 to 2 on the Ethics Committee, with the two dissenters arguing only that Myers should not be expelled while criminal charges were pending against him.[cii] On Oct. 2, 1980, this H. Res. 794 passed the House by the vote of 376 to 30, far more than the two-thirds vote required, and Michael Myers became the first Member of Congress expelled from Congress since the Civil War.[ciii] Myers stood for re-election the following month, and he was defeated. In 1981, he was convicted of bribery and conspiracy, and sentenced to three years in prison.[civ]

One Senator and six others also were convicted in Abscam.[cv] Most of them left Congress at the end of their terms. Senator Williams (D-NJ) and Rep. John Jenrette (D-SC) resigned before the Congressional votes on their expulsion. (Jenrette told an FBI undercover agent, "I've got larceny in my blood. I'd take it [the bribe] in a goddamn minute.")[cvi]

James Traficant

Congressman. Charge: Bribery. Expelled from the U.S. House of Representatives on July 24, 2002, by a vote of 420 to 1.

James Traficant

Congressman James Traficant was expelled from Congress, following is criminal conviction for corruption. Traficant began his political career as a sheriff who refused to enforce eviction orders (good politics) and who allegedly took bribes (bad politics). Charged with racketeering as a sheriff, Traficant testified in his own defense that he actually had been conducting a secret sting operation to identify persons offering bribes – to him. The jury either swallowed this hook, line and sinker, or they were charmed by Traficant's audacity. Either way, he was acquitted.[cvii]

Traficant then was elected to Congress in 1984. (Why Congress? Perhaps because of Mark Twain's observation: "There is no distinctly native American criminal class except Congress."[cviii]) In Congress, Traficant demonstrated that he had learned his lesson, the lesson being that he could get away with anything. He fought against IRS overreach (good politics) but defended Nazis against what he called "the powerful Jewish lobby" (bad politics). He somehow managed to antagonize both parties so much that in 2001, neither the Democrats nor the Republicans would assign him to any House Committee.[cix]

On May 4, 2001, Traficant was indicted again. The indictment alleged that "while he was a congressman, Traficant demanded thousands of dollars in goods and services from businesses in return for official favors, including contacting the Director of the Federal Aviation [Authority], the Secretary of State, and the King of Saudi Arabia; paid inflated salaries to his staffers, who were required to kickback the difference to their boss; and forced his congressional staffers to bale hay, repair plumbing, and reinforce barns at his show-horse farm." Traficant probably regarding the hay-bailing and plumbing-repair as constituent service; after all, he was a constituent. And, to be fair, Traficant's staffers only had to bail his hay, not bail his toupee. On April 11, 2002, a jury convicted Traficant on all ten counts.[cx]

The House Ethics Committee issued a report ruling that by the same misconduct, Traficant had also violated the House Rules. On July 24, 2002, the House voted 420 to 1 in H. Res. 495 to expel him:

"Resolved, *That, pursuant to Article I, Section 5, Clause 2 of the United States Constitution, Representative James A. Traficant, Jr., be, and he hereby is, expelled from the House of Representatives.*"[cxi]

Adding injury to insult, Traficant was sentenced to eight years in prison. He ran for Congress twice again (once from prison), and lost. After his release, he joined the Tea Party, perhaps in the hope that they would bale his hay. A few years ago, at his show-horse farm, Traficant managed to overturn his tractor, the tractor fell on his chest, and he died of suffocation.[cxii]

There is little doubt that if Traficant had been subject to impeachment rather than expulsion, he would have been impeached, convicted and removed from office. Bribery, kickbacks and "forcing his congressional staff to bale hay" clearly qualify as impeachable offenses, as any Congressional staffer will confirm.

William Belknap

Former Secretary of War. Charge: Bribery. Resigned but nevertheless impeached unanimously by the U.S. House of Representatives on March 2, 1876. Senate voted 35-25 (less than 2/3 vote) to convict Belknap on April 5, 1876, so he was acquitted.

William Belknap

The fact that all three Vice Presidents who faced impeachment for bribery and corruption did so for acts *before* they took office suggests that as Vice Presidents, they really didn't have much to sell. (You can't be a sell-out if no one is buying.) As for our two Congressmen-bribees, Myers was sucked into a sting operation, and Traficant had to resort to auctioning off low-ticket bribe items like contacting the Director of the FAA. This illustrates a maxim among Members of Congress: On one hand, if they do *quid pro quo* favors for people, it's a felony. On the other hand, most of them have very few favors to do.

Members of the Executive Branch, on the other other hand (you know, the third hand), they have lots of favors to do, from the President on down. This is illustrated well by William Belknap, a very entrepreneurial Secretary of War, and the third Secretary of War (along with Calhoun and Colfax, when they were Veeps) to face possible impeachment.

"War is a racket."

— Major General Smedley Butler.[cxiii]

In the 1860s and 1870s, the U.S. Army had trading posts at military bases throughout the American West. (The modern-day equivalent is the commissaries of the Defense Commissary Agency.) Soldiers were required to buy supplies there, often at exorbitant prices. Native Americans found that they could buy rifles and ammunition there, sometimes more modern and better than the weapons supplied to the soldiers at whom they might aim. The operators of the trading posts were civilians appointed by the military. William Belknap, the U.S. Secretary of War in 1870, arranged to appoint these operators, called "sutlers," personally.[cxiv]

Belknap and his wife Carita had a well-known taste for expensive clothing, and they hosted lavish and expensive parties at their Washington, D.C. home. This created cash-flow issues for Belknap.[cxv]

Belknap's wife Carita prevailed upon Belknap to appoint Caleb Marsh as the sutler for Fort Sill, a new military base in Indian Territory. The Ft. Sill trading post already was being managed by one John Evans, however. Evans worked it out with Marsh that Evans could continuing managing the trading post if he gave $12,000 a year to Marsh. Marsh, in turn, committed to give half of that to Carita.

Marsh made his first quarterly payment, but then Carita died, shortly after childbirth. What to do? Belknap continued to accept the payments, supposedly for the benefit of Carita's newborn child, making the infant possibly the youngest person ever to participate in a federal bribery scheme.

But then, a few months later, the precocious little imp died. What to do now? Carita's sister Amanda had been living with Belknap and Carita. After

Carita died, Belknap married Amanda.[cxvi] The trading post payments then went to Amanda. (Apparently, for bribery purposes, all Mrs. Belknaps are equal.) This went on for six years.[cxvii]

The game was exposed by none other than Gen. George Armstrong Custer. Custer published an anonymous letter in the *New York Herald,* charging Belknap and President Grant's brother with trading post corruption.[cxviii] On Feb. 29, 1876, the U.S. House took testimony from Belknap's Ft. Sill appointee Caleb Marsh, flushing out the scheme. (Marsh produced the written agreement between him and Evans, the original sutler.) Marsh's testimony was given to Rep. Heister Clymer (D-PA), who happened to be Belknap's college roommate, but that wasn't enough to save Belknap.

Within 48 hours after Marsh's testimony, Belknap submitted his resignation to President Grant. Within 24 hours after that, the House unanimously impeached Belknap, his resignation notwithstanding. (The impeachment resolution referred to Belknap as the "late Secretary of War," as though he were dead. It was novel enough to impeach someone who already had left office, but impeaching a dead person would have been the bee's knees.)[cxix]

The five articles of impeachment against Belknap all concerned the Ft. Sill bribery payments. They enumerated the 17 payments: 14 for $1500, one for $1700, one for $1000 and one for $750. They explicitly charged Belknap with "basely prostituting his high office to his lust for private gain,"[cxx] which is easily one of the worst mixed metaphors in Congressional history. (A "prostitute" generally doesn't engage in his or her profession for the sake of "lust.")

In the U.S. Senate, the debate was never over Belknap's guilt or innocence, but whether it made sense to impeach and convict an official who had already resigned. When Belknap appeared before the Senate, his statement urged that the Senate:

"ought not to have or take further cognizance of the said articles of impeachment exhibited and presented against him by the House of Representatives of the United States, because, he says, that before and at the time when the said House of Representatives ordered and directed that he, the said Belknap, should

be impeached at the bar of the Senate, and at the time when the said articles of impeachment were exhibited and presented against him, the said Belknap, by the said House of Representatives, he, the said Belknap, was not, nor hath he since been, nor is he now an officer of the United States; but at the said times was, ever since hath been, and now is a private citizen of the United States. . . .[cxxi]

The impeachment managers sent by the House asserted that the Senate should carry on, because the acts charged in the articles of impeachment all occurred while Belknap was in office, and that he had resigned "with intent to evade the proceedings of impeachment against him."[cxxii]

On May 29, 1876, the following resolution passed the Senate by the relatively narrow vote of 37 to 29:

"Resolved, That in the opinion of the Senate William W. Belknap, the respondent, is amenable to trial by impeachment for acts done as Secretary of War, notwithstanding his resignation of said office before he was impeached."[cxxiii]

This resolution passed, but it did not garner the two-thirds vote that would be necessary for conviction, which did not bode well for anyone but Belknap.

The Senate then received evidence in Belknap's impeachment. On August 1, 1876, the Senate voted on the five articles of impeachment. Each article drew between 35 and 37 votes in favor; every article drew 25 votes against. These votes closely shadowed the earlier vote on jurisdiction. Since no article reached the required two-thirds affirmative vote for conviction, Belknap was formally acquitted.

At the time of the vote, each Senator was allowed to provide a brief explanation of his vote. Of the 25 Senators who voted "not guilty," 22 said that they did so because the Senate had no impeachment jurisdiction of an official who had resigned, three said that they did so on the evidence, and zero attributed their vote to Belknap's copious ZZ Top beard, easily one of the most awesome chin supplements in all of American history. (A squirrel could hide in there.)[cxxiv] Notably, these acquitting Senators were not willing to accept the judgment of the majority of the Senate that there was jurisdiction to impeach a former official; they voted on the articles based on their personal views instead.

Alcee Hastings

Federal Judge. Charge: Bribery. Impeached on 17 articles of impeachment by the U.S. House of Representatives on Aug. 3, 1988, by vote of 413 to 3. Convicted by the Senate on Oct. 20, 1989, on nine charges (between 67 and 70 Senate votes in favor, between 25 and 28 against), acquitted on three charges, and no vote on five charges.

Alcee Hastings

Article III judges, like Article I elected officials and cabinet members, have a lot to offer in exchange for a bribe. How that works is illustrated by the recent impeachment and conviction of Judge Alcee Hastings, and the not-recent impeachment and conviction of English Lord Chancellor Francis Bacon.

Although you won't see it in your Twitter feed, our nation has faced a crime wave of impeachable offenses during the last three decades. Five federal judges have been impeached, and four of them convicted. Those four convictions equal the number of judges impeached and convicted during the previous two centuries.[cxxv]

What is most notable about this rise in lawlessness — among those who determine the law — is that it has obliterated the argument that an impeachable act is a violation of official duties solely *while in office*. Only the Alcee Hastings impeachment and conviction fully fits that mold. The other

34

recent four federal judge impeachments – Harry Claiborne, Walter Nixon, Samuel Kent and Thomas Porteous – all arise from acts preceding office, or other unofficial acts.

As to Alcee Hastings, he was appointed a federal judge in November 1979. His impeachment alleged that in 1981, he conspired with a criminal defense attorney, William Borders, to avoid a prison sentence and return forfeited property for two criminal defendants, in exchange for $150,000. This turned out to be a sting operation, initially against Borders and then against Hastings. Hastings was charged criminally with bribery. In February 1983, the criminal jury acquitted Hastings when Borders refused to testify, and Hastings testified that he did not know about the deal. But then in 1988, five years later, after an investigation by the Judicial Conference, Hasting faced a new, unrelated charge: leaking wiretapped information. The U.S. House of Representatives impeached Hastings. In 1989, the U.S. Senate convicted him, removing Hastings from office.[cxxvi]

The House impeached Hastings by a vote of 413 to 3. It leveled 17 Articles of Impeachment against Hastings. The first Article was for conspiring with Borders to obtain the bribe. Articles 2 through 15 were for Hastings perjuring himself at the criminal trial. Article 16 was for leaking wiretap information that he had received, as a judge, to the Mayor of Dade County, when the mayor was a target of the investigation. That was in 1985, after Hastings' criminal acquittal. Article 17 was a catch-all Article, claiming that by these actions, Hastings did "undermine confidence in the integrity and impartiality of the judiciary and betray the trust of the people of the United States, thereby bringing disrepute on the Federal courts and the administration of justice by the Federal courts."[cxxvii]

On the charge of Hastings conspiring to take a bribe (Article I), the Senate voted in favor of conviction by a vote of 69 to 26, more than a two-thirds vote. This first vote ended Hastings' judicial career. The Senate continued to vote, however. On seven of the first eight perjury charges, the vote was essentially the same. Between 67 and 70 Senators voted for conviction, and between 25 and 28 voted against conviction. (The exception was Article 6, regarding Hastings's criminal testimony that he had not expected Borders to appear at his hotel room to strike a deal, which mustered a vote of only 48 "guilty" and 47 "not guilty.") The Senate chose not to vote on the last five perjury Articles, since they had become moot. The Senate then proceeded to the charge that Hastings had leaked wiretap information, and the Senate unanimously *acquitted* Hastings on that, by a vote of 95 to 0. On the catch-all Article, the Senate voted 60 to 35 for conviction, short of the necessary two-thirds majority. Hence the Senate convicted Hastings on the charge of conspiracy to take a bribe, and on eight counts of perjury regarding that bribe.[cxxviii]

In essence, the Senate found Hastings guilty, after a criminal jury had found him not guilty, because the "burden of proof" is different. This demonstrates that an impeachment and conviction need not be predicated on criminal legal standards like "beyond a reasonable doubt," much less on a criminal conviction.

It's no surprise that Hastings was convicted on the first Article of Impeachment, since bribery is enumerated in the U.S. Constitution as grounds for impeachment, and attempted bribery is no less serious. Nor is it any surprise that Hastings would be convicted of perjury, since other officials have been impeached and convicted of that. It is interesting, nevertheless, that Hastings was impeached and convicted after a criminal acquittal. It is also notable that Hastings was impeached and convicted after ten years as a federal judge (and two years before that as a state judge) for misconduct on a single case, albeit the worst kind of misconduct. Noteworthy as well is the fact that he was removed from office *eight years* after the misconduct, demonstrating again that there is no statute of limitations for an impeachable offense.

IMPEACHMENT INSIGHT—

AS IN THE *HASTINGS* CASE, IMPEACHMENT DOES NOT HAVE TO CONFORM TO THE STANDARDS OF CRIMINAL LAW.

Shortly after the Hastings impeachment and conviction, another Southern African-American judge nominated by President Jimmy Carter, Robert Collins of Louisiana, was charged with bribery, and convicted on

June 29, 1991.[cxxix] Collins tried to retain his position even after he went to prison. Almost a year later, the House Judiciary Committee scheduled impeachment hearings on Collins. Collins resigned on Aug. 6, 1993, the day before the hearings were to start, and thus avoided the fate of Alcee Hastings.[cxxx]

Sir Francis Bacon

Lord High Chancellor of England. Charge: Bribery. Impeached and convicted by Parliament; pardoned by the King.

Sir Francis Bacon

Likely the most famous of all Englishmen to be impeached was Sir Francis Bacon, philosopher and scientist. He served as Lord Chancellor, the English equivalent of our Chief Justice of the Supreme Court. In 1621, he was charged with taking bribes from litigants – sometimes on both sides of the case. Bacon's creative defense was that the bribes never influenced his judgment: *"With respect to this charge of bribery I am as innocent as any man born on St. Innocents Day. I never had a bribe or reward in my eye or thought when pronouncing judgment or order."*[cxxxi] To which Parliament replied, "Oh, well then, never you mind. Terribly sorry to interrupt your fine day. Cheerio!" No, that's not what happened. What actually happened was that Bacon was impeached, convicted, and sentenced to imprisonment in the Tower of London.

The King pardoned Bacon shortly thereafter, however – he saved Bacon's bacon.[cxxxii] The Bacon case may be one reason why our Constitution provides that our President's power to pardon does not extend to impeachment cases.

Donald Trump

Trump Fun Fact: When the rapper Eminem ran for President in 2004, Trump gave his nomination speech. Impeachment Charge: Bribery.

Donald Trump[cxxxiii]

To judge whether Donald Trump can be impeached for bribery, it's necessary to zoom in first on what constitutes bribery. Bribery, like treason, is defined narrowly. Although the Criminal Code is not binding in impeachment proceedings, the definition of bribery that it provides is instructive. Under 18 U.S.C. § 201(b)(2), it's when someone:

> *being a public official or person selected to be a public official, directly or indirectly, corruptly demands, seeks, receives, accepts, or agrees to receive or accept anything of value personally or for any other person or entity, in return for:*
>
> *(A) being influenced in the performance of any official act;*
>
> *(B) being influenced to commit or aid in committing, or to collude in, or allow, any fraud, or make opportunity for the commission of any fraud, on the United States; or*
>
> *(C) being induced to do or omit to do any act in violation of the official duty of such official or person.*

The Calhoun, Agnew, Myers, Traficant, Belknap, Hastings and Bacon cases all involved: (i) seeking or accepting, (ii) things "of value," (iii) in return for, (iv) being influenced, (v) in the performance of an official act. They conformed to the statutory definition of bribery.

Traficant, Hastings and Bacon all played with the elasticity of the concept of "being influenced." And that is exactly what Donald Trump would do, if faced with a charge of bribery. "Yes, I took the money with both hands. In fact, I stuck some under my extra chins, and more under my belly roll and my sagging man-boobs. BUT the money never *influenced* me."

For instance, it is a well-documented fact that governments and officials of Saudi Arabia, Kuwait, the Philippines, Malaysia, China and Poland have spent massive amounts of money at Trump properties since his inauguration.[cxxxiv] In the case of Saudi Arabia, has Trump supported the Saudi-UAE intervention in Yemen and the Saudi-UAE embargo against Qatar, and avoided criticism of the Saudi murder of *Washington Post* columnist Jamal Khashoggi, because of the money that The Saudis put in his pocket at his properties? Or has he done this to spur military weapon sales by the United States to Saudi Arabia (which is Trump's stated explanation)?

In the case of the Philippines, dictator Rodrigo Duterte has promised to "slaughter" drug addicts like Hitler massacred Jews, called Barack Obama a "son of a whore," and threatened to assassinate journalists.[cxxxv] Trump has flattered Duterte profusely. Did Trump do this because of the money that the Government of the Philippines put in his pocket at his U.S. properties, and to protect and promote Trump Tower Manila? Or is this simply an example of "great minds think alike"?

Trump is on record as asking Argentine and British officials for favors relating to his properties there, following his election.[cxxxvi] Has he taken some official act in return, or does he, like Sir Francis Bacon, profess to enjoy such largesse for free?

(Of course, if a whistleblower were to step forward to connect the dots, or a stash of e-mails regarding these interactions were to connect the dots, then the dots would then be connected. Who would blow the whistle? Maybe Trump's counterparties. When a Government official tries to extort bribes, sometimes the victims accept their fate with stoic grace and aplomb, and sometimes, they don't.)

The statutory definition of bribery requires a *quid pro quo*. As the Mueller Report of Trump-Russia illustrates, proving a *quid pro quo* is not an easy thing.[cxxxvii] This constraint, however, does not apply to bribery's kid-sister, corruption. There have been a number of cases of impeachment for corruption where the standard was much looser than I'll-give-you-this-if-you'll-do-that. In other words, corruption is an impeachable offense, even when it does not satisfy the narrow statutory definition of bribery.

CHAPTER

CORRUPTION

In the Venn diagram for corruption, bribery is a circle inside. Although corruption is not expressly listed in the Impeachment Clause, corruption is an impeachable "high crime or misdemeanor." Like bribery, corruption is a Hamiltonian violation of the public trust, a misuse of the authority of public office. Historically, any significant case of corruption, like bribery, leads to impeachment and conviction.

David Butler

Governor of Nebraska. Charge: Corruption. Impeached by the Nebraska Legislature, and removed from office by the Nebraska Supreme Court on June 2, 1871.

d Butler

David Butler (R-NE) was the first Governor of Nebraska. In his third term, in 1871, he was charged with taking $16,000 from the state school fund, and misusing it personally to buy real estate lots in Lincoln, Nebraska. Butler had made Lincoln the state capital in his second term, and it also was a new stop for the railroads. (The Burlington & Missouri River Railroad arrived in Lincoln on June 26, 1870, followed by the Midland Pacific in 1871 and the Atchison & Nebraska in 1872.) Butler was impeached by the Nebraska Legislature for corruption in 1871, and removed from office by vote of the Nebraska Supreme Court on June 2, 1871. (That's how they do it in Nebraska.) In 1877, however, the Nebraska Senate expunged its record of Butler's impeachment, and Butler was re-elected to the Nebraska Senate in 1882. In any case, Butler's impeachment and conviction makes it clear that benefiting personally from directing government funds is an impeachable offense – not "bribery," but rather, corruption.

Robert Archbald

Federal Judge (U.S. Commerce Court). Charge: Corruption (before and in office). Impeached by the U.S. House of Representatives on 13 articles on July 13, 1912, by vote of 223 to 1. Convicted by the Senate on five articles, by votes ranging from 68-5 to 42-20.

Robert W. Archbald

Robert Archbald was a judge on the U.S. Commerce Court, which heard appeals from the decision of the Interstate Commerce Commission (ICC). Previously, he had served for ten years as a federal judge in the U.S. District Court for the Middle District of Pennsylvania. In his impeachment proceedings, he was charged with corruption in both of those judicial positions, including accepting a free trip to Europe for himself and his family from a litigant, and also accepting a "purse" from members of the Commerce Court bar. The thirteen articles of impeachment against Archbald specifically accused him of having used his judicial office for personal financial gain in a wide variety of forms, such as making "side deals" with litigants, discussing bribes, and accepting bribes from both litigants and attorneys. His defense was that these benefits came to him out of friendship, not in return for official acts.[cxxxviii] (And with friends like that, who needs real friends, right?)

On July 13, 1912, the U.S. House of Representatives impeached Archbald by a vote of 223 to 1. In the Senate votes on the articles of impeachment, the Senate showed remarkable attention and discernment, with results on Jan. 13, 1913 ranging from 68-5 in favor of conviction to 65-1 against. All told, Archbald was convicted on five articles of impeachment, four alleging corruption and one for bringing the judiciary into disrepute.[cxxxix] Archbald was also barred from holding federal office.[cxl]

Notably, the U.S. House Judiciary Committee directly addressed whether Archbald could be impeached for conduct preceding his service on the ICC, and concluded that he could:

"It is indeed anomalous if the Congress is powerless to remove a corrupt or unfit Federal judge from office because his corruption or misdemeanor, however vicious or reprehensible, may have occurred during his tenure in some other judicial office under the Government of the United States prior to his appointment to the particular office from which he is sought to be ousted by impeachment, although he may have held a Federal judgeship continuously from the time of the commission of his offenses. Surely the House of Representatives will not recognize nor the Senate apply such a narrow and technical construction of the constitutional provisions relating to impeachments."[cxli]

Harold Louderback

Federal Judge. Charge: Corruption. Impeached by the House on five articles of impeachment on Feb. 24, 1933, by vote of 183 to 142. On May 24, 1933, the Senate voted 45 to 34 (less than 2/3 vote) to convict Louderback on the charge that he had "brought the judiciary into disrepute," and in his favor on the other four charges, so he was acquitted.

Harold Louderback and Halsted Ritter

Harold Louderback, a federal judge in California, was impeached for misconduct "prejudicial to the dignity of the judiciary. All to the scandal and disrepute of said court and the administration of justice therein." This was later described in the U.S. House of Representatives Precedents as "general misbehavior."[cxlii] Halsted Ritter, a federal judge in Florida, was impeached on the same grounds in an investigation started five days after the Senate issued judgment on Louderback.

Louderback escaped conviction when the Senate voted 45 to 34 against him, less than the two-thirds voted needed to convict him. Ritter was less fortunate; the Senate voted 56 to 28 to convict him, exactly the two-thirds vote needed, on one count only.

The Louderback and Ritter impeachments demonstrate that when an official is impeached for corruption and abuse of power, and there are two genuine sides to the story, the outcome is uncertain.

The allegation against Louderback, as reported in San Francisco newspapers, was that he had appointed several friends as bankruptcy "receivers," and then he received some of the receivers' fees as kickbacks. (Bankruptcy receivers distribute the assets in a bankruptcy, and generally receive a percentage of the value of the assets they distribute.)[cxliii] Louderback had been recommended for the judicial appointment by Senator Samuel Shortridge. Many of Louderback's bankruptcy trustee appointments went to Shortridge's son.[cxliv] After the San Francisco newspaper exposés, the San Francisco Bar Association reported the allegations against Louderback to President Hoover, and later to the House Judiciary Committee.[cxlv]

The House Judiciary Committee appointed five Members to investigate the charge, and they reported to the Committee. On Feb. 6, 1933, the Committee voted 10 to 5 to censure Louderback, not to impeach him, for "conduct prejudicial to the dignity of the judiciary in appointing incompetent receivers, for the method of selecting receivers, for allowing fees that seem excessive, and for a high degree of indifference to the interest of litigants in receiverships."[cxlvi] The five investigating Members, however, recommended impeachment. [cxlvii] This led the House Speaker, John Nance Garner, to suggest unanimous consent to a vote by the full House on impeachment notwithstanding the censure vote, which was given.[cxlviii] On Feb. 24, 1933, the House voted 183 to 142 in favor of impeachment.

The House voted out five articles of impeachment. Article I was the only article to charge Louderback expressly with personal corruption. That article claimed that one Sam Leake paid for Louderback's room at the Fairmont Hotel, Louderback appointed Douglas Short as a trustee and awarded him fees, and that Short paid Leake $1200 to reimburse him for the Louderback room at the Fairmont. Article II claimed that Louderback had awarded excessive bankruptcy fees to Marshall Woodward, his friend, and Samuel Shortridge, Jr., the son of the U.S. Senator who had arranged for Louderback's appointment, but omitted a charge of kickbacks. Articles III and IV accused Louderback of appointing Guy Gilbert as a bankruptcy receiver even though Gilbert was incompetent – again, omitting a charge of kickbacks. (Louderback had appointed both Leake and Gilbert to be paid appraisers when Louderback had been a state court judge.) The last Article charged that Louderback had brought the judiciary into disrepute, i.e., that he had acted in such a way as:

"to excite fear and distrust and to inspire a widespread belief in and beyond said northern district of California that causes were not decided in said court according to their merits, but were decided with partiality and with prejudice and favoritism to certain individuals, particularly to receivers and attorneys for receivers by him so appointed, all of which is prejudicial to the dignity of the judiciary. All to the scandal and disrepute of said court and the administration of justice therein."

This Article was later amended to be more specific, largely limiting it to a recapitulation of the first four articles.[cxlix] Notably, all five articles of impeachment accused Louderback of a "misdemeanor," not treason, bribery or a high crime. [cl]

Louderback appeared before the Senate, testified, and vigorously disputed the allegations against him. In fact, he filed a lengthy "Answer" that not only asserted legal defenses, but rebutted the specific allegations in the Articles of Impeachment.

The Senate conducted a trial, which one of the Senators later described as "dreary, involved and protracted."[cli] On May 24, 1933, a majority of Senators voted against impeaching Louderback on all four of the bankruptcy trustee articles. (The vote on Article I, alleging corruption, was the closest, at 34 to 42.) As to the catch-all, he-must-be-guilty-of-something Article, a majority of Senators (45 to 34) voted in favor of that article of impeachment, but not enough to reach the two-thirds threshold to convict Louderback and remove him from office.[clii] Louderback continued to serve as a federal judge until the day he died, on Dec. 11, 1941.[cliii]

IMPEACHMENT INSIGHT—

AS IN THE *LOUDERBACK* CASE (AND ALSO NIXON IMPEACHMENT ARTICLES IV AND V), IT'S DIFFICULT TO IMPEACH AND CONVICT ON HONESTLY DISPUTED FACTS.

The Louderback impeachment demonstrates that it's difficult to obtain an impeachment conviction when a government official claims that he is being impeached "merely" for poor decisions in office. When the House decided to omit the explosive charge of kickbacks from Louderback's articles of impeachment, it reduced the gravity of the charges by several orders of magnitude. In Louderback's case, the Senate seemed reluctant to delve into the details of Louderback's judicial decisions, much less second-guess him. Also, Louderback clearly helped himself by disputing the facts, and by testifying under oath as to his side of the story. There may not be two sides to every story, but there were two sides to this story, and the proponents of Louderback's impeachment could not muster the two-thirds vote that they needed to convict him.

Halsted Ritter

Federal Judge. Charge: Corruption. Impeached on four articles by the House on Mar. 2, 1936, by vote of 181 to 146, and three more on Mar. 30, 1936. On Apr. 17, 1936, the Senate voted 56 to 28 (exactly 2/3) to convict Ritter on the charge that he had brought his court "into scandal and disrepute," and by less than 2/3 on the other six articles.

Not so in the Ritter impeachment. On March 2, 1936, three years after a Member of Congress requested an investigation, the U.S. House of Representatives voted 181 to 146 to impeach Ritter. The vote in the House was nearly identical to the Louderback impeachment vote.[cliv]

The charges were superficially similar to Louderback's, but they focused much more heavily on corruption. There were four initial Articles of Impeachment against Ritter. Articles I and II alleged that Ritter had raised the attorney's fees awarded to Ritter's former law partner from $15,000 (as determined by another judge) to $90,000, and that the former law partner had given Ritter a $4500 kickback. (The initial payment of $2500 was given on the same day as the fees were received.) The case in question was the bankruptcy case for the Whitehall Hotel (formerly the posh 75-room Henry Flagler mansion, which has its own Wikipedia page[clv]). The judge, his family and his secretary all had enjoyed free food and lodging at the luxurious hotel during the hotel's bankruptcy proceedings. (Article II of the Articles of Impeachment alleged Ritter's participation in a conspiracy to commit Article I.)

Article III alleged that Ritter had requested and received a $2000 payment from a client 45 days after he became a judge, telling the client that he was "assuming to continue [his] interest in [the case] until finally closed up." Federal judges are not allowed to practice law.[clvi]

Article IV alleged that Ritter had helped his sister-in-law be appointed manager of a hotel in a case before him, although she had no hotel manager experience. It also alleged that Ritter had received another $7500 and $2000 in mystery payments in the two months following his appointment as a federal judge, which were later clarified as alleged payments for Ritter improperly practicing law during his judgeship.

On March 30, 1936, the Ritter Articles of Impeachment were amended to add three more Articles. Article V complained that Ritter had not paid taxes on the $7500 and $2000 payments, allegedly for practicing law. Article VI complained that Ritter had not paid taxes on the alleged kickback from his former law partner, and other concurrent income. [In 1927, the U.S. Supreme Court had ruled in *United States v. Sullivan,* 274 U.S. 259 (1927), that illegal income was subject to income tax, and Al Capone had been convicted of this in 1931,[clvii] so such claims were *au courant*.] Article VII was a catch-all Article (like the final Article lodged against Judge Louderback). It claimed that the misconduct of the first six Articles was such as "to bring his court into scandal and disrepute, to the prejudice of said court and public confidence in the administration of justice therein, and to the prejudice of public respect for and confidence in the Federal judiciary, and to render him unfit to continue to serve as such judge."[clviii] Ritter's attorneys moved to strike Article VII, arguing that a catch-all article of impeachment was improper. The Senate, fatefully, voted to deny that motion.[clix]

Ritter, like Louderback, testified before the Senate.[clx] Regarding the $75,000 increase in fees for his former law partner, he testified that he was told that all the parties agreed to it, adding this (which aptly illustrates the potential difficulty in bad-decision impeachment charges that fall short of establishing corruption):

"I respectfully submit that there was no corruption, there was nothing back of it; and if there was no corruption, if I used my best judgment, as I did, at the time, I claim that I ought not to be criticized for it."[clxi]

Regarding the money that he had received from his former law partner (Articles I and II), Ritter testified that when he was appointed a federal judge, his partner agreed to pay him $5000 "when he could," and his partner had, in fact, paid him "when he could." Regarding the fees that Ritter had collected after his appointment (Article III), he testified that it was "some money that was due for work which had been fully performed prior to my going on the bench.... I never did a single thing on that case after this payment.... I was not practicing law. I was simply trying to close up a matter in which I had been interested and in which I thought some money was coming to me...."[clxii] Ritter claimed that the $7500 (Article IV) was a gift from a friend for whom he had done a lot of unpaid legal work before becoming a judge, and the money was to help Ritter buy a home lot in Coconut Grove. (Ritter conceded under examination that he also had made suggestions on some deeds and addressed a business dispute for this "friend" while Ritter was in office.) Ritter testified that he had reported and paid taxes on the initial $2500 from his law partner; that he hadn't paid taxes on the $7500 at the time because it was a gift, not income, and that he hadn't paid taxes on the other payments because he had offsetting deductions (Article V and VI). Regarding the free hotel stays at the bankrupt hotel, he testified that he had stayed at the hotel twice, as a guest of the manager: the first time to assess what fix-up work he would need to approve in court, and the second time with other local honorees in celebration of Washington's Birthday.

The Q&A by the Senators was much the same, like this:

> *"[Q.] Did you anticipate, when the fee of $75,000 was allowed, that Judge Rankin would pay you from the proceeds? A. I never thought a thing about it. I never anticipated it, never thought about it.* "[lxiii]

The transcript resembles a fine, long volley at Wimbleton:

> Q. *And so your declination to allow him to stop his suit was based upon your interpretation of article 7 of the deed of trust and that part of it which you have just read [rather than based on the payments Ritter had received]?*
> A. *How can a judge proceed in a case unless he uses his judgment and does the best he can? Yes, sir.*
> Q. *I think, in answer to your question, that many times they proceed otherwise [meaning, they proceed corruptly].*
> A. *You charged it in this case, and I would like to have you prove it.*[clxiv]

Regarding the $7500 "gift," Ritter said modestly, "it was the first time in my life that anybody in my acquaintance thought well enough of me to give me anything." He testified that it was from someone who "had no litigation before my court."[clxv]

Two sides to the story.

After deliberating privately for more than ten hours, the Senate voted on the Articles of Impeachment. The vote on the first Article, the alleged kickback from Ritter's former law partner, went strongly against Ritter, but fell one vote short of conviction – 55 "guilty" to 29 "not guilty." (56 to 28 would have been enough to convict.) On the second Article, conspiracy regarding the kickback, the vote was 52 guilty, 32 not guilty. On the third Article, regarding Ritter taking $2000 from a former client a month and a half after his ascension, the vote was 44 guilty, 39 not guilty. On the fourth Article, which had focused on Ritter taking $7500 from a friend as a supposed gift, most of the Senators concluded that it was, in fact, a gift: the vote was 36 guilty, 48 not guilty. On the fifth and sixth Articles, regarding alleged tax evasion, the votes were 36 guilty, 48 not guilty, followed by 46 guilty, 37 not guilty.

One can picture spectators – including Ritter – holding their breath when the catchall Article, the final Article, came to a vote. Article I had fallen just short of a two-thirds vote for conviction. The votes on the other Articles varied, and they were less harsh toward Ritter. Two of the votes had not even mustered a majority against Ritter. But it showed that different Senators held different views of the various accusations. Would at least one of the Senators who had been a "not guilty" vote on Article I become a "guilty" vote on the catch-all Article?

The answer was "yes." Article VII drew one more vote to convict than Article I had drawn, and that was exactly enough. By a vote of 56 guilty to 28 not guilty, the U.S. Senate convicted Halsted Ritter, and removed him from office.

This was followed by a vote on disqualifying Ritter from future office which, remarkably, failed unanimously – 0 for disqualification, 76 against it.[clxvi]

Ritter did not go gentle into that good night.[clxvii] He wrote a book in his defense, called "The Strange Impeachment of Halsted L. Ritter." Ritter noted that for much of his testimony, there had been a grand total of three Senators present to hear it.[clxviii] Ritter also filed a lawsuit in the U.S. Court of Claims, asserting that if the Senate had been unable to convict him on Articles I through VI, it could not convict him on Article VII, which he said was simply Articles I through VI added up. Although Ritter's argument had a certain mathematical appeal, the Court of Claims ruled that it had no jurisdiction to review the actions of the U.S. Senate in an impeachment trial.[clxix]

Both the Louderback and the Ritter impeachments could be called "he said, she said" proceedings. Both judges testified; neither had an airtight case against him; each had some kind of explanation for every allegation against him; and both generated substantial support for their alibis. What they said was not, patently, a fish story, a song and dance, a cock and bull tale, or jive talking. Both could claim plausibly, as Ritter did, "if there was no corruption, if I used my best judgment, as I did, at the time, I claim that I ought not to be criticized for it." Which meant that in both cases, the outcome was not a foregone conclusion, and couldn't be. In cases like these, the Senate has to do what juries do: listen to the evidence, weigh it, and then decide.

The difference – probably, the difference that made a difference – is that the Louderback charges were, at root, charges of poor performance in office, with a heavy coat of indignation slathered all over them. The Ritter charges, in contrast, were corruption charges. Corruption is an impeachable offense; poor performance in office generally is not.

In 1970, Congressman Frank Thompson, Jr., attempted a comprehensive review of charges against federal judges. He found that up to that time, eight judges had been impeached, with four of them convicted (Pickering, Humphreys, Archbald and Ritter) and four acquitted (Chase, Peck, Swayne and Louderback).

Thompson found that 47 other judges had been questioned by the U.S. House of Representatives, and their conduct provides a good indication of what *might* constitute an impeachable offense.

Thirty-three out of 47 (70 percent) had been accused of bribery or corruption. (As I said, American history provides a plethora of examples of official greed.) Twenty-two of those 33 had resigned. Five were censured but not impeached. The House of Representatives investigated and acquitted four of them, and two others were referred to the Attorney General for prosecution.

Six of the remaining judges among the 47 had been investigated for overbearing conduct or flagrant bias on the bench, but none of them was impeached. Five were accused of making unusually bad decisions; none was impeached. Two had been investigated for alcoholism, but not impeached. One judge had been charged with treason, and cleared. Mississippi Judge Herald Cox was investigated for referring to African-American litigants as "chimpanzees," but he wasn't impeached.

It seems to come down to this. There are Seven Deadly Sins: pride, greed, lust, envy, gluttony, wrath and sloth.[clxx] Of those, the only impeachable sin is greed.

Donald Trump

Trump Fun Fact: Trump once questioned whether the Mashantucket Pequot tribe should be able to open a casino that would compete against his because they didn't "look like Indians to me." "I think I might have more Indian blood than a lot of the so-called Indians," said Trump. Charge: Corruption.

Donald Trump[clxxi]

Having covered the territory of the bribery/corruption and impeachment of Vice Presidents, Members of Congress, a Secretary of War, federal judges and an English Lord Chancellor, we now turn to Donald Trump. When it comes to bribery, Trump stands accused of a unique perspective, since he may have been on both sides of the art of that particular deal.

The Trump Organization owns two golf courses in Dubai. _Transparency International_ published a report last year entitled _"Dirty Money Hub Dubai_

Must Clean Up Its Real Estate Sector," claiming that Dubai real estate is home to "vast amounts of dirty money."[clxxii] Trump's Dubai business partner, Hussain Sajwani, was sentenced to five years in prison in Egypt for corruption, and he paid a $15 million fine.[clxxiii]

The Foreign Corrupt Practices Act (FCPA) is the law that prohibits Americans from bribing foreign officials.[clxxiv] In 2012, on CNBC, Trump labeled it "ridiculous" and "a horrible law."[clxxv] In 2013, Trump and Sajwani announced the Trump International Golf Club in Dubai.

Trump colleague Felix Sater planned to give the $50 million penthouse in Trump Tower Moscow to Russian President Vladimir Putin, and Trump attorney Michael Cohen says that the offer was conveyed to Putin's staff. Trump signed the letter of intent for that project during the Presidential campaign.[clxxvi]

Trump evidently has remained concerned about the FPCA – I wonder why? — during his Presidency. When Trump met with Secretary of State Rex Tillerson to discuss an entirely different subject, Trump began "fulminating" against laws that prevent Americans from bribing foreign officials.[clxxvii]

So Trump thinks that bribery is, you know, a good thing. Let he who is without sin cast the first shekel.

As for Trump bribery here in the good ol' U. S. of A., the Trump Foundation gave an illegal $25,000 campaign contribution to a group supporting Florida Attorney General Pam Bondi. Bondi had personally asked Trump for the donation. Four days after the contribution, Bondi announced that she would not investigate Trump University. *Propter hoc, ergo propter hoc.* Texas Attorney General Greg Abbott also decided not to investigate Trump University, and when Abbott ran for Governor, Trump rewarded Abbott with a $35,000 contribution to Abbott's campaign.[clxxviii]

On the subject of bribery, Trump, as usual, has left nothing to the imagination. In 2015, Trump told the *Wall St. Journal,* "as a businessman and a very substantial donor to very important people, when you give, they do whatever the hell you want them to do. As a businessman, I need that." In 2016, during his Presidential campaign, Trump said "when I want something, I get it. When I call [officials to whom he has contributed], they kiss my ass. It's true." Bribery, for Trump, is just a cost of doing business.

So when it comes to bribery and corruption, does Donald Trump, against all appearances, believe that it's better to give than to receive? C'mon, it's Donald Trump we're talking about. Trump and members of his immediate family have benefited financially from his office to a staggering degree, as follows:

- Trump has solicited and received business and financial benefits from foreign leaders.[clxxix]
- The Trump International Hotel, on property leased from the federal government, went from $2 million in the red each quarter to $40 million in the black during Trump's first year in office. The hotel received six-figure amounts from the Trump inaugural committee, and from foreign governments, embassies and agencies hosting events there. William Barr, Trump's Attorney General, has booked a $30,000 party there.[clxxx]
- Trump visited his own golf clubs and resorts 150 times in his first year in office.[clxxxi] Trump refers to his Florida resort Mar-a-Lago as the "Southern White House," and he has hosted official visits by the Prime Minister of Japan and others there. Mar-a-Lago doubled its membership fee from $100,000 to $200,000 the same month that Trump took office,[clxxxii] and it has become a magnet for persons seeking access to Trump.[clxxxiii] Trump has named eight current and former members of the club as ambassadors.[clxxxiv]
- The U.S. Department of Defense has spent hundreds of thousands of dollars at Trump properties,[clxxxv] and the Secret Service an unknown amount. The Secret Service paid $54,020 for tents at last year's New Year's Eve party at Mar-a-Lago. (Mar-a-Lago charged members of the public $1000 to attend.)[clxxxvi]
- Trump's son-in-law Jared Kushner and Kushner's father sought and obtained a billion-dollar refinancing of a Kushner property. This refinancing was indirectly funded by the Government of Qatar. The Government of Qatar sought Trump's help when Saudi Arabia and the U.A.E. (which surround Qatar on three sides) instituted an embargo.
- The Trump inauguration committee paid a friend of Trump's wife Melania $26 million.[clxxxvii] (That is not a misprint.)

Which raises an interesting question: how can someone so rich be so greedy?

If Schuyler Colfax, Michael Myers, James Traficant, William Belknap, Alcee Hastings, David Butler, Robert Archbald and Halsted Ritter and others could be impeached or expelled from office because of bribery and corruption, then shouldn't Donald Trump?

*C*HAPTER III:

EMOLUMENTS

Peter Oliver

Massachusetts Judge. Charge: Emoluments. Faced impeached by the Massachusetts House of Representatives and forced into exile in 1776.

Peter Oliver

Justice Peter Oliver served on the Superior Court of Judicature, the highest court in colonial Massachusetts. During the War of Independence, the Massachusetts House of Representatives began impeachment proceedings against Oliver, for taking a salary supplement from Britain during the

Revolutionary War, and for disloyalty to the cause. His side of the story: he felt that he was underpaid.[clxxxviii] (But then again, who doesn't?)

Massachusetts had paid Oliver £120 per year. The Crown had offered him another £200 on top of that (which would have a purchasing power of approximately $32,000 today[clxxxix]). Judge Oliver was all for that. He found, however, that not only did he face impeachment on account of this kind gratuity, but the colonists were unwilling to serve as jurors before a judge who was on the payroll of King George. The good people of Massachusetts had reached the startling conclusion that if Oliver were paid by the Crown, then he was biased in favor of the Crown.

In 1774, Oliver was forced to seek the protection of British troops. Oliver fled Boston when the British troops left, and he died in exile.[cxc]

We can probably thank Peter Oliver for the Emoluments Clauses that we find not only in the U.S. Constitution, but also in the earlier Articles of Confederation. Their purpose was obvious: to make officials "independent of external influence."[cxci]

Article V of the Articles of Confederation prevented delegates to the Confederation Congress from "holding any office under the united states, for which he, or another for his benefit receives any salary, fees or emolument of any kind," and Article VI prohibited "any person holding any office of profit or trust under the united states, or any of them, [from] accept[ing] of any present, emolument, office, or title of any kind whatever, from any king, prince, or foreign state"[cxcii]

The former evolved into Article I, Section 6, clause 2 of the U.S. Constitution. The latter became the Foreign Emoluments provision in Article I, Section 9, clause 8: "no Person holding any Office of Profit or Trust under the [United States], shall, without the Consent of the Congress, accept of any present, Emolument, Office, or Title, of any kind whatever,[cxciii] from any King, Prince, or foreign State."

The fear among the Founders was that if foreign emoluments "were allowed to be received without number, and privately, they might produce an improper effect, by seducing men from an honest attachment for their country, in favor of that which was loading them with favors."[cxciv] Therefore, the Founders prohibited receiving anything that would have even the "potential of influencing or corrupting the integrity of the recipient."[cxcv] Or, as recently summarized:

> The Clause's purpose is "to exclude corruption and foreign influence," 3 *Elliot's Debates* 465 (Randolph), and its adoption was prompted by "the necessity of preserving … officers of the U.S. independent of external influence," 2 *Convention Records* 389 (Pinckney). Federalists trumpeted the Clause as "a wholesome provision" made against the "influence which foreign powers may attempt to exercise in our affairs," Tench Coxe, *An Examination of the Constitution for the United States of America*, No. 4 (Oct. 21, 1787), proclaiming that it was "impossible to guard better against corruption," 3 *Elliot's Debates* 486 (Randolph). From the Republic's earliest days, it was acknowledged that the Clause was meant to "lock up *every* door to foreign influence," 5 *Annals of Cong.* 1584 (1798) (Claiborne), and was "founded in a just jealousy of foreign influence *of every sort*," 3 Joseph Story, *Commentaries on the Constitution of the United States* § 1346 (1833) (emphases added). By preventing "undue influence and corruption by foreign governments," 18 Op. O.L.C. at 15, it seeks to ensure "the undivided loyalty of individuals occupying positions of trust under our government," 10 Op. O.L.C. 96, 100 (1986), including, of course, the President—who "surely" occupies such a position, *Memorandum Opinion for the Counsel to the President*, Office of Legal Counsel, 2009 WL 6365082, at *4 (Dec. 7, 2009); *cf. Nixon v. Fitzgerald*, 457 U.S. 731, 752 (1982) (presidents "must make the most sensitive and far[-]reaching decisions entrusted to any official under our constitutional system").[cxcvi]

Article II, Section 1 added the Domestic Emoluments provision regarding the President only: that other than his salary, he "shall not receive within that Period [of election] any other Emolument from the United States, or any of them," "any of them" meaning any State.[cxcvii] In plain English, this means that neither the federal government nor any state government can pay a President anything other than his salary set by law.

Trump Fun Fact: Trump had four student deferments during Vietnam War, and medical deferment for undocumented bone spurs. Charge: Emoluments Violations.

Donald Trump

The issue regarding Donald Trump's violation of the Emoluments Clauses can be boiled down to this: has Trump "accepted any present [or] Emolument ... of any kind whatever, from any ... foreign State," or from the United States or any State of the United States? Answer: Yes.

Regarding Trump accepting an "emolument" from any foreign state, the *Washington Post* reported that the Kingdom of Saudi Arabia picked up the tab of $270,000 for lobbyists staying at the Trump International Hotel in Washington, D.C., as they lobbied in Congress against a bill that would allow 9/11 lawsuits against Saudi Arabia. Trump made Saudi Arabia the destination for his first international trip as President, shortly thereafter. [cxcviii]

The Embassies of Kuwait and the Philippines have held celebrations at the same hotel, and the Prime Minister of Malaysia and his entourage stayed there during a visit to Washington, D.C. [cxcix]

In the first quarter of 2018, revenue at the Trump International Hotel in New York was up by 13 percent, primarily because of a single five-day visit to New York (March 26-30) by the Crown Prince of Saudi Arabia, even though the Crown Prince himself didn't stay at the Trump hotel.

Trump's Mar-a-Lago Club in Florida has hosted a Polish-American Leadership Summit, organized by the Government of Poland.[cc]

Trump has promised to donate to the U.S. Treasury any of what he deems *profits* made by the Trump hotel from foreign governments, but not to donate the *revenue.* For 2017, the donation was $151,470,[cci] and for 2018, $191,538.[ccii] But the Foreign Emoluments Clause prohibits "accepting" an emolument (without prior Congressional permission) – it doesn't forgive the sin if you donate the emolument to the U.S. Treasury.

In the first few months of Trump's Presidency, the Trump International Hotel in Washington, D.C, went from a projected $2 million loss to a $2 million profit.[cciii] Trump reported income of *$40 million* from the hotel in 2017.[cciv] That hotel is located in a building leased from the federal government, the Old Post Office Pavilion at 1100 Pennsylvania Ave., N.W., Washington, DC. (For several years in the 1980's, when I was a mere tadpole, I worked across the street. FBI HQ is on the next block over.) The Trump International Hotel profit is an "emolument" that Trump receives from the federal government, in addition to his Presidential salary. In fact, the hotel's mere existence arguably violates the Domestic Emoluments Clause. This should come as no surprise; the U.S. Criminal Code prohibits Members of Congress from contracting with the U.S. Government (18 U.S.C. § 431-32), so why should the President be allowed to do it?

There are more Trump foreign emoluments to emol. In New York, the Governments of Saudi Arabia and China pay rent at Trump properties. The amount of the rent is unknown.[ccv]

The Trump Organization owns three golf properties in Scotland, one in Ireland, and two in Dubai.[ccvi] Whenever the Trump Organization receives any land, tax abatements or tax breaks, zoning or permit concessions, or subsidies of any kind from national or local governments there, then that appears to violate the Foreign Emoluments Clause. The same thing is true of Trump-licensed properties in Indonesia, Canada, Turkey, South Korea, Panama, the Philippines, India and Uruguay.[ccvii] In fact, Trump has been accused of promoting those properties in conversations with foreign leaders, while serving as President.[ccviii] China mysteriously reversed itself and granted Trump valuable trademarks, after Trump tilted U.S. policy on Taiwan away from the Government of Taiwan, and toward China.[ccix]

Trump hasn't even bothered to deny the conflict of interest. On the contrary, he has admitted to "a little conflict of interest" regarding Turkey because he has "a major, major building in Istanbul." Trump also conceded that he "get[s] along" with Saudi Arabians because "[t]hey buy apartments from me. They spend $40 million, $50 million. Am I supposed to dislike them?"[ccx] Trump shamelessly has proposed holding the next international G-7 summit at a Trump property in Florida.[ccxi]

Notably, Trump has made no effort whatsoever to obtain "the Consent of Congress" for these emoluments, as the Constitution requires.

There have been three major lawsuits filed against Trump regarding violations of the Emoluments Clause: *Blumenthal v. Trump,* No. 1:17-CV-01154 (D.D.C. 2017), *D.C. and Maryland v. Trump,* No. 8:17-CV-01596 (D. Md. 2017) and *CREW v. Trump,* No. 1:17-CV-00458 (S.D.N.Y. 2017). These lawsuits were filed by Members of Congress, two States, and hotel/restaurant owners competing against Trump properties. In the D.C. case, it was alleged that the Trump International Hotel in D.C. is charging three times the market rate. The case in Maryland has been dismissed by the Federal Appeals Court, and a rehearing has been requested. Trump, however, has sought to dismiss all these lawsuits, primarily on the basis that it is not appropriate for the courts to try to enforce these Constitutional clauses against the President of the United States. Which leaves only one remedy: impeachment.

If Judge Oliver was removed from office for the modern equivalent of $32,000 in emoluments, then shouldn't Donald Trump be removed from office for profiting to the tune of $40 million in emoluments from one property alone?

$\mathcal{P}$ART II – HIGH CRIMES

$\mathcal{C}$HAPTER IV:

OBSTRUCTION OF JUSTICE

Aside from treason and bribery/ corruption, the U.S. Constitution authorizes impeachment for 'high crimes' and misdemeanors. These terms were added to the Constitution by Founder George Mason, in lieu of the broader term "maladministration."[ccxii] 'High crimes' sometimes has been taken to mean crimes made possible, or made worse, when cloaked in official authority. For instance, obstruction of justice. Anyone can try to obstruct justice, but very few of us can do it by calling on the CIA to kill an FBI investigation . . . .

Richard Nixon

Tyrant and King. Charges: Abuse of Power, Obstruction of Justice. On July 27-30, 1974, the House Judiciary Committee voted in favor of three articles of impeachment against Nixon, by votes of 27 to 11, 28 to 10 and 21 to 17. Recognizing that he would be impeached by the House and convicted by the Senate, Nixon resigned on Aug. 9, 1974.

Richard Nixon[ccxiii]

When this humble scribe was but a young lad, he attended the Hampshire College Summer Studies in Mathematics program, a sort of a boot camp for nerds. The program was divided into multiple classes ("sections"), meeting at different locations on campus. The campus was set in a rural area, but there was one outpost of civilization, the campus newspaper stand. Each morning, that newspaper stand was restocked with a few copies of a fresh edition of the New York Times, which is how people learned about the news in the mid-1970s (especially when some idiot had broken the rabbit-ears antenna on the black-and-white TV, which never worked well anyway because the channel tuning knob was loose, but don't get me started).

Classes ended at 12:30 p.m. each day. As the Watergate scandal became hot and heavy, one of the sections broke at 12:20 p.m. Those fortunate few then ran to the newspaper stand, took out their quarters, got their nickels in change, and captured all of the copies of that day's New York Times.

Well, we weren't going to let them get away with that. So the next day, we quit at 12:10 p.m., and we all ran to the newspaper stand.

We found that another section had been there for ten minutes already, and they had bought up all the copies before we could.

Even if you are not a mathematics scholar, you can see where this is heading. Within a couple of days, classes were canceled.

It's difficult to overstate the political electricity in the air during the Summer of '74, whether you were 16 years old or 60. The Watergate scandal was rooted in a group of Nixon operatives — blue-collar-ly named "The Plumbers" — breaking and entering the Democratic National Committee headquarters at the Watergate in the middle of the night, trying to steal records, and getting caught, plus the ensuing cover-up. (Yes, children, this is how people "hacked" back then. It seems very Fred Flintstone, I know.) The file cabinet that Nixon's "Plumbers" jimmied at the Watergate now resides in the lower level of Democratic National Committee headquarters, on South Capitol St. in Washington, D.C. Your humble scribe has seen it many times, but it's always still a thrill for me.

Between August 5, 1974, when the Watergate "smoking gun" recording was released revealing that Nixon had ordered the cover-up,[ccxiv] and August 9, 1974, when President Nixon resigned, we all watched, listened, ate, breathed and dreamt the Watergate scandal. As to impeaching Nixon, many of us felt this way:

Andrew Johnson came closer than Richard Nixon to impeachment and conviction, it's true. But nevertheless, there are many impeachment lessons to learn from political *denouement* of that "two-bit burglary," as Nixon's White House Spokesperson described the Watergate break-in.[ccxv]

Before the Watergate impeachment process took hold in the House, there were four unsuccessful impeachment resolutions, including one seeking to impeach Nixon for the secret bombing of Cambodia (secret to us, anyway; less secret to the Cambodians). But after Nixon's "Saturday Night Massacre" on Oct. 20, 1973, when Nixon fired the Special Prosecutor and both the Attorney General and the Deputy Attorney General resigned, numerous impeachment resolutions were introduced, including 14 in one day.[ccxvi]

Impeachment hearings began before the House Judiciary Committee on May 9, 1974. They covered a wide range of Presidential misconduct. At the end of July, 1974, the committee voted on five Articles of Impeachment against Nixon.

In Article I, the House Judiciary Committee alleged obstruction of justice regarding the Watergate break-in, *i.e.,* that Nixon, "using the powers of his high office, engaged personally and through his close subordinates and agents, in a course of conduct or plan designed to delay, impede, and obstruct the investigation of such illegal entry; to cover up, conceal and protect those responsible; and to conceal the existence and scope of other unlawful covert activities."[ccxvii] This Article alleged nine specific "means" by which Nixon had done this.[ccxviii]

Article II charged Nixon with abuse of power, *i.e.,* "violating the constitutional rights of citizens, impairing the due and proper administration of justice and the conduct of lawful inquiries, or contravening the laws governing agencies of the executive branch and the purposed of these agencies." This gist of this charge was that Nixon had used his control over federal agencies for improper, illegal and unconstitutional political purposes. The first specifics regarding Nixon's abuse of power alleged that Nixon had, essentially: [1] weaponized IRS audits; and [2] misused electronic surveillance "for purposes unrelated to national security, the enforcement of laws, or any other lawful function of his office." The latter was referred to as "bugging," which led to this memorable bumper sticker:

Impeach Nixon...
He Bugs Me.

This abuse of power Article also condemned Nixon for [3] "maintain[ing] a secret investigative unit within the office of the President," — "the Plumbers" — "which unlawfully…engaged in covert and unlawful activities"; and for Nixon allowing his "close subordinates" to [4] cover up the Watergate break-in and "other unlawful activities including those relating to [5] the confirmation of Richard Kleindienst as Attorney General of the United States, [6] the electronic surveillance of private citizens, [7] the break-in into the offices of Dr. Lewis Fielding, and [8] the campaign financing practices of the Committee to Re-elect the President"; and [9] for Nixon "interfering with" the FBI, the Department of Justice, the Special Prosecutor and the CIA.[ccxix]

Article III charged Nixon with obstruction of justice for refusing to comply with House Judiciary Committee subpoenas during the impeachment investigation.[ccxx]

Note that Nixon was *not* charged with ordering the Watergate break-in himself. Somehow, as the articles of impeachment against Nixon were unveiled, Nixon managed to avoid tweeting out: "NO COLLUSION! NO COLLUSION! NO COLLUSION!" Also, no inside-the-Beltway simpletons put it out there that Nixon really wanted to be impeached, or that impeachment would motivate Nixon's "base." Those were simpler times.

The House Judiciary Committee passed those three Articles of Impeachment against Nixon. The votes were 27 to 11, 28 to 10, and 21 to 17. There were only two Democratic "no" votes, both against Article III. The Republicans, in contrast, were seriously split on Articles I and II, voting 6 to 11 and then 7 to 10 against the Articles. The Republicans were more united against Article III, voting 2 to 15 against it.[ccxxi]

Articles I and II, regarding obstruction of justice and abuse of power, clearly alleged major misuse of public office for personal political advantage, *i.e.,* "high crimes." In Nixon's case and in many other cases of impeachment, there has been no real debate about whether these charges technically qualified as "high crimes or misdemeanors" or not. On the contrary, Nixon's dictatorial misconduct seemed to exemplify a violation of "the public trust," as Alexander Hamilton had put it in 1788.[ccxxii] Nixon's defenders were left to argue what might be called the *"l'état, c'est moi"*[ccxxiii] defense, as Nixon himself did in an interview with David Frost, where he said "when the President does it, that means that it is not illegal."[ccxxiv] That argument, however, is a tough row to hoe in any democracy. As President Theodore Roosevelt said, "no man is above the law and no man is below it, nor do we ask any man's permission when we ask him to obey it."[ccxxv]

The third Nixon impeachment article was, in essence, for failure to provide accurate information in a legal proceeding. This Article was somewhat different from the first two. Although the failure to provide accurate information in a legal proceeding has been judged an impeachable offense on multiple occasions, here (using our Constitutional scorecard) the Article I House Judiciary Committee was employing compulsory process against the Article II President. Although the Article III Supreme Court weighed in against the President to demand his compliance,[ccxxvi] Nixon provided more than a fig leaf to his supporters when he said Constitutional separation of powers provided him an "executive privilege" against forced compliance.

In any event, the House Judiciary Committee passage of Article III of the Nixon Articles of Impeachment stands for the principle that a President can be impeached for failing to provide information to Congress, even (or, perhaps, especially) information relating to his own potential impeachment.

President Nixon escaped impeachment on two other Articles. Article IV charged Nixon with lying to Congress about the bombing of Cambodia, in derogation of Congress's Constitutional power to declare war. Article V charged Nixon with financial misconduct in two respects. The first was government funds spent improving Nixon properties at San Clemente and Key Biscayne. The second was Nixon filing false income tax returns during his first four years as President, primarily because he took large, questionable deductions for charitable contributions for the donation of his records in office.[ccxxvii] IRS and Congressional audits showed that Nixon had backdated some documents to try to qualify for the charitable deduction, and the IRS had assessed him $432,000 due in back taxes, including a negligence penalty.[ccxxviii]

The primary arguments against Article IV were that in secretly bombing Cambodia, Nixon had been exercising (not abusing) his Constitutional authority as Commander-in-Chief to protect U.S. troops elsewhere in Indochina, that uncharacteristic honesty by Nixon would have comprised the military operation, and that Congress's War Powers Resolution rendered the issue moot. The primary arguments against the San Clemente and Key Biscayne Article V financial misconduct allegations were that the Secret Service itself had requested the improvements for security reasons, and that Nixon might not have known that government funds would be spent. The primary arguments against the tax allegations in Article V were that Nixon's actions may have been mistaken but were not necessarily dishonest, and that such matters should be resolved administratively, civilly or even criminally, but not through impeachment.[ccxxix]

Articles IV and V were defeated in the House Judiciary Committee votes by a wide margin, 12 in favor and 26 against. The Democrats voted 12 to 9 in favor of these Articles, and 17 Republicans voted unanimously against them.[ccxxx]

It's fair to say that these Articles may have been voted down because with respect to these allegations, many Members of Congress believed that Nixon had done nothing wrong, much less committed impeachable offenses. Regarding these two Articles, Nixon crossed the "two-sides-to-every-story" threshold, providing nonculpable explanations. In other words, if you haven't done anything wrong, you can't be impeached. The evidence has to lead firmly to a conclusion of guilt.

There also is the question of whether these were impeachable offenses under the Constitutional standard. In the somewhat-cynical judgment of some, lying to Congress simply may not have been a high crime or a misdemeanor. The same thing is true of using government funds to make home improvements (especially security-related improvements), or erring in one's tax returns, however "shabby" and "disgraceful" those acts may have been, as they were characterized at the time.[ccxxxi]

Or maybe the Judiciary Committee believed that it had reached the point of diminishing returns. As one commentator said:

"In the circumstances, the decision to reject these articles was probably sound. The most compelling reason for doing so, however, was not that the wrongdoing they charged had no place in an impeachment proceeding or was too trivial to warrant impeachment, but rather that these charges would have complicated the case enormously without adding much weight to the allegations against President Nixon."[ccxxxii]

A week after these votes, the White House released the Watergate "Smoking Gun" recording, showing Nixon and his aide John Haldeman scheming to have the CIA tell the FBI that "national security" precluded an investigation of the Watergate break-in. Support for Nixon collapsed. Two Senate Republicans told Nixon privately that he could expect no more than 15 acquittal votes in the Senate on the three Articles of Impeachment. Three days later, on Aug. 8, 1974, President Nixon announced his resignation. The impeachment machinery then ground to a halt, sparing Nixon the seemingly inevitable indignity of being the only President to be impeached, convicted and removed from office.[ccxxxiii]

Bill Clinton

President. Charges: Obstruction of Justice, Lying Under Oath. On Dec. 19, 1998, the U.S. House of Representatives voted by 228 to 206, and 221 to 212, in favor of two articles of impeachment against Bill Clinton. On Feb. 12, 1999, the Senate voted against conviction, by votes of 45 to 55, and 50 to 50.

Bill Clinton

Late in his second term as President, Bill Clinton was impeached by the U.S. House of Representatives, and acquitted by the Senate. The two charges against Clinton that made it to the Senate were lying under oath in the Monica Lewinsky matter, and obstruction of justice (_i.e.,_ witness tampering and hiding evidence) in the Paula Jones case.

Those charges flowed from Special Counsel Ken Starr's "Whitewater" investigation, even though the charges had nothing to do with Whitewater itself. Whitewater was a real estate investment by Bill and Hillary Clinton when Bill Clinton had been Governor of Arkansas. David Hale, an Arkansas banker facing criminal charges, claimed that in 1986, then-Governor Clinton had pressured him to make a $300,000 loan to Susan McDougal, Clinton's Whitewater partner. Shortly after Hale made his accusation, the Attorney General appointed Special Prosecutor Ken Starr to investigate it, in 1994.[ccxxxiv]

Starr's investigation of Whitewater pushed the envelope, then gnawed at the envelope, then shredded the envelope, and then burned the contents of what remained of the envelope, reclaimed from the shredder bin. The investigation went far and wide and then further and wider, eventually extending to Clinton's extramarital relationship with White House intern Monica Lewinsky; and even the pre-Presidential sexual harassment claim by Arkansas state employee Paula Jones, filed in 1994 after Starr's appointment, regarding an encounter with then-Governor Clinton in 1991. All of the details in the two Senate impeachment charges concerned Clinton's alleged obstruction of justice, in one form or another, regarding Lewinsky and Jones. But neither charge alleged any obstruction of justice by Clinton *using his official authority*, either as Governor or as President.[ccxxxv]

IMPEACHMENT INSIGHT—

AS THE *CLINTON* AND *NIXON* CASES SHOWED, OBSTRUCTION OF JUSTICE CHARGES ARE MORE LIKELY TO JUSTIFY REMOVAL FROM OFFICE WHEN THE OBSTRUCTION EMPLOYED THE POWER OF THE OFFICE.

On Dec. 11-12, 1998, the House Judiciary Committee voted in favor of four Articles of Impeachment against Bill Clinton. Article I accused Clinton of lying under oath to a grand jury on Aug. 17, 1998, regarding his relationship with Lewinsky, and the Paula Jones case. Article II accused Clinton of lying in written answers to interrogatories in the Paula Jones case on Dec. 23, 1997, and in a deposition in that case on Jan. 17, 1988. Article III accused Clinton of obstructing justice in the Paula Jones case in several ways, allegedly by trying to get other witnesses to lie and by hiding evidence. Article IV accused Clinton of lying and withholding evidence in the House's own impeachment investigation. Each Article argued that Clinton's conduct "has undermined the integrity of his office, has brought disrepute on the Presidency, has betrayed his trust as President, and has acted in a manner subversive of the rule of law and justice, to the manifest injury of the people of the United States."[ccxxxvi]

The House Judiciary Committee votes were 21 to 16 on Articles I, III and IV, and 20 to 17 on Article II. The four votes were entirely on party lines, except for Rep. Lindsey Graham's (R-SC) vote on Article II, regarding Clinton's answers to interrogatories, where Graham said that he was giving President Clinton "the benefit of the doubt."[ccxxxvii]

Notably, the House Judiciary Committee did not attempt to impeach Clinton regarding the underlying sexual misconduct – allegedly exposing himself to Arkansas state employee Paula Jones, or alleged sexual activity in the Oval Office with White House intern Monica Lewinsky. Perhaps that was too Victorian for House Republicans, or perhaps glasshouse dwellers Newt Gingrich and Bob Livingston, leading the charge on impeachment, recognized that it would be imprudent to throw that particular stone.[ccxxxviii]

One week later, on Dec. 19, 1998, the U.S. House of Representatives voted on the four Clinton Articles of Impeachment. The Democrats were steadfast against all four Articles. They voted 200 to 5 against Articles I and II, 199 to 5 against Article III, and 203 to 1 against Article IV. The Republicans voted largely as a bloc on Articles I and III, but not on Articles II and IV. They voted 223 to 5 on Article I, 200 to 28 on Article II, 216 to 12 on Article III, and 147 to 81 on Article IV.

As a result, Articles I and III passed, on votes of 228 to 206 (52% to 48%) and 221 to 212 (51% to 49%). This made President Clinton the second President to be impeached by the full House (after Andrew Johnson). But due to Democratic unity and GOP defections, Article II failed, 205 to 229, and Article IV also failed by a wide margin, 148 to 285.[ccxxxix]

Regarding the failed Articles, Article II was defeated in large part because Clinton could argue that those litigation decisions in the Paula Jones case (interrogatory answers prepared by counsel) were made on advice of counsel. Article IV was defeated because Clinton could argue that when he allegedly withheld evidence from the House in his own impeachment inquiry, he was defending the prerogatives of the Presidency and the Constitutional separation of powers. In other words, Clinton could offer a nonculpable explanation, which sufficed to carry the day in the House.

The Clinton obstruction of justice charges in Article I and Article III were arguably in line with impeachment precedents, where public officials had been impeached and convicted for lying under oath and obstructing justice, and they lacked any convincing explanation. (Although, as noted above, the other cases generally involved obstruction employing the power of public office, like Nixon asking the CIA to shut down an FBI investigation.) In successful obstruction-of-justice impeachments, however, members of *both* parties generally found the evidence and argument persuasive. The combined Democratic vote on the four Articles of 802 to 16 here – 2% in favor, 98% against – demonstrated that that was not the case here. It certainly did not bode well for any vote in favor of conviction of President Clinton in the Senate. The House Democrats evidently concluded, as a group, either that Special Counsel Ken Starr's investigation was politically motivated and fundamentally illegitimate, or that Clinton's actions were not an impeachable violation of public trust in the Hamiltonian sense, or both. In the Senate, where the Republicans could not afford to eschew Democratic votes, that would prove to be decisive.

On Feb. 12, 1999, the Senate voted on the two Clinton Articles of Impeachment. All 45 Democratic Senators voted against both Articles, which ensured their defeat. (Clinton needed 34 votes to avoid conviction.) Among Republicans, the votes were 45 to 10 on Article I (lying under oath to a grand jury regarding Monica Lewinsky and Paula Jones) and 50 to 5 on Article III (obstructing justice by lying and witness tampering regarding Paula Jones). But it simply didn't matter. Even if all the Senate Republicans had voted to convict, their votes would have been insufficient, because they had failed to make a convincing case to Senate Democrats.

This was not like the Nixon impeachment, where Nixon was told that he could expect no more than 15 Senate votes from his own party. Nor was it like the Andrew Johnson impeachment, where Johnson's own party could provide only nine Senate votes, and he had to win 10 Senate votes from the other party (the Republicans) to survive. The opposition to Nixon came to be bipartisan, while the support for Johnson was bipartisan enough (9 Democrats and 10 Republicans voted against Johnson's impeachment, while 35 Republicans voted in favor of it). In Clinton's case, in contrast, in the end, both his support and his opposition were partisan.

As explained above, the Clinton obstruction-of-justice charges were anomalous from the start, because they never had any material connection to Bill Clinton's official acts as Governor or President. Clearly, lying under oath and obstructing justice are impeachable offenses; Bill Clinton was impeached for them. But when such charges arise from something other than official acts, they may not be perceived as "high crimes," and a conviction in the Senate may not be forthcoming.

Also, the actual charges against Clinton seemed to be thinly-veiled and disingenuous proxies for underlying putative misconduct (Clinton's actions with Lewinsky and Jones, or his helping Susan McDougal to get her loan) that just couldn't be proved as a high crime or even a low crime. (If unseemliness alone were a crime, Donald Trump would already be serving 800+ consecutive life sentences. For goodness sake, Trump even qualifies as the "world's worst cheat" at *golf*.[ccxl])

Walter Nixon

Federal Judge. Charge: Perjury. Impeached by the U.S. House of Representatives on three articles of impeachment on May 10, 1989, and convicted by the Senate on two articles on Nov. 3, 1989, by votes of 89 to 8, and 78 to 19.

Walter Nixon

What is it about public officials named Nixon, and obstruction of justice charges? They attract them like flies on ... sherbet. (We're still striving for a PG rating here.)

Walter Nixon, a federal judge in Mississippi, was convicted of misconduct that occurred when he wasn't wearing his robes, so to speak. Outside
the courtroom. Nixon, a federal judge, misused his influence with the district attorney, a state official and a friend, and then lied about it. Judge
Nixon thus conjured up a sort of gray area between the obstruction charges
against President Nixon (gross misuse of the powers of his public office) and
the obstruction charges against President Clinton (lying under oath and witness tampering, which you surely do not have to be POTUS to do).

Judge Nixon knew Wiley Fairchild, who owned a construction company. In 1980, Fairchild's son Drew was arrested during the seizure of more
than a ton of marijuana, flown in from Colombia on an airplane. According
to Judge Nixon's later indictment, in February 1981, Wiley Fairchild asked
Nixon to help his son avoid a conviction, and in order to motivate Nixon,
Fairchild gave him $60,000 in royalties from three oil and gas wells. Judge
Nixon then asked his friend, the state district attorney, to "do what he could"
to help young Drew Fairchild.

Nixon blatantly lied to the FBI about his conversation with the district
attorney. Then Nixon lied to the grand jury. Nixon said that he "didn't even
know Mr. Fairchild had a son when I was dealing with him" on the oil and
gas royalties, which Nixon claimed he had bought from Fairchild (albeit at
"an extremely modest price")[ccxli]. When asked about whether he had discussed Drew's case with the state district attorney, he said, "no, not to the
best of my recollection," and then added this:

*"I have had nothing whatsoever officially or unofficially to do with the Drew
Fairchild criminal case in federal court or state court. I don't need to reconstruct
anything with reference to that. I've told you that from the beginning. I have
never talked to anyone about the case, any federal judge or state judge, federal
prosecutor or state prosecutor, and I never handled any aspect of this case in
federal court. As you said, Judge Cox handled it. I don't know where—someone
told me maybe Judge Russell handled one of the other defendants also and—but
I never handled any part of it, never had a thing to do with it at all, and never
talked to anyone, state or federal, prosecutor or judge, in any way influence anybody with respect to this case. Didn't know anything about it until I read that
account in the newspaper. Didn't even know Mr. Fairchild had a son when I was
dealing with him in the business transaction."[ccxlii]*

In a very creative flourish, Nixon testified that the state district attorney had *offered* to discuss the case with him, but Nixon had politely declined, because "it takes Bud an hour to tell you what anybody else could tell you in a minute."

Unfortunately for Nixon, the state district attorney, "Bud," testified directly to the contrary (and remarkably succinctly). Bud said that when he and Nixon were out "picking up the turkeys" (whatever that is), it went down like this:

"He [Nixon] said [to Bud], 'I was out at Mr. Fairchild's and he asked me to put in a good word for his boy, or would I say something to you about Drew.' — I think, I don't think he said 'Drew,' I think he said 'his boy.'. . . . So, I took it on myself, said, 'well, judge, hell, I'm district attorney, I'll pass it to the files [meaning that he would make the case inactive].' And he said 'no, I'm not asking you to do that. Now, I'm not asking you to do anything now.'"[ccxliii]

Together, the state district attorney and Nixon then called Wiley Fairchild, the father, from the district attorney's house, and told him that his son wouldn't be going to prison. Fairchild's testimony confirmed that the two had called him, and that Nixon had said to Fairchild, on the phone, "everything [is] going to be taken care of to your satisfaction." The state district attorney told Fairchild, "when this man [Nixon] asks me to do something, I don't ask no questions, I just go ahead and do it."

Nevertheless, during the FBI investigation, Nixon said, twice, that "he never talked to anyone at any time about the case."

Wiley Fairchild, the father, was indicted on perjury charges, and pled guilty to giving a gratuity to a public official, *i.e.,* Nixon. Drew Fairchild, the son, pled guilty to conspiring to smuggle marijuana into the United States, but his sentencing was delayed for *five years,* having spent several years "passed to the files" after the conversation between Judge Nixon and the state district attorney.

On August 29, 1985, Judge Nixon was indicted on four criminal counts, one of bribery and three of perjury.[ccxliv] Nixon was acquitted on the bribery charge and one of the perjury charges, and found guilty on the two charges of lying to the grand jury.[ccxlv] Nixon was sentenced to five years in prison.[ccxlvi] The conviction was affirmed on April 30, 1987.

Judge Nixon, like Judge Harry Claiborne a few years later, refused to resign from office, despite his conviction. So the U.S. House of Representatives voted three Articles of Impeachment against Judge Nixon. The first two tracked his convictions on the two successful criminal charges, for lying to the grand jury. The third sought to impeach Nixon for lying to the investigators, a charge for which Nixon had escaped conviction.

The Senate vote against Judge Nixon mirrored the later Senate vote against Judge Claiborne.[ccxlvii] On the first two counts, tracking the two criminal charges, the Senate voted 89 to 8 and 78 to 19 to convict and remove Judge Nixon. The Senate voted in favor of the last count, 57 to 40, but not by the two-thirds vote required to convict.[ccxlviii] In any case, Nixon was removed from office on Nov. 4, 1989, just 23 days before he was due to be released from prison.[ccxlix] Judge Nixon's conviction on the criminal charges consolidated the Senate vote against him on the two corresponding impeachment counts.

IMPEACHMENT INSIGHT—

AS THE *JUDGE NIXON* CASE SHOWED, CRIMINAL CHARGES ARE NOT A CONDITION PRECEDENT TO IMPEACHMENT, BUT THEY MAKE IMPEACHMENT AND CONVICTION VERY, VERY LIKELY.

Whatever it is that Judge Nixon was doing when he was "picking up the turkeys," it's safe to say that he wasn't wearing black robes when he was doing it. Nixon exploited his influence with the district attorney, but that district attorney was a state official, and Nixon very likely had no way to exercise any authority or influence over him as a federal judge. The district attorney might have done the same thing for a justice of the peace or a notary public, or for any other friend like Judge Nixon. (That's what "picking up the turkeys" with someone does to you, I guess.) The same thing is true about Nixon's false testimony before the grand jury – during his testimony, it's very unlikely that he was wearing anything but a business suit, and his official duties as a federal judge had little or nothing to do with his false testimony.

Yet here again, the U.S. House did not hesitate to impeach Judge Nixon, and the Senate convict him, for criminal misconduct even though it was outside his official duties.

Evan Mecham

Governor of Arizona. Charges: Campaign Finance Violation, Misuse of Public Funds, Obstruction of Justice. Impeached by the Arizona House of Representatives on three articles of impeachment on Feb. 8, 1988 by a vote of 46 to 14, and convicted by the Arizona Senate on Apr. 4, 1988, on obstruction of justice (21 to 9) and misuse of government funds (26 to 4).

Evan Mecham

Governor Evan Mecham (R-AZ) was elected in 1986, and impeached and removed from office in 1988. The Arizona House impeached Mecham for three reasons: (1) failing to report a $250,000 campaign loan, (2) directing $80,000 in state funds to his auto dealership (which Mecham repaid with interest), and (3) directing his Director of Public Safety not to report an alleged death threat by one of Mecham's staffers, which was characterized as obstruction of justice. The Arizona House vote was 46 to 14.

The Arizona Senate dismissed the failure-to-report charge, by a vote of 16 to 12. The Senate convicted Mecham on the misuse of public funds charge by 26 to 4, and convicted him of the obstruction of justice charge, by 21 to 9. Since the Arizona Senate had only 11 Democratic members, the Senate votes in favor of convicting Mecham were bipartisan.

Mecham also was criminally indicted for his failure to report the campaign loan, but a jury acquitted him.

Mecham diverted the $80,000 from a "protocol" fund, which evidently was meant to cover official expenses of the Governor's office. He claimed that he lent this money to his dealership because the dealership would pay higher interest on the loan that the fund could obtain otherwise.

The obstruction-of-justice charge came out of a grand jury investigation of Mecham. A state official allegedly threatened to kill a witness testifying before the grand jury. This death threat was reported to Ralph Milstead, the Arizona Director of Public Services, who reported it to Mecham. Mecham told Milstead not to report the death threat to the Arizona Attorney General. When Mecham was questioned on this, Mecham testified that he "could have" said that to Milstead.

Note that Mecham tried to cover up obstruction of justice by a member of his administration, and in doing so, Mecham committed obstruction himself. Far worse would be obstruction of justice regarding charges against one's self, as in the impeachment case of Governor William Sulzer, three-quarters of a century earlier (discussed in detail in a separate chapter below). Sulzer was impeached and removed from office, in part, for "prati[cing] deceit and fraud and us[ing] threats and menaces" against three witnesses who were to testify *against him,* before the Joint Legislative Committee established by the New York Legislature to investigate Sulzer.[ccl] But in both cases, the obstruction of justice resulted in impeachment and conviction.

Let's summarize what history tells us about obstruction of justice as an impeachable offense. Article I of President Nixon's articles of impeachment accused Nixon of "using the powers of his high office, engag[ing] personally and through his close subordinates and agents, in a course of conduct or plan designed to delay, impede, and obstruct the investigation of such illegal entry [the Watergate break-in]; to cover up, conceal and protect those responsible; and to conceal the existence and scope of other unlawful covert activities." Article III, a closer vote, accused Nixon of obstruction for withholding information from the House during its impeachment investigation. Judge Nixon was impeached and convicted for lying to a grand jury about a single act of interference in a criminal proceeding, not before him as a judge. Governor Mecham was impeached and convicted for trying to cover up a single act of misconduct (a death threat to a grand jury witness) by a colleague. In all three cases, obstruction of justice resulted in impeachment, and resignation or removal from office.

Article I of President Clinton's articles of impeachment accused Clinton of lying under oath to a grand jury regarding Monica Lewinsky and Paula Jones. Article III accused Clinton of obstructing justice in the Paula Jones case, by witness-tampering and hiding evidence. These articles resulted in impeachment, but not conviction. Clinton was not impeached on the charge of withholding evidence from the House during its impeachment investigation.

So, to sum up. Obstruction of justice is an impeachable offense. Multiple acts of obstruction, instigating obstruction by others or using the power of public office to obstruct, are aggravating factors. Obstruction in the name of asserting "executive authority" against an impeachment investigation appears to be a mitigating factor.

Donald Trump

Trump Fun Fact: Trump filed for bankruptcy for his business properties six times. Impeachment Charge: Obstruction of Justice.

Donald Trump

The primary charge of obstruction of justice against Donald Trump is set forth, at length, in Volume 2 of the Mueller Report – at least regarding

Trump's obstruction of justice as to the Trump-Russia investigation. Here are the highlights:

- During his Presidential campaign, on July 27, 2016, at the last news conference of his campaign, Trump said, "Russia, if you're listening, I hope you're able to find the 30,000 emails that are missing," evidently referring to Hillary Clinton's deleted e-mails. Russia did, in fact, hack the Democratic National Committee's e-mails, and then released them through Wikileaks in coordination with Trump agent Roger Stone. Trump, however, falsely suggested that Russia was not responsible for the DNC hacking. At the Presidential Debate on Sept. 26, 2016, Trump suggested that the hacker actually may have been "somebody sitting on their [sic] bed that weighs 400 lbs." Trump also tweeted "I HAVE NOTHING TO DO WITH RUSSIA – NO DEALS, NO LOANS, NO NOTHING!"[ccli] (Would someone *please* fix the Caps Lock on Trump's phone?) In fact, Trump has sought to do business in Russia since 1987, when he met with Mikhail Gorbachev and discussed Trump property development in Russia.[cclii] In 2008, Donald Trump, Jr., said at a real estate conference that "Russians make up a pretty disproportionate cross-section of a lot of our assets .... We see a lot of money pouring in from Russia."[ccliii] And according to the Mueller Report, Trump had pursued the Trump Tower Moscow project "as late as June 2016."[cccliv]

- In a one-on-one meeting in the Oval Office on Feb. 14, 2017, three weeks after taking office, Trump asked FBI Director James Comey to end the investigation of National Security Advisor Michael Flynn. Flynn had failed to register as a foreign agent, and had lied to investigators about it. Trump later tried to bully Comey about the meeting, suggesting there might be tapes of the meeting, to which Comey replied "Lordy, I hope there are tapes."[cclv] (By the way, why hasn't anyone tried to subpoena such Trump tapes? Do people just assume that Trump is lying?)

- Trump directed White House counsel Don McGahn to prevent Attorney General Jeff Sessions from recusing himself from the Russia investigation, because Trump wanted an Attorney General who would "protect" him. (Sessions recused himself from the Trump-Russia investigation because he had met with the Russian Ambassador during the campaign, among other reasons.) Trump then bitterly and publicly criticized Sessions for recusing himself.[cclvi] (For instance, Trump criticized Sessions in a *New York Times* interview, and Trump tweeted that Sessions "should be ashamed of himself" and that Sessions should have warned Trump that Sessions would recuse himself.)[cclvii] At Mar-a-Lago, in March 2017, Trump demanded to Sessions that Sessions un-recuse himself.

- In March 2017, Trump asked CIA Director Mike Pompeo to state publicly that the Trump campaign had not coordinated with the Russians. Pompeo had no basis to make such a statement.[cclviii]
- Trump asked FBI Director Comey to "lift the cloud" of the investigation by stating publicly that Trump was not being investigated. Comey refused.[cclix]
- Trump then fired Comey on May 9, 2017 – because of, as Trump said on national TV, "this Russia thing." The day after Trump fired Comey, he told the Russian Foreign Minister and Ambassador that he had "faced great pressure because of Russia," and the pressure had been 'taken off' by his firing Comey. [cclx]
- After Robert Mueller was appointed as Special Counsel, Trump repeatedly ordered White House Counsel Don McGahn to have Mueller fired. McGahn refused to do so. Trump made similar efforts in June and July 2017 through his former campaign manager, Corey Lewandowski.[cclxi]
- On July 8, 2017, the media was about to report on a meeting that Donald Trump, Jr. had arranged at Trump Tower during the campaign, on June 9, 2016, with a Russian lawyer/agent who claimed to have damaging information on Hillary Clinton ("if it's what you say, I love it"). Trump "personally dictated" a false response to the report.[cclxii]
- Trump engaged in wholesale witness tampering, most notably in the investigation of his personal attorney, Michael Cohen (who pled guilty to multiple felonies). In the Trump-Russia investigation, Trump publicly and privately complimented some witnesses, hoping that they would testify favorably toward Trump, while castigating

others, trying to discredit them or deter negative testimony, or even make them feel unsafe. Trump dangled pardons, and in Cohen's case, after Cohen started to cooperate with investigators, Trump called him a "rat" and tried to instigate an investigation of Cohen's father.[cclxiii] Cohen testified before Congress that Trump had intimidated him.

In sum, #WorseThanWatergate. And far worse than the obstruction of justice by Judge Nixon and Governor Mecham, which resulted in their impeachment, conviction and removal from office.

The one common form of obstruction of justice that is missing from the Mueller Report is one that the Mueller Report itself notes. Trump refused to testify in person, and thus avoided perjuring himself. Trump's lawyers referred to this as "the perjury trap," and a trap it would be – for a pathological liar. It would not be a trap for anyone who was ready, willing and able to tell the truth, the whole truth, and nothing but the truth.

It seems obvious that Trump's obstruction of justice in the Trump-Russia investigation not only matches but, if anything, exceeds the obstruction in other cases of impeachment that were based on obstruction of justice. In fact, Trump has employed many Nixonian obstructive tactics, like dangling pardons and trying to enlist the help of the CIA. Indeed, of the nine, specific means of obstruction of justice alleged in Article I of the Nixon Articles of Impeachment, Trump is guilty of eight of them.[cclxiv] Trump, like Nixon:

> *"using the powers of his high office, engaged personally and through his close subordinates and agents, in a course of conduct or plan designed to delay, impede, and obstruct the investigation of such [Russian interference in the election]; to cover up, conceal and protect those responsible; and to conceal the existence and scope of other unlawful covert activities . . . ."*

Some of the Nixon means of obstruction bear an almost eerie resemblance to present Trumpist Trumpery, like the last two:

8. *making or causing to be made false or misleading public statements for the purpose of deceiving the people of the United States into believing*

that a thorough and complete investigation had been conducted with respect to allegations of misconduct on the part of personnel of the executive branch of the United States and personnel of the Committee for the Re-election of the President, and that there was no involvement of such personnel in such misconduct: or

9. *endeavouring to cause prospective defendants, and individuals duly tried and convicted, to expect favoured treatment and consideration in return for their silence or false testimony, or rewarding individuals for their silence or false testimony.[cclxv]*

Article III of the Nixon impeachment articles charged Nixon with obstruction of justice for failing to comply with a Congressional subpoena. Trump hasn't been charged with that – yet. But the House Ways and Means Chairman has requested Trump's tax returns, something that he has an absolute right to obtain under Title 26, Section 6103(f) of the U.S. Code.[cclxvi] Trump's Chief of Staff says that Trump will "never" provide those returns. Trump's Treasury Secretary has defied a subpoena for them.[cclxvii]

After the Mueller Report was released, Trump tried to prevent Congress from obtaining the unredacted report and the grand jury evidence behind it. Trump directed former White House counsel Don McGahn, former Security Director Carl Kline, DOJ Official John Gore and White House Advisor Stephen Miller not to testify before Congress. (Trump tried to rationalize this obstruction by saying, "the Democrats [asking for this information] are trying to win 2020.")[cclxviii] So it probably won't be long before an impeachment article for obstruction of justice mirroring Nixon Article III can be lodged against Trump, too.

Measuring Trump's obstruction versus the allegations against President Clinton, it's clear that Trump's obstruction far exceeds anything alleged against Clinton. As noted above, the House voted in favor of two Clinton articles of impeachment. Article I accused Clinton of lying under oath to a grand jury regarding his relationship with Monica Lewinsky, and the Paula Jones case. Article II accused Clinton of lying in written answers to interrogatories and in a deposition in the Paula Jones case.

So Clinton was faced with the charge that he had lied three times; the *Washington Post* has enumerated that Trump has lied more than 10,000 times.[cclxix] Clinton was charged about lying about alleged sexual encounters ("I did not have sexual relations with that woman")[cclxx]; Trump has lied about anything and everything, including where his father was born.[cclxxi] And the fact that Trump often lies via Twitter rather than under oath is no shield for Trump; the Nixon impeachment articles made "making or causing to be made false or misleading public statements for the purpose of deceiving the people of the United States" an impeachable offense.[cclxxii]

In any event, the obstruction charge in the Mueller Report rests on Trump lying about the influence of a hostile foreign power to sway a Presidential election in his favor – a matter seemingly of substantially greater international, political and historic importance than a stain on a blue dress. Finally, Clinton *himself* was charged with lying, while Trump (like President Nixon) appears to have demanded that everyone and anyone lie about Trump-Russia.

Trump's obstruction of justice in the Trump-Russia investigation, as documented in the Mueller Report, vastly exceeds the obstruction of justice for which Judge Walter Nixon was impeached and removed from office. As noted above, Judge Nixon committed obstruction of justice in lying to the grand jury about *one conversation* regarding sentencing *in one criminal case:*

> *"I have had nothing whatsoever officially or unofficially to do with the Drew Fairchild criminal case in federal court or state court.... I've told you that from the beginning. I have never talked to anyone about the case, any federal judge or state judge, federal prosecutor or state prosecutor...."*

Trump, in contrast, erected a Great Wall of obstruction that fenced in virtually anyone who had anything to do with Trump-Russia: his former campaign manager, his other former campaign manager, his son, his son-in-law, his personal attorney, his White House attorney, his Attorney General, his National Security Advisor, the then-current FBI Director, the former FBI Director, 28-year-old Hope Hicks, and on and on and on. (Trump has so far left the White House Gardener out of it – as far as we know.)

As for Gov. Mecham, as noted above, he tried to squelch obstruction of justice by a member of his administration, and in doing so, Mecham committed obstruction of justice himself. Mecham tried to fend off trouble for someone he worked with, who was someone he presumably liked. It was obstruction, but obstruction with no apparent direct selfish benefit to Mecham (except possibly the avoidance of public embarrassment). You can make this argument for Trump when he interceded on Michael Flynn's behalf, perhaps. But not when Trump fired the FBI Director, sought to fire the Special Counsel, tried to enlist the CIA and the FBI to whitewash the record, tampered with witnesses, lied about the Trump Tower meeting, lied about Russian interference in the Presidential election, *etc., etc.* Donald Trump didn't do these things for anyone but Donald Trump.

Mecham was impeached and removed from office for obstruction that consisted of a *single conversation,* and an *unsuccessful attempt* to obstruct justice. In Trump's case, however, you could make the case that thwarting the Trump-Russia investigation has been the primary focus of his Presidency until the Mueller Report was released – judging by his tweets, for instance – and that as the Mueller Report itself makes clear, Trump's obstruction *succeeded* in preventing the Special Counsel from obtaining information that should have been available to him. In other words, in terms of the federal omnibus statute on obstruction of justice, Trump not only "endeavor[ed] to influence, obstruct, or impede, the due administration of justice," [a crime], but *acutally did* "influence[], obstruct[], or impede[]" the due administration of justice [also a crime].

The Mueller Report addressed obstruction of justice not under an impeachment standard – Mueller would have had no authority to do that – but rather under the criminal standard of a violation of the U.S. Criminal Code, "beyond a reasonable doubt." (Nevertheless, the Mueller Report has been characterized as an "impeachment referral" to the House.)[cclxxiii] Although the Criminal Code's obstruction-of-justice statutes are drawn narrowly, they certainly resonate with much of the Trump misconduct that Mueller laid out:

Criminal prosecutions for obstruction of justice often are based on what is known as the "omnibus clause" of Title 18, Section 1503 of the U.S. Code. This provides that anyone who "corruptly or by threats or force, or by any threatening letter or communication, influences, obstructs, or impedes, or endeavors to influence, obstruct, or impede, the due administration of justice" commits obstruction of justice, and may be imprisoned for up to ten years. According to the U.S. Department of Justice Manual, "it is no defense that such obstruction was unsuccessful, *United States v. Edwards*, 36 F.3d 639, 645 (7th Cir. 1994)."[cclxxiv] In a criminal prosecution, the "weight of authority" is that there has to be "a specific intent to obstruct or impede a pending judicial proceeding" in order to violate this statute.[cclxxv]

There is a similar omnibus clause under Title 18, Section 1505. It prohibits "corruptly, or by threats or force, or by any threatening letter or communication influenc[ing], obstruct[ing], or imped[ing] or endeavor[ing] to influence, obstruct, or impede the due and proper administration of the law under which any pending proceeding is being had before any department or agency of the United States."

There are also sections of the Criminal Code on obstruction of criminal investigations (Section 1510), and witness tampering (Section 1512). The witness tampering statute prohibits "knowingly us[ing] intimidation, threatens, or corruptly persuad[ing] another person, or attempt[ing] to do so, or engag[ing] in misleading conduct toward another person, with intent to—(1)influence, delay, or prevent the testimony of any person in an official proceeding."

There is ample evidence that Trump is "Guilty, Guilty, GUILTY" of all of these criminal statutes. These all are tightly-drawn rules for criminal prosecution, moreover, not for impeachment. Trump appointee Attorney General Barr said that he would not bring any criminal prosecution for obstruction of justice based on the Mueller Report, but he did not – and could not – preempt an impeachment by the U.S. House of Representatives for obstruction of justice.

Following the issuance of the Mueller Report, Trump dug in his heels. Less than a month after the report was released, the *Washington Post* reported that Trump was obstructing 20+ probes by House Democrats, "in an all-out war with Congress."[cclxxvi] "Unprecedented stonewalling" throughout the Trump Administration is now official policy.[cclxxvii]

If President Clinton could be impeached and President Nixon referred for impeachment for obstruction of justice, and if Judge Nixon and Governors Mecham and Sulzer could be impeached and removed from office for obstruction of justice, then shouldn't Donald Trump also be impeached and removed from office for obstruction of justice?

*C*HAPTER V:

OFFICIAL MISCONDUCT

(ABUSE OF POWER)

Andrew Johnson

President. Charges: Official Misconduct and Disgracing the Office. The U.S. House of Representatives voted on Feb. 4, 1868 to impeach Johnson on eleven articles, by a vote of 126 to 47. On May 16-26, 1868, the Senate voted 35 to 19 in favor of conviction on three articles, but by less than a 2/3 majority, so Johnson remained in office.

Andrew Johnson – Illegal Appointment and "Disgracing the Office"
On the subject of impeachment, the case of President Andrew Johnson deserves a great deal of attention, not only because Johnson came closest

among all the Presidents to being impeached and convicted, but also because the Johnson case addressed the crucial question of what happens when the person with the Constitutional responsibility to see that "the Laws be faithfully executed" unfaithfully breaks one.

One of the oddities of American law is that there is no prescribed punishment for violating most laws. In most cases, the law says X, but it doesn't say that a specific person must (or cannot) Y, and that if that person does (or doesn't), then the punishment is Z. The great majority of laws on the books do not demand any action or inaction on the part of specific people, and do not prescribe any punishment for violating them.

This incompleteness of "positive law" is outside the experience of most people; violate the speed limit, get caught, and you'll get a ticket. The truth, however, is that most law says what ought to be, not how to make it that way.

The federal Criminal Code (Title 18) is an exception to this incompleteness. It is exhaustive about punishing violators. But it is one title out of 50+.

The duties of Presidents, and some other high officials named in federal statutes, are another exception to this rule. When someone is charged with enforcing the law, he had better not break it. Thus the U.S. Constitution prescribes a loyalty oath, in Article VI, for high officials in all branches of government, and even state legislators: "The Senators and Representatives before mentioned, and the Members of the several State Legislatures, and all executive and judicial Officers, both of the United States and of the several States, shall be bound by Oath or Affirmation, to support this Constitution ...." And for the President, alone, the terms of the oath are spelled out in Article II, Section 1: "I do solemnly swear (or affirm) that I will faithfully execute the Office of President of the United States, and will to the best of my Ability, preserve, protect and defend the Constitution of the United States." On this score, for the hard of seeing, the Constitution repeats itself in Article II, Section 3: the President "shall take Care that *the Laws be faithfully executed.*" That's "faithfully executed" times two. The President, alone in the Constitutional scheme, has a personal responsibility to see that the Laws be faithfully executed.

Which brings us to the case of President Andrew Johnson. Johnson was impeached for violating a federal law that he considered unconstitutional and that had vetoed (with his veto being overridden). Despite those extenuating circumstances, Johnson escaped conviction by just one vote.

The Johnson impeachment centered on the President's appointment authority over the Cabinet. Article II, Section 2 of the U.S. Constitution gives the President the authority to appoint numerous federal officials, with the advice and consent of the U.S. Senate: The President "shall nominate, and by and with the Advice and Consent of the Senate, shall appoint Ambassadors, other public Ministers and Consuls, Judges of the supreme Court, and all other Officers of the United States, whose Appointments are not herein otherwise provided for, and which shall be established by Law." The Constitution does not say, however, whether the President needs the consent of the Senate in order to *remove* "Officers of the United States." That's a blind spot in the Constitution. It was debated in Congress from the first year that Congress convened.[cclxxviii]

Much later, in *Myers v. United States*, 272 U.S. 52, 117 (1926), former President Taft, then Chief Justice, issued a U.S. Supreme Court opinion holding that: "in the absence of any express limitation respecting removals, that, as his selection of administrative officers is essential to the execution of the laws by him, so must be his power of removing those for whom he cannot continue to be responsible." But no one could foresee that Supreme Court holding during the administration of Andrew Johnson, sixty years earlier. Johnson's impeachment revolved around the then-legitimate Constitutional question of whether a President could dismiss appointed Officers of the United States at will, when a duly-enacted statute said that he could not.

Of course, Johnson's political opponents despised him, and *vice versa.* They said so, and so did he. Many regarded him as an illegitimate President, since he had come to power only as a result of the first Presidential assassination in our history. Neither Democrats nor Republicans, neither Northerners nor Southerners, neither abolitionists nor slave-owners, trusted Johnson. So when Johnson committed what many regarded as an impeachable act, his numerous opponents did not shed any tears. But the impetus to Johnson's impeachment remained the underlying legal question: did Johnson have the legal authority to dismiss Members of the Cabinet, notwithstanding the Tenure in Office Act?

There seems to be a common impulse to question the motives of impeachment proponents, and that certainly was the case with the impeachment of Andrew Johnson. His impeachment often has been depicted as a power grab by Radical Republicans against Johnson, a Democrat. Honestly, if you resurrected the Radical Republicans from the dead, administered the sodium pentothal (not yet discovered in their time) and hooked them all up to lie detectors (not yet invented in their time), shined a bright light in their eyes (also not yet invented) and gave them all the third degree,[cclxxix] we don't/ can't know what they would say about their motives. However, we can say for a fact that Johnson's Presidential authority to dismiss Cabinet members without the Senate's consent was a real issue at that time.

During the Civil War, Andrew Johnson was the only U.S. Senator from a Confederate State not accused of disloyalty. In fact, Johnson unequivocally opposed secession, and he served the military governor of his home State of Tennessee when it became the first Confederate State occupied by Union forces (not counting the border states of Missouri and Kentucky, which remained largely under Union control throughout the entire Civil War). As Military Governor, Johnson punished support for succession as treason. Lincoln then rewarded Johnson for his service to the Union by elevating him to the Vice Presidency, in 1864.

On the other hand, Johnson was an unapologetic slave-owner who may have had three children with his first slave, a 14-year-old girl. Johnson had supported slavery for decades before the War Between the States, as he would have called it. Johnson was no abolitionist, for sure.

Andrew Johnson became President on April 14, 1865, when Lincoln was assassinated. [FWIW, Lincoln's assassin also conspired to kill Johnson. [cclxxx] Johnson's would-be assassin lost his nerve, but that would-be assassin was hanged anyway. If that assassin had succeeded, next in line for President under the Presidential Succession Act of 1792 was the otherwise un-notable President Pro Tempore of the Senate, one Sen. Lafayette S. Foster (R-CT). The alternative history in which President Foster, a New Englander, presided over Reconstruction remains to be written.][cclxxxi]

After Andrew Johnson assumed the Presidency, he used the Presidential pardon power to grant amnesty to most former Confederates, which was an extremely unpopular move in the North. He allowed Confederates to participate in the new state governments. He did nothing to quell widespread violence in the South against freed slaves. He vetoed major Reconstruction legislation, although Congress often overrode his vetoes (15 times out of 29, both the highest number and the highest percentage of overrides in history)[cclxxxii].

Notably, Johnson was not impeached for any of this.

Illustrating the total breakdown in relations between President Johnson and the Radical Republican Congress, Congress enacted three Constitutional Amendments during Johnson's Administration, in part because Johnson was "out of the loop" on amending the Constitution. (Constitutional amendments require only Congressional and state legislative approval.) The feeling was mutual. In the run-up to the Congressional Mid-Term Elections of 1866, Johnson suggested hanging his opponents. When his own supporters suggested that he show more dignity, he replied, "I don't care about my dignity."[cclxxxiii]

Johnson's abandonment of his dignity was not a successful campaign strategy for him. In the 1866 Election (and ensuing special elections), the first post-Civil War elections, the Republicans added 37 seats to their majority in the U.S. House of Representatives, controlling it by a supermajority of 175 to 47. In the Senate, the Republican majority rose to 37 to 10. Johnson lost all eight House seats in his home state of Tennessee to Republicans.

The Union Army was the strongest force in the South during Reconstruction. Johnson theoretically was in charge of it, as Commander-in-Chief, but real power was wielded by the Secretary of War. That was Edwin Stanton, a Radical Republican and a holdover from the Lincoln Administration. Johnson resolved to get rid of Stanton. The question was whether he could remove a Cabinet member without the consent of the Senate.

Following the overwhelming defeat of Johnson's allies in the 1866 Election, the Reconstruction Congress rushed to answer that question in the negative. A week after the new U.S. Senate took office, it enacted the Tenure of Office Act. A month later, the House followed suit. President Johnson then vetoed the law, and *on the same day*, both the House and the Senate overrode the Presidential veto.

Section 1 of the Tenure of Office Act provided that civil officers appointed with the advice and consent of the Senate remained in office *until their successors* received the advice and consent of the Senate. That no-vacancy rule may have seemed innocuous, but it gave the Senate *de facto* veto power over replacing a civil officer. Section 1 also established a special rule for six Cabinet Members including the Secretary of War, stating that they remained in office throughout a Presidential administration and for one month afterward, "subject to removal by and with the advice and consent of the Senate." Section 2 of the Tenure of Office Act allowed the President to suspend Executive Branch officers during Senate recesses if, and only if, they committed "misconduct in office, or crime, or for any reason shall become incapable or legally disqualified to perform [their] duties." Section 9, the last section, prescribed up to 10 years in prison and a fine of up to $10,000 for anyone who performed official duties in violation of the Act.[cclxxxiv] (That's equivalent to approximately $180,000 today.)[cclxxxv] The Act did not prescribe any punishment for a *President who made such an appointment,* however.

Johnson came up with a scheme to get rid of Stanton while *appearing* to comply with the Act. Johnson suspended Stanton during a U.S. Senate recess on August 5, 1867 under the putative authority of Section 2 of the Act, although it was quite a stretch to say that Stanton had become "incapable" of performing his duties. Showing that he wasn't a complete idiot when it came to politics, Johnson then appointed the extremely popular Commanding General of the Union Army in the Civil War, Gen. Ulysses S. Grant, to fill the position. When the Senate recess ended in December 1867, however, the Senate adopted a resolution of non-concurrence. Under the Tenure of Office Act, that put Stanton back in office.[cclxxxvi]

Johnson evidently believed that Grant would try to remain in office after the Senate vote. Grant, however, had no interest in potentially spending ten years in prison. When Grant resigned, the ever-tactful Johnson called Grant a liar, claiming that Grant had promised that he would remain in office. Grant was easily the most popular political figure in the country, soon to be elected President. (Grant would win 26 states, his opponent 8.[cclxxxvii]) When Johnson's attack on Grant became public, it did not help Johnson's reputation.[cclxxxviii]

On Feb. 21, 1868, Johnson's frustration reached the boiling point. He appointed Lorenzo Thomas, the U.S. Army's Adjutant General, to replace Stanton. Since the Senate was in session, this appointment clearly violated the Tenure of Office Act. Stanton barricaded himself in his office, and ordered Thomas arrested.

Three days later, the U.S. House of Representatives voted on party lines, 126 to 47, to impeach Johnson. Emotions ran high in the House. One of the founders of the Republican Party, Congressman Kelley of Pennsylvania, declared: "*Sir, the bloody and untilled fields of the ten unreconstructed states, the unsheeted ghosts of the two thousand murdered negroes in Texas, cry, if the dead ever evoke vengeance, for the punishment of Andrew Johnson.*"

The House voted 11 articles of impeachment against Johnson. The first nine involved Johnson's so-far unsuccessful effort to dismiss Stanton, who remained in office (literally). The last two articles of impeachment addressed Johnson's disastrous campaigning before the 1866 Congressional Mid-Term Elections, which the House said "attempt[ed] to bring into disgrace, ridicule, hatred, contempt and reproach, the Congress of the United States," and had brought disgrace and ridicule to the Presidency.[cclxxxix] These articles of impeachment offered lengthy excerpts from Johnson's speeches, in which Johnson generally had played a whiny victim, and condemned him for speaking "with a loud voice certain intemperate, inflammatory and scandalous harangues, and did therein utter loud threats and bitter menaces as well against Congress as [well as] the laws of the United States duly enacted thereby, amid the cries[,] jeers and laughter of the multitudes then assembled."[ccxc] In sum, Johnson was impeached for violating the Tenure of Office Act, an actual crime, and also for making three awful public speeches, in which he acted like a jerk.

Following Johnson's ascent to the Presidency, the Republicans had made a key substitution in the Senate, sending in a tough-as-nails pinch-hitter as Senate President Pro Tempore. If the U.S. Senate had voted for impeachment, then Senate President Pro Tempore Benjamin Wade (R-OH), a Radical Republican, would have risen to the Presidency for the rest of Johnson's term, which had less than one year to go.[ccxci] Even for a Radical Republican, Wade was radical. Highly critical of what he regarded as Lincoln foot-dragging on slavery, he had once referred to President Lincoln as "poor white trash."[ccxcii]

During Johnson's Senate impeachment trial, there was evidence of bribery or attempted bribery by both sides. A later investigation by Rep. Ben Butler, one of the House impeachment prosecutors, found evidence that Johnson's side had offered patronage appointments and cash for votes in the Senate. On the other hand, anti-Johnson forces had offered certain Senators the Ambassadorship to Great Britain, appointment as Secretary of State, and "a bushel of" money.[ccxciii]

On May 16, 1868, after the trial in the Senate, the Senate skipped over the first ten Johnson articles of impeachment, and took a vote on the 11th. This was the charge that Johnson's speeches during the 1866 Elections had disgraced the Presidency. Thirty-five Republicans voted to convict Johnson. Ten Republicans joined with nine Democrats to vote "not guilty." This 35-to-19 vote was one vote short of the two-thirds majority needed to convict Johnson and remove him from office. It was very fortunate for Johnson that post-Civil War Tennessee representatives had been restored to Congress; both Tennessee Senators voted "not guilty." Without their votes, Johnson would have been convicted and removed from office.

Ten days later, the Senate voted on Articles II and III of the Johnson Articles of Impeachment, which claimed that Johnson's letter of authority appointing Thomas in place of Stanton, and the appointment itself, were each a "high misdemeanor in office." The vote was the same. Unable to reach a two-thirds majority to remove Johnson, the Senate discontinued impeachment proceedings, and Stanton resigned.

The impeachment of Andrew Johnson, however, certainly did his political reputation no good. Soon thereafter, Johnson was defeated in his campaign to be the Democratic Party nominee for President. (The convention motto was: "This is a White Man's Country, Let White Men Rule."[ccxciv] Apparently, subtlety had not been invented yet, and dog whistles were still just for dogs.) The Republican convention unanimously chose Grant as the Republican nominee, Grant won the election in a walk, and Grant replaced Johnson as President nine months after the impeachment vote. The Tenure of Office Act was repealed in 1887.

Assuming *arguendo* that the outcome of the Johnson impeachment proceedings was not colored by corruption or power-politics, these proceedings stand for the proposition that the President is not above the law, and a clear-cut case of his violating the law can and should result in his impeachment. With the constitutionality of the Tenure of Office Act in question, however, Johnson escaped conviction, albeit barely.

Rod Blagojevich

Governor of Illinois. Charges: Official Misconduct (attempting to sell an appointment, and pressuring the media). The Illinois House of Representatives voted on Jan. 9, 2009 to impeach Blagojevich on 13 articles, by a vote of 114 to 1. On Jan. 29, 2009, the Illinois Senate voted 59 to 0 to convict him on all counts.

Rod Blagojevich – Selling an Appointment and Pressuring the Media[ccxcv]

Governor Rod Blagojevich (D-IL) was elected in 2002, reelected in 2006, and impeached and removed from office in 2009. He was later found guilty in two criminal trials, and sentenced to 14 years in prison.

The infamous ground for impeaching Blagojevich and removing him from office was Blagojevich's effort to "sell to the highest bidder" Barack Obama's Senate seat, after Obama was elected President. As Governor, Blagojevich had the authority to fill Obama's seat by appointment.

Blagojevich initially came under criminal investigation because his "bagman" for campaign contributions, Tony Rezko, was demanding "pay to play" kickbacks from Illinois government contractors. In connection with the Rezko investigation, prosecutors obtained court permission to record Blagojevich's conversations. After Obama's Senate seat opened, and Blagojevich realized that he could appoint Obama's Senate successor, Blagojevich delivered this eloquent soliloquy, recorded in full:

""I've got this thing, and it's f**king golden. I'm just not giving it up for f**king nothing. It's a f**king valuable thing, you just don't give it away for nothing. If I don't get what I want [...] I'll just take the Senate seat myself."

In exchange for the Senate appointment, Blagojevich sought $1.5 million in supposed "campaign contributions," which was a bit odd, because Blagojevich was not running for reelection. According to the *Chicago Sun-Times,* other contemplated *quid pro quos* for the Senate appointment included:

- A substantial salary for himself, at either a non-profit foundation or an organization affiliated with labor unions.
- Placing his wife on paid corporate boards where, he speculated, she might garner as much as $150,000 a year.
- Promises of campaign funds—including cash up front.
- A Cabinet appointment.
- The U.S. ambassadorship to Serbia, where his parents were from (or actually, in the case of his mother, Serbian Bosnia).

Blagojevich was indicted and arrested on corruption charges on Dec. 9, 2008. Exactly one month later, the Illinois House voted 114 to 1 to impeach him. Far from limiting itself to the sale of the Obama Senate seat, however, the Illinois House enumerated 13 separate grounds of impeachment. The impeachment resolution charged Blagojevich with seven different "plot[s] to trade official acts in exchange for campaign contributions."

The Illinois Senate then voted unanimously (59 to 0) to convict Blagojevich on all 13 charges.

Regarding the criminal charges running parallel to the impeachment proceedings, the first trial resulted in Blagojevich being found guilty of only one charge – lying to the FBI – and a hung jury on the other 23. In a second trial, however, Blagojevich was found guilty of 11 charges related to selling the Senate seat, and six related to interfering in state payments to a hospital in order to obtain a $50,000 campaign contribution. On appeal, the U.S. Court of Appeals for the Seventh Circuit had these choice words about the case:

> *"Blagojevich now asks us to hold that the evidence is insufficient to convict him on any count. The argument is frivolous. The evidence, much of it from Blagojevich's own mouth, is overwhelming."*[ccxcvi]

Almost overlooked in the midst of Blagojevich's campaign finance criminal bacchanal was one charge of abuse of power. The second impeachment charge against Blagojevich read as follows:

"The Governor's plot to condition the awarding of State financial assistance to the Tribune Company on the firing of members of the Chicago Tribune editorial board . . . ."

According to the corresponding elements of Blagojevich's criminal indictment, the Tribune Co. owned both the *Chicago Tribune* and the Chicago Cubs, as well as Wrigley Stadium. It was looking for $150 million in state aid from the Illinois Finance Authority to sell the stadium. While this request for state aid was pending, Blagojevich told John Harris, his Chief of Staff: "Our recommendation is to fire all these [expletive] people, get 'em the [expletive] out of there and get us some editorial support." Harris conveyed that to the Tribune. There was later back-and-forth between Blagojevich and Harris that focused on dismissal of the Tribune Editorial Board, and specifically Deputy Editorial Page Editor John P. McCormick. (McCormick wears the badge of honor that Blagojevich called him "a bad guy.")

As noted above, threatening to withhold state aid in exchange for more favorable media coverage was one of the grounds of impeachment on which the Illinois Senate convicted Blagojevich. In other words, the Blagojevich case demonstrates that not only are seven different "plot[s] to trade official acts in exchange for campaign contributions" impeachable offenses, but so is plotting to trade an official act for more favorable media coverage.

Corrupt politician Donald Trump has indicated that he may pardon corrupt politician Rod Blagojevich, proving that it takes one to know one, and also to let-go one. Blagojevich's wife evidently has fooled Trump into thinking that Blagojevich somehow was set up by Trump foe former FBI Director James Comey, demonstrating that it takes one to snow one, too.[ccxcvii]

James Ferguson

Governor of Texas. Charges: Corruption and Abuse of Power. In July 1917, the Texas House of Representatives voted 85 to 51 in favor of impeachment. On Sept. 22, 1917, the Texas Senate convicted him on seven counts of corruption and three of abuse of power.

James Ferguson – Pressuring an Independent Gov't Authority
James Ferguson's impeachment and removal from office was flavored not only by his abuse of power but also his corruption. We address him in the context of abuse of power because, frankly, in American history, corruption cases are a dime a dozen, run-of-the-mill, and par for the course, while abuse of power cases are a needle in a haystack, as scarce as hen's teeth, or as common as a 3-leaf clover. [End metaphor.]

Governor James Ferguson (D-TX) was elected Governor of Texas in 1914, reelected in 1916, and impeached and removed from office in 1917. He was convicted on ten articles of impeachment. Seven of them involved corruption, and three involved abuse of power, based on his effort to remove political opponents from the faculty at the University of Texas.[ccxcviii]

Ferguson led a colorful life before taking office. He was the son of a preacher, and yet he was expelled from school for disobedience. (He did manage to make it through sixth grade.)[ccxcix] He left home at the age of 16, taking jobs at a mine, a barbed-wire factory, a ranch and a vineyard. He came back home and was admitted to the bar to practice law (without the benefit of having ever attended middle school, high school, college or law school), but he couldn't find full-time work as an attorney. So he started a bank – that's where the money is, after all – he sold it, and then he started another bank. That second bank, the Temple State Bank, was the focus of corruption charges against Ferguson as governor. Basically, Ferguson directed state funds to Temple, and then used Temple as his piggy bank.

For some reason, Ferguson had the nickname "Pa," even though he was all of 44 years old when he was elected Governor.

Ferguson is a fascinating case study in impeachment because, more than anyone else who has ever been impeached, he publicly and constantly employed the power of his office for personal financial and political gain – and he always claimed otherwise. With Ferguson, the impeachable offenses were in broad daylight.

When Ferguson ran for Governor, he defeated the incumbent Lieutenant Governor, William Harding Mayes. Mayes turned out to be an implacable opponent. Mayes used his platform as the founder and dean of the University of Texas School of Journalism, and his ownership of Texas newspapers, to foment opposition to Ferguson as Governor. U.T. was a public institution – actually a very notable one, whose existence is enshrined in the Texas Constitution. Ferguson asked the trustees of U.T. to relieve him of this Mayes headache.

"Will no one rid me of this turbulent priest?" – King Henry II (1170) regarding Archbishop of Canterbury Thomas Becket, who was killed shortly thereafter by four noblemen in the king's service.

Ferguson actually asked for the dismissal of not only Mayes, but rather a total of six faculty members. Ferguson's complaint against them was that "they had skinned him from hell to breakfast,"[ccc] which apparently was a thing in Texas in 1916.

The answer to Governor Ferguson, unlike to the answer to King Henry II, was "no." The U.T. trustees refused to remove Mayes and his allies. So Ferguson demanded the resignation of the U.T. Regent, whom Ferguson hoped to replace with someone more compliant, or at least more pliant. "No," again.

To add insult to injury, U.T. students soon were marching under the Governor's window, waiving their fists at him and accusing him of "Kaiserism" (dictatorship).[ccci]

And then Ferguson had this "brilliant" – seven-foot-tall air-quotes around the word "brilliant" – idea. Ferguson realized that if he vetoed *the entire U.T. appropriation,* then there would be no money to pay Mayes. So U.T. was the baby, and Mayes was the bathwater.

By this time, Ferguson already had survived one impeachment vote for corruption and abuse of office. In the earlier case, the Texas House had found that impeachment charges against Ferguson had been substantiated, but not to the point that he should suffer the "severe pains and penalties of impeachment."[cccii] So one would think that Ferguson would be on best behavior. *Mais non.* Ferguson vetoed the appropriation for U.T.

Major uproar.

Note that Ferguson clearly had the legal authority to veto U.T.'s appropriation. The problem was that Ferguson did so for *an improper purpose, i.e.,* to remove it as a launchpad for Mayes's political attacks on Ferguson. That's what made this an abuse of power.

But Ferguson did not try to justify his funding veto on that basis; instead, he attacked higher education itself. As for the scientific research that the University conducted, for instance, Ferguson reported that "it took a teacher in the University three years to learn that wool would not grow on an armadillo's back."[ccciii]

With its state funding zeroed out, U.T. caved in, dismissing the six faculty members.[ccciv] Ferguson then called a special session of the Texas

Legislature to fund U.T. But that session did not go quite as Ferguson had planned.

> *"People of the same trade seldom meet together, even for merriment and diversion, but the conversation ends in a conspiracy against the public, or in some contrivance to raise prices."* – Adam Smith, "Wealth of Nations" (1776).

By that point, members of the Texas Legislature seldom met together, even for merriment and diversion underwritten by lobbyists, but the conversation ended in a conspiracy to impeach "Pa" Ferguson.

In July 1917, a grand jury in Austin, Texas indicted Ferguson. The indictment ultimately was dropped, but in the meantime, it spurred the Texas House to initiative impeachment proceedings against Ferguson. The House voted 82 to 51 in favor of impeachment.[cccv]

Following this action by the House, the Texas Senate drew up 21 articles of impeachment against Ferguson. Ferguson "demurred" to (requested dismissal of) the charges for several reasons, one of which is particularly interesting. Ferguson claimed that he could not be impeached for anything that happened before his reelection in 1916, because the voters had had their say in that election, and the Legislature could not reverse the decision of the voters.[cccvi] Of course, the voters had not had the benefit of Texas House investigation of Ferguson, nor were they sitting as an impeachment jury judging high crimes and misdemeanors. (Voting is so much easier.) The Texas Senate rejected that argument.

IMPEACHMENT INSIGHT—

AS IN THE *FERGUSON* CASE, IMPEACHMENT CANNOT BE THWARTED BY CLAIMING THAT IT WOULD REVERSE THE JUDGMENT OF THE VOTERS, BECAUSE IMPEACHMENT OF AN ELECTED OFFICIAL *ALWAYS* REVERSES THE JUDGMENT OF THE VOTERS.

There were 32 witnesses, including Ferguson himself. Ferguson testified for five days. He defended himself forcefully, even giving a two-hour closing argument on his own behalf.[cccvii] Ferguson's testimony rendered impeccable examples of what we, today, would call "whataboutism." On the subject of diverting state funds to his bank, for instance, Ferguson asked why he was being impeached for that, when U.T. Regent George Washington Littlefield had done the same thing (or so Ferguson claimed).[cccviii]

Limiting ourselves to the charges actually sustained by the Senate, the corruption charges against Ferguson were extensive and substantial. Ferguson was convicted on four separate impeachment counts regarding his misdirection of state funds to his own bank, the Temple State Bank. Ferguson owned one-quarter of the shares of the bank. Specifically, Ferguson was found guilty of:

- Depositing $101,000 in general state funds in the bank, so that he would profit on those funds;
- Depositing $60,000 of funds of the Texas Secretary of State;
- Having a Temple State Bank official deposit $250,000 of state funds at the American National Bank of Austin, which shared the profits on that deposit with the Temple State Bank, and
- Inducing the Temple State Bank to exceed the limit on its loans to Ferguson personally (Articles 2, 6, 7 and 14).

The lending limit that Ferguson somehow managed to exceed with his own personal borrowing (from his own personal bank, at least as he saw it) was the astoundingly high 30 percent. So not only did Ferguson use Temple as his piggy bank, but he also was just a pig.

Ferguson's Temple Bank boho dance wasn't the only kind of corruption for which he was convicted. Ferguson also violated state law by transferring money from the Adjutant General's department fund to the Canyon City Normal School fund, and then simply snatching $5000 of that (Articles 1 & 12).

This may not seem like a lot of money today, but a century ago, it was. Ferguson's salary as Governor, set by the Texas Constitution of 1876, was $4000 a year.[cccix] So the $5000 that he grabbed from the Canyon City

Normal School fund was more than what he made as Governor in a year. And if Ferguson had purloined merely 30% of the $161,000 in state money that he deposited in his own bank, or $48,300, that would have been twelve times as much as his annual salary.

But the big-ticket item in the impeachment of James Ferguson was Charge No. 11:

> *"That, before the recent house committee, he refused to divulge the source of the $156,000 which he received from certain parties immediately after the adjournment of the regular session of 1917...."*

That $156,000 in mystery money is equivalent to more than $3 million today.[cccx] The rumor was that the liquor companies had given this money to the staunchly anti-Prohibitionist Governor, for fending off all Prohibitionist attacks until after the Legislature left town, [cccxi] the liquor companies apparently being familiar with the words of Gideon Tucker:

> *"No man's life, liberty, or property are safe while the legislature is in session."* – New York Judge Gideon J. Tucker (1866). *"No man's wife or property is safe while the Legislature is in session."* The *New York Times* (Feb. 6, 1977) at 24, misquoting Tucker.

It's hard to say what incensed the Texas Legislature more, the fact that Ferguson may have received an enormous bribe from the liquor companies, or the fact that he didn't share it with them.

Note, however, that Ferguson was under no legal duty to divulge to the Texas House from whence this money came. Note, also, that Ferguson didn't lie to the Texas House; he simply refused to answer the question. Note, further, that the Texas House never voted to hold Ferguson in contempt of the House for refusing to answer its question. Note, finally, that there was no indication that Ferguson had taken any official action during the legislative session of 1917 to benefit the liquor companies (for instance, a veto). There was no direct evidence that Ferguson violated any law. Nevertheless, Ferguson was impeached and convicted for this – basically, circumstantial evidence of bribery. In fact, the Texas Senate vote on this impeachment count was the most lopsided of all: 27 to 4.

What the Ferguson case means is that when judging impeachment, the Senate is allowed to count to four. As in 2 + 2 = 4. The Texas Senate could *infer* an impeachable offense, from Ferguson's refusal to explain from whence the money came. In the law, this principle is popular enough to have acquired its own Latin saying: *"qui tacet consentire videtur,"* or "he who is silent is taken to agree." The refusal to provide information – like Donald Trump's tax returns, for instance – is always suspicious, and sometimes impeachable.

IMPEACHMENT INSIGHT—

AS IN THE *FERGUSON* CASE, IMPEACHMENT
NEED NOT BE BASED ON DIRECT EVIDENCE, BUT
RATHER ON CIRCUMSTANTIAL EVIDENCE, OR
EVEN THE WITHHOLDING OF EVIDENCE.

As noted above, the first seven impeachment charges on which Ferguson was convicted can fairly be described as charges of corruption. The last three, in contrast, were charges of abuse of power. These are the charges that related to Ferguson's successful effort to remove U.T. faculty members. Emphasizing the element of abuse of power, they refer to Ferguson's "despotic will," and his "imperious will."[cccxii] In other words, they focus not on whether Ferguson had the *power* to do what he did, but rather, whether Ferguson *abused* it.

The U.T. impeachment charges represent an interesting and subtle series of decisions by the Texas Senate. Article 15 of the articles of impeachment against Ferguson charged him with threatening to veto, and vetoing, funding for U.T. The Texas Senate actually exonerated Ferguson on that charge, by vote of 6 to 24. The Senate's view was that Ferguson had acted well within his authority as Governor to veto the university funding, so he shouldn't be impeached for that.

Similarly, Article 18 accused Ferguson with making "vile charges … criminal libel, and slander," against "the fair name of Texas and one of its most cherished institutions" when he had campaigned around the state attacking U.T., trying to justify his veto to The People. That article was defeated by a vote of 9 to 20. The Senate's view, evidently, is that Ferguson had the right to freedom of speech, the right to take his case to the public. In other words, free speech is neither a high crime nor a misdemeanor.

The Senate voted that Ferguson had crossed the line, however, and abused his power, when he did the following:

- Trying to substitute his "will" for the "will" of the Texas Board of Regents in dismissing faculty members;
- Trying to remove Regents without legal authority to remove them, and forcing them to vote as he wished; and
- "remit[ing] a forfeiture of $5,000 for W.P. Allen, who was a surety on a bail bond, and thereby attempt[ing] to control the actions and votes of the said Allen, who was a member of the board of regents."[cccxiii]

(The last, pressuring a member of the board of regents by using the governor's power to impose a $5000 bond forfeiture on him, surely earns an "A" for creativity.) Two-thirds of the Senate (or more) voted in favor of these three abuse-of-power articles of impeachment.

Basically, the Texas Senate concluded that the Texas Constitution established checks and balances between the governor and the U.T. Board of Regents, even though both the Governor and the Regents were part of the Executive Branch. By law, the Governor had the power of appointment, subject to the advice and consent of the Texas Senate. But the governor did not have the power of removal, nor could he make decisions (or even try to make decisions) for the Board of Regents against its will.

[The same checks and balances considerations would come into play when a President tries to dictate to Congress, or the courts, or an independent agency or organization like the Federal Trade Commission or the Post Office, or the Federal Reserve Board, or a special prosecutor or DOJ executing its prosecutorial function.]

Ten of the 23 Ferguson articles of impeachment earned the required two-thirds vote in the Texas Senate: Articles 1, 2, 6, 7, 11, 12, 14, 16, 17 and 19. The votes on seven corruption counts were overwhelming, ranging from 24-7 to 27-4. The votes on three abuse-of-power counts were less one-sided, being 22-8, 22-9 and 21-10.

Historian Cortez A.M. Ewing proposed this epitaph on Ferguson's term as Governor, and the impeachment and conviction that ended it: "politics, as is usually the case in impeachment trials, contributed more than evidence or legal definition in the final decision of the court."[cccxiv] That seems perhaps too kind to Ferguson. At Ferguson's trial, evidence of high crimes and misdemeanors was not in short supply.

The Texas Senate barred Gov. Ferguson from any future "office of honor, trust or profit under the State of Texas."[cccxv] Ferguson had the last laugh, however, although his impeachment and removal certainly slowed him down. Ferguson:

- ran against his successor in 1918 (ignoring the disqualification from office) and lost the primary,
- ran as the American Party candidate for President in 1920 and lost (appearing on the ballot only in Texas, and drawing less than ten percent of the vote there), and
- ran for the U.S. Senate in 1922 and lost in the Democratic Primary runoff.

In 1924, however, Ferguson became the "First Gentleman" of Texas (The very first? Ever? Was it really that hard to find a gentleman in Texas?) by helping his wife to be elected Governor of Texas. Their memorable campaign slogan was "Two Governors for the Price of One," appealing to smart shoppers around the state.

Ferguson actually became the first "First Gentleman" in the history of the United States. Wyoming swore in Nellie Tayloe Ross as the first female governor in American history two weeks before Miriam Ferguson took office in Texas. But Nellie Ross's husband suffered from a serious character flaw that disqualified him from serving as "First Gentleman": he was dead.

Inevitably, since James Ferguson was known as "Pa" Ferguson, Miriam was known as "Ma" Ferguson. She/he/they also won the Texas Governor's race in 1932.

So, to summarize regarding impeachable abuse of power, President Andrew Johnson was impeached and almost convicted for making a Cabinet appointment that was contrary to law. Governor Blagojevich was impeached primarily for corruptly trading official acts for campaign contributions, but also for withholding state aid from a media company while seeking dismissal of staff and more favorable coverage. Governor Ferguson was impeached primarily for corruption, but also for undermining the independence of a separate government institution for the sake of more favorable media coverage. As to abuse of power, in each case, a single "bad act" was the basis for impeachment.

Donald Trump

Trump Fun Fact: Trump's ex-wife, Ivana, says that Trump keeps a book of Adolf Hitler's speeches, *My New Order,* by his bed, and reads it from time to time for inspiration. Impeachment Charge: Official Misconduct (Abuse of Power).

Donald Trump[cccxvi]

When it comes to abuse of power, American elected officials fall into two categories:

1. Donald Trump.
2. Everyone else.

Even with 230 years of American Constitutional experience through which to comb, when it comes to abuse of power, historical analogies fail. In fact, they pale. Which is why Donald Trump belongs in jail. There has never been anyone else in high office in America with the rape-and-pillage, slash-and-burn mentality of Donald Trump.

The thing about Donald Trump and abuse of power is that he *wants* to abuse power. Also, he enjoys it. In fact, he delights in it. Donald Trump has been manipulating, bullying, insulting, cheating and exploiting people throughout his whole adult life. Presidential abuse of power is simply an extension of that, on a grand scale.

If Donald Trump took a multiple-choice test – correction, if Donald Trump could read, and he took a multiple-choice test — and the choices were:

A. Abuse power.
B. Don't abuse power.
C. Covfefe.

…Trump would choose (A), every time. If Trump's limo came to a fork in the road, and the road sign said:

← Don't Abuse Power   Abuse Power →

…Trump would order his chauffeur to turn right. Loudly and pro-fanely. Every time.

Maybe the reason why Trump so consistently blows kisses to dictators is that they get to abuse power all the time, and then, as a bonus, they get to punish journalists, dissidents and political opponents ("Lock her up! Lock her up!") who criticize them for that abuse of power. *Of course,* Trump didn't punish Saudi Arabia for murdering reporter Jamal Khashoggi and then chopping him up into little pieces; Trump would love to do the same to Jim Acosta and Anderson Cooper.

We've never had a President like that before. Sort of like Dennis the Menace, but with nukes.

That's what makes it possible to come up, in less than an hour, with this very incomplete list of examples of Donald Trump's abuse of power:

- Repeatedly demanding that the Attorney General and the FBI investigate and indict Hillary Clinton, evidently for her crime of getting three million more Presidential votes than Trump did.[cccxvii] (And isn't this a hallmark of abuse of power – employing the power of government to try to punish political adversaries simply for being political adversaries, when they've done nothing wrong? Check out the Declaration of Independence.)

- Ordering security clearances for Jared Kushner and Ivanka Trump after, among other things, Jared met with the Russian Ambassador to set up a "back channel" to the Kremlin, sought foreign sources to bail him out of a billion-dollar bad investment, and lied repeatedly about foreign contacts on his application for access to classified material. Trump overturned the decision of the national security staff to deny the application, and then ordered Security Director Carl Kline to refuse to testify to Congress about it.[cccxviii] Trump also revoked the security clearance of former FBI Director John Brennan because Brennan publicly criticized Trump.

- Providing classified information to the Russian Foreign Minister and the Russian Ambassador in the Oval Office. Possibly doing the same thing in meetings with Russian President Vladimir Putin, and then confiscating the notes of Trump's own interpreter in order to cover his tracks. Selectively declassifying the FBI's warrant application on Carter Page, in order to try to support his claim that the Trump-Russia investigation was politically motivated. Tweeting out a classified photo of an Iranian missile launch.[cccxix]

- Pardoning Trump campaign surrogate Joe Arpaio for political reasons,[cccxx] and pardoning Dinesh D'Souza for political reasons.[cccxxi] (This is particularly odd when one considers that Trump has granted clemency to only 21 people so far. Obama granted clemency to 1927 people, George W. Bush 200 and Clinton 459. Trump hasn't even filled the position of DOJ Pardon Attorney yet.[cccxxii]) Trump also dangled pardons in front of Trump-Russia witnesses, and Trump told the Commissioner of Customs and Border Protection that he would pardon him if he went to prison for illegally preventing asylum seekers from entering the United States.[cccxxiii] The Mueller Report specifically pointed to Trump campaign chair Paul Manafort being led to believe that Trump would pardon him, and therefore refusing to cooperate with the investigation.[cccxxiv]

- Burying, mangling, silencing and censoring Government data and analysis on climate change, while deriding climate change as "Fake Science."[cccxxv]

- Banning or attempting to ban Muslims, Mexicans and asylum-seekers from entering the United States, whether or not they had a legal right to do so. (The right to seek asylum is not only reflected in U.S. law, but also in the United Nations Universal Declaration of Human Rights.[cccxxvi]) Declaring a baseless "state of emergency" to try to justify misappropriating earmarked military funds to build a wall on the Mexican border, and then misappropriating those funds – billions of dollars.

- Abusing his power as Commander in Chief to ban transgendered soldiers from the military.

- Declaring war on the media, and misusing the power of the Presidency to try to punish media critics. Trump ordered the Postmaster General to come to the White House "several times" (in meetings omitted from his public schedule), and demanded that she double shipping rates on Amazon packages, because the largest shareholder in Amazon also owns the *Washington Post* (*i.e.,* the "lying, failing" *Washington Post*, as Trump calls it).[cccxxvii] Trump's ally the *National Enquirer,* which agreed to make hush-money payments during the Trump Presidential campaign, also spied on that Amazon shareholder, Jeff Bezos. It threatened to report his extramarital affair and publish a "dick pic" unless Bezos made certain public statements and complied with the *Enquirer's* demands.[cccxxviii] Trump has repeatedly threatened to deprive NBC of its broadcast licenses, specifically because he dislikes NBC's coverage of him.[cccxxix]

The Trump Administration has approved the Sinclair takeover of Tribune Media (Sinclair having run heavily favorable coverage of Trump), while trying to thwart the merger of AT&T and Time Warner (which have not). Trump sought an FBI investigation of the *New York Times* op-ed entitled "I Am Part of the Resistance inside the Trump Administration." Trump threatened a *Time* reporter with a prison sentence for taking a picture of a letter from Kim Jong Un that Trump himself showed to the media.[cccxxx] Trump's Press Secretary deprived CNN reporter Jim Acosta of his White House Press credentials, until a court ordered them restored. The Trump Administration ordered a huge rise in tariffs on Canadian newsprint (for "national security" reasons, no less), which substantially increased the cost of printing newspapers in the United States. The tariffs eventually were reversed by Trump's own appointees to the International Trade Commission.

But the most disturbing Trump abuse of power in the eyes of the public has been Trump's separation of immigrant children from their families, and the imprisonment of those children in cages. If there is any single incident that sums up the utter repulsiveness of the Trump Administration, it is the death of 8-year-old Felipe Gomez Alonzo, who died on Christmas Eve last year, in the custody of the U.S. Customs and Border Protection (CBP), after receiving improper medical treatment from the CBP.

Four days later, Trump tweeted: "Any deaths of children or others at the Border are strictly the fault of the Democrats and their pathetic immigration policies."[cccxxxi] Six migrant children now have died in the custody of the Trump Administration.[cccxxxii] Is kidnapping an impeachable offense? What about negligent homicide?

In the first year of the Trump Administration alone, the American Civil Liberties Union filed more than 100 lawsuits against the Trump Administration for abuse of power, and otherwise acting contrary to law.[cccxxxiii]

Every example of abuse of power, whether large or small, is a violation of Trump's Constitutional oath of office: "I do solemnly swear (or affirm) that I will *faithfully execute* the Office of President of the United States, and will to the best of my Ability, preserve, protect and defend the Constitution of the United States."^{cccxxxiv}

The very areas in which Trump has abused his power, or tried to – investigation, prosecutorial discretion, security clearances, declassification, pardons, licensing, military organization and border security – are precisely the areas where Executive Branch authority is least likely to be checked. When it comes to an issue like healthcare, the President, the Executive Agencies, Congress, the courts and the States all have their say, but when it comes to an issue like pardons, Trump can say, "*L'état, c'est moi.*" ("The Government is me.")^{cccxxxv} We may have a Constitutional system of checks and balances in general, but these types of Presidential abuse of power cannot be checked effectively by judicial review, or legislation, or Congressional oversight, or Senate "advice and consent" on appointments, but *only* by impeachment and removal from office.

Blagojevich and Ferguson attacked the independent media *once;* Trump has attacked it dozens of times – not to mention all of the other abuses of power. When you measure Trump's abuse of power against President Johnson's flouting of the Tenure of Office Act, or Governor Blagojevich's sale of an appointment or pressuring of the media, or Governor Ferguson's pressuring of University of Texas Regents (all of which resulted in impeachment, and all of which were nowhere near as serious), the conclusion is inescapable.

If President Johnson was impeached and almost removed from office for insisting on his choice for Secretary of War, and Governor Blagojevich was impeached and removed from office for trying to benefit from a Senatorial appointment and trying to condition state funds on favorable media coverage, and Governor Ferguson was impeached and removed from office for interfering in University of Texas governance to try to silence his critics, then shouldn't Donald Trump be impeached and removed from office for his severe and relentless abuse of the power of the Presidency?

CHAPTER VI:

CAMPAIGN MISCONDUCT

Several impeachment cases have revolved around the charge that because of misconduct when seeking public office, the official shouldn't (or might not) have held the office in the first place. In the law, this would be called "fraudulent inducement."

For elected officials, this issue arises in election fraud cases. For appointed officials, it has arisen regarding the "job application," *i.e.,* the representations made as a candidate for appointment.

In cases like this, defenders have counter-argued that actions before holding office, even actions to acquire the office, do not qualify as "high crimes or misdemeanors." That argument generally has been rejected, sometimes with scorn. Certainly, the veil of legitimacy that an election or Senate confirmation confers on an official is torn to shreds by any credible charge of fraudulent inducement that did affect, or even could have affected, the outcome.

William Sulzer

Governor of New York. Charges: Campaign Finance Violations and Obstruction of Justice. The New York Assembly voted on Aug. 13, 1913 to impeach Sulzer on eight articles, by a vote of 79 to 35. On Oct. 16, 1913, the Court of Impeachment cleared Sulzer unanimously on five articles, but convicted him (by votes of 39 to 18, twice, and 43 to 14) on three.

William Sulzer – Campaign Misconduct

William Sulzer was elected Governor of New York in 1912. He was sworn into office on January 1, 1913, and impeached and removed from office on October 17, 1913. Notably, he was impeached entirely for his actions *before* he took office.

Sulzer was a remarkably successful elected official. He was hired by the Tammany Hall Democratic political machine in New York City, at the age of 21, as a stump speaker and surrogate campaigner for other candidates, like President Grover Cleveland.[cccxxxvi] Tammany Hall soon found him an elected position in the New York State Assembly, the lower house of the New York Legislature, to which elections take place each year. Sulzer won election five times, from 1890 through 1894. In his fourth year, he was elected Speaker. At age 30, he was the youngest New York Assembly Speaker in history.

In the Assembly, Sulzer never was shy about expressing his loyalty to the Tammany Hall machine. While Speaker, he was quoted as saying that "all legislation came from Tammany Hall and was dictated by that great statesman, Richard Croker," the boss of Tammany Hall.[cccxxxvii]

Sulzer then was elevated to the U.S. House of Representatives, whereupon the leopard changed its spots. For the next 18 years, from 1894 to 1912, Sulzer was no longer a machine politician, but rather an outspoken progressive champion. He rose to be Chairman of the House Committee on Foreign Affairs, where he was a forceful advocate for human rights, national self-determination and peace.

During his time in Congress, Sulzer sought the governorship of New York over and over again, but the Tammany Hall machine delivered the nomination to Democrats it deemed more reliable, and the Republican and Progressive Parties had no interest in nominating a Democrat. Going into the election of 1912, it looked like the Republican and Progressive Parties would split the non-Democratic vote (just as they did in the Presidential election that year). That bode well for the Democratic candidate. Within the Democratic Party, however, reformers threatened to put up a candidate against Tammany Hall's choice, founding the competing "Democracy Party." In order to avoid a split, the Democratic reformers and Tammany Hall agreed on Sulzer as a compromise Democratic candidate. Sulzer defeated the incumbent Democratic Governor, upstate Democrat John Alden Dix, on the third ballot at the New York Democratic Convention.[cccxxxviii]

As expected, the Republican Party and the Progressive Party divided the anti-Democratic vote in November. Sulzer was elected Governor with 41% of the vote, the Republican winning 28% and the Progressive 25%.[cccxxxix] This mirrored the Presidential election in New York, where the Democrat won 42%, the Progressive 27% and the Republican 23%.[cccxl]

After being sworn in, Sulzer allied himself with the Progressive Party and Democratic reformers, for instance by pushing hard for selection of party candidates in primaries rather than conventions controlled by machine politics. Sulzer also refused to populate New York State public works projects with Tammany Hall selections, denying Tammany Hall a very important source of patronage.

Tammany Hall returned the favor by putting the New York Legislature, which it controlled, on lockdown against Sulzer's initiatives. The Speaker of the Assembly was Al Smith, future Governor and Presidential candidate. The President of the New York Senate was Robert F. Wagner, Sr., future four-term U.S. Senator. Sulzer was outmatched.

As soon as Tammany Hall saw which way the wind was blowing in the Sulzer Administration, it ensured that Sulzer became mired in scandal. This was, perhaps, an early example of what Bill Clinton called "the politics of personal destruction." Sulzer was accused of committing perjury in a lawsuit *23 years earlier*. He was accused of involvement in fraudulent companies in Cuba before he was elected Governor.[cccxli] Also, Sulzer was sued for $30,000 ($764,000 in today's money) by Mignon Hopkins (really, that was her name), a cloak model at a department store in Philadelphia (John Wannamaker's, possibly the only time that chain was ever featured in the news section of the newspaper) for Sulzer's breach of a *promise to marry her,* ten years earlier. It would have been difficult for Ms. Mignon to obtain specific performance of that promise, however, because Sulzer had married the prosaically named "Clara" five years earlier. The July 13, 1913 edition of the front page of the *Philadelphia Inquirer* breathlessly reported that "missives burning with love will be introduced when the breach of promise suit … is called for trial." The cover page featured a picture of Miss Mignon, in profile.[cccxlii]

Sulzer's response was less than compelling:

- the lawsuit was "rot: r-o-t," (Sulzer spelled it out for the benefit of his supporters who might have difficulty spelling the word "rot").
- It was all a plot by Tammany Hall to destroy him, because he refused to be their "kind of a Governor."
- Mignon Hopkins had sued him six years earlier on the same grounds, and lost the case.

As this dirt dust devil swirled around Governor Sulzer, the New York State Assembly brought eight articles of impeachment against him. Article I and II alleged that Sulzer had sworn to two false campaign fund disclosures, one on Nov. 5, 1912 (election day) and one on Nov. 13, 1912. Sulzer had reported $5460 in contributions, but he had omitted $8500, from 11 different sources. (It was widely alleged that Sulzer had used the extra money to play the stock market, but that allegation wasn't part of the articles of impeachment. These articles didn't focus on Sulzer's misuse of campaign funds, but rather, his dishonesty in misreporting them.) Article IV alleged that Sulzer had obstructed justice by threatening three witnesses who were to testify before the Joint Legislative Committee established by the Legislature to investigate Sulzer (the Frawley Committee). Specifically, Suzler was charged with "prati[cing] deceit and fraud and us[ing] threats and menaces" against these witnesses.[cccxliii] (Sulzer would be acquitted on the other five articles.)

The question arose as to whether Sulzer could be impeached and convicted for actions he took before he was Governor. Sulzer's lawyers seized on the fact that a New York State statute, the Code of Criminal Procedure, prescribed impeachment for "wilful and corrupt misconduct *in office.*" New York formed a Hamiltonian "Court of Impeachment" including six judges from its highest court and three lower court judges. (Alexander Hamilton thought that judges should be involved in impeachment proceedings.) This Court of Impeachment ruled on legal issues arising in the Sulzer proceedings. They voted 5 to 4 that the limitation in the Code of Criminal Procedure did not prevent the Legislature from acting on impeachment for acts committed before public office.[cccxliv]

IMPEACHMENT INSIGHT—

AS IN THE *SULZER* CASE, IMPEACHMENT CAN BE BASED ON CAMPAIGN-RELATED MISCONDUCT BEFORE TAKING OFFICE.

It would have been very hard to argue that the unreported campaign funds actually determined the outcome of the election (especially if Sulzer did, in fact, blow them on the market). Sulzer had won 650,000 votes; his closest competitor received only 444,000 votes. Every New York Democrat statewide candidate won office that year by similar margins, regardless of what money was spent on their individual campaigns.[cccxlv] The argument against Sulzer was not that "he won only because he cheated." The argument was that he *was* a cheater, and therefore he shouldn't be Governor.

The Court of Impeachment, now including the New York Senate, unanimously found in Sulzer's favor on five of the Sulzer impeachment articles. Sulzer was less fortunate on Articles I, II and IV. The Court of Impeachment voted 39 to 18 to convict Sulzer on Articles I and II, and 43 to 14 to convict Sulzer on Article IV, thus removing him from office. Hence Sulzer was impeached and convicted for campaign finance violations (which preceded his term in office) and for obstruction of justice in his own impeachment investigation.

Sulzer wasn't done with public life. *Eighteen days* after he was removed from office, he was elected to the New York State Assembly, as a Progressive Party candidate. In the following year, in 1914, he ran for Governor again. His path to the Progressive Party nomination was blocked by the Progressive Party's 1912 Presidential nominee, former President Teddy Roosevelt, who wrote to party members that "the trouble with Sulzer is that he does not tell the truth."[cccxlvi] Still seeking to thwart the candidacy of Gov. Martin Glynn, the Democratic Party *apparatchik* who had succeeded him, Suzler won the American Party and the Prohibition Party nominations for Governor. Although it can't be said that Suzler alone caused Glynn's defeat, Suzler did have an impact. The Republican nominee won 48% of the vote, Democrat Glynn won 37%, and Suzler won 9%.[cccxlvii] Two years later, the American Party nominated Sulzer for President, but he declined the nomination.[cccxlviii] [The American Party seems to have had a thing for impeached ex-Governors; in the following Presidential election, it nominated former Gov. Ferguson (D-TX) after his impeachment.]

In 1917, five years after he was impeached, Sulzer returned to his roots, as a stump speaker surrogate campaigner for reformist New York Mayor John Purroy Mitchel. Mitchel paid Sulzer $5000, demonstrating that reform does not come cheaply.[cccxlix]

Sulzer wasn't the only public official who faced impeachment for campaign irregularities. Governor Eric Greitens (R-MO) was indicted for taking a contribution list from a charity he founded, to use it for fundraising for his campaign. Greitens faced impeachment, but he resigned as part of his criminal plea agreement. Governor Rob Blagojevich (D-IL) was impeached and removed from office for trading official acts for campaign contributions. And then there was that Watergate thing.....

Thomas Porteous

Federal Judge. Charges: Kickbacks, Gifts from Bail Bondsmen, Misrepresentation in Bankruptcy Proceeding and Judicial Application. On March 11, 2010, the U.S. House voted unanimously in favor of the four articles of impeachment (412, 410, 416 and 423 to 0). On Dec. 8, 2010, the Senate convicted Porteous on all four counts (96 to 0, 69 to 27, 88 to 8, 90 to 6).

Thomas Porteous – Lying to Get the Job, etc.

Thomas Porteous, Jr., was elected a state judge in Louisiana in 1984, and he was appointed a federal judge in 1994. In 1999, five years after his federal appointment, the FBI and the Department of Justice (DOJ) opened an investigation of him. By that time, the statute of limitations already had run on crimes that Porteous was suspected to have committed as a state judge. Nevertheless, DOJ continued to investigate Porteous for eight years, through 2007, and then DOJ submitted a formal complaint of judicial misconduct to the Chief Judge of the Fifth Circuit, the federal circuit in which Porteous served. (Such complaints have no limitations period.)

The Fifth Circuit's Special Investigative Committee reviewed DOJ's allegations and issued a rather foggy report, concluding that Porteous "might" have committed impeachable offenses. In Sept. 2008, the Fifth Circuit's Judicial Council ordered that Porteous could no long employ any staff, and would not be assigned any new cases, for two years. The Judicial Conference, a panel of federal judges from around the country, asked the U.S. House to consider impeaching Porteous.[cccl]

And what had Porteous done? According to the Articles of Impeachment, when Porteous had been a state court judge, *two decades earlier,* he had had the power to appoint a "curator" (apparently, a guardian) in certain cases. In hundreds of cases over Porteous's ten years as a state judge, he had appointed the law firm Amato & Creely, P.C., to serve as curator. This had generated around $40,000 in fees for the law firm, which had kicked back around $20,000 to Porteous.[cccli]

The only connection drawn to Porteous's service as a federal judge was that in a 1993 case, *fifteen years earlier, Lifemark Hospitals of La., Inc. v. Liljeberg Enterprises, Inc.,* Civ. Action No. 93-1794 (E.D. La.), Amato & Creely, P.C. represented one of the parties, Porteous refused to recuse himself, and Porteous had ruled in favor of the party represented by Amato & Creely, P.C. (Article I).[ccclii]

Separately, and again largely as a state judge, Porteous had aided a brother-and-sister bail bonds company (the Marcottes) with bond rulings, expunging two convictions, and "us[ing] the power and prestige of his office to assist the Marcottes in forming relationships with State judicial officers," in exchange for meals, trips, home repairs and car repairs for Porteous (Article II). [cccliii] This had happened from around 1990 through "approximately 2004," the focus clearly being on the period when Porteous had been a state judge. "Judge Porteous's conduct while a Federal judge [*i.e.,* for the previous 14 years] did not involve taking judicial actions to benefit the Marcottes...."[cccliv]

Porteous also "committed numerous acts of misconduct in the course of his personal bankruptcy," in 2001, *eight years earlier.* The misconduct involved misrepresenting assets and liabilities. The House Judiciary Committee characterized this as "dishonesty under oath in arguably personal and/or financial matters." (Article III)[ccclv] Of course, this was conduct outside the Porteous courtroom; Porteous was a party in his bankruptcy case, not the judge. And FWIW, the year of the Porteous bankruptcy filing, 2001, set an all-time national high in bankruptcy filings, at 1.5 million.[ccclvi]

The House also charged Porteous with committing "fraud" on his Senate Judiciary Committee Questionnaire, *fifteen years earlier,* because he was asked the general question of whether there was anything in his past that could be used to blackmail or coerce him, and he answered "no," notwithstanding his kickbacks from Amato & Creely, P.C., and accepting "gifts" from the Marcottes (Article IV).[ccclvii]

In essence, Articles I & II charged Porteous with the crime, and Article IV charged him with the cover-up. To be fair, however, expecting a federal judicial nominee to confess to kickbacks and bribery on his job application is expecting a lot; when has that ever happened? In any case, Article IV of the Porteous Articles of Impeachment establishes a clear precedent that a federal official's misrepresentation while seeking public office is an impeachable offense. Porteous's misrepresentation on his Senate Judiciary Committee Questionnaire was analogous to Sulzer's failure to disclose campaign contributions – both are cases of obtaining a position through false pretenses.

The Judiciary Committee Report makes it clear beyond any reasonable doubt that Porteous had taken a lot of "gifts" from a lot of people.[ccclviii] Porteous, unlike many other federal officials facing impeachment, didn't try to offer any innocent explanation. Instead, he engaged in highly obstructive and utterly unsuccessful litigation against House investigators, which did not endear him to them.[ccclix]

But by the time that the U.S. House voted on the Porteous Articles of Impeachment, the misconduct at issue had taken place:

- Between 16 and 26 years earlier (the kickbacks, and Marcotte rulings);
- 15 years earlier (failure to recuse himself);
- More than 6 years earlier (making introductions for Marcotte business development);
- 8 years earlier (the bankruptcy filings); and
- 16 years earlier (answers to the Senate questionnaire).

Clearly, Porteous was not likely to be facing any criminal charges over this; the statute of limitations for most federal crimes is five years. The

Porteous case established the precedent that *there is no statute of limitations for an impeachable offense.*

Explaining why the House was relying heavily on conduct before Porteous had risen to the federal court, and conduct outside the courtroom, the House Judiciary Committee quoted liberally from the testimony of Constitutional scholars who had testified against Porteous, establishing what might be called the "Who Cares?" Principle:

IMPEACHMENT INSIGHT—

AS IN THE *PORTEOUS* CASE, THERE IS NO STATUTE OF LIMITATIONS FOR AN IMPEACHABLE OFFENSE.

"*[t]he critical questions are whether Judge Porteous committed such misconduct and whether such misconduct demonstrates the lack of integrity and judgment that are required in order for him to continue to function' as a Federal judge. The reason for considering pre-Federal bench conduct in appropriate circumstances is evident from very basic examples. Take the situation where the individual committed a truly heinous crime prior to becoming a Federal judge: 'Say, for instance, that the offence was murder—it is as serious a crime as any we have, and its commission by a judge completely undermines both his integrity and the moral authority he must have in order to function as a Federal judge. The timing of the murder is of less concern that the fact of it; this is the kind of behavior that is completely incompatible with the public trust invested in officials who are sufficiently high-ranking to be subject to the impeachment process.' However, the crime or misconduct need not be comparable to homicide to justify impeachment. As another professor testified: 'Let's take bribery. Imagine now a person who bribes his very way into office. By definition, the bribery here occurs prior to the commencement of office holding. But surely that fact can't immunize the briber from impeachment and removal. Had the bribery not occurred, the person never would have been an officer in the first place.... Who cares if it occurred before?' ... Now what is true of bribery is equally true of fraud. A person who procures a judgeship by lying to the President and lying to the Senate has wrongly obtained his office by fraud and is surely removable via impeachment for that fraud.*"[ccclx]

That is certainly how the House saw it. On March 11, 2010, the House voted unanimously in favor of the four Porteous Articles of Impeachment, by votes of 412 to 0, 410 to 0, 416 to 0 and 423 to 0.[ccclxi] The Senate vote was less numbingly uniform, but still overwhelming. On Article I, regarding the kickbacks, the vote was unanimous: 96 to 0. On Article II, regarding the bail bond gifts, the vote was 69 to 27. On Article III, regarding the bankruptcy proceedings, the vote was 88 to 8. On Article IV, Porteous lying on his judicial job application, the vote was 90 to 6. Clearly the Senate, like the House, was not overly concerned with the long period of time that has passed since the misconduct at issue, nor the fact that most of the charges concerned misconduct before Porteous took federal office, nor the fact that some of it (like his personal bankruptcy filing) had nothing to do with his conduct as a judge.

They just didn't think that Thomas Porteous should be a federal judge anymore. He lacked the "integrity and the moral authority he [had to] have in order to function as a Federal judge," and the evidence against him was "completely incompatible with the public trust invested in officials who are sufficiently high-ranking to be subject to the impeachment process."

Now ask yourself: how much "integrity" and "moral authority" does Donald Trump have?

Donald Trump

Trump Fun Fact: In 1990, *Spy* magazine sent checks for 13 cents to 13 rich people. Only two cashed them: an arm's dealer, and Trump, whom *Spy* called a "demibillionaire casino operator and adulterer." Impeachment charge: Campaign Finance Violations.

"Individual-1"[ccclxii]

Karen McDougal, a 1997 Playboy centerfold model, had an alleged affair with Trump in 2006-07,[ccclxiii] and Stormy Daniels, an adult-film actress, had an alleged affair with Trump in 2006[ccclxiv]. Neither one claims that the relationship was non-consensual, but both were paid "hush money" during the Trump Presidential campaign ($150,000 to McDougal, $130,000 to Daniels) to avoid their discussing what happened.

The payments were arranged by Michael Cohen, Trump's personal attorney. This led to Michael Cohen's indictment for campaign finance violations, in which Trump is named as "Individual-1."[ccclxv]

Specifically, Cohen "was able to arrange for the purchase of two stories [the Trump-Daniels and Trump-McDougal relationships] so as to suppress them and prevent them from influencing the election." For the $130,000 hush payment, the Trump Organization "reimbursed" Cohen $420,000. This was characterized as both an illegal corporate campaign contribution, and a contribution in excess of legal limits.[ccclxvi]

Cohen stated in his Sentencing Memorandum (where Trump is referred to as 'Client-1') that Cohen had made the hush money payments "in coordination with and at the direction of" Trump.[ccclxvii]

> *Michael made a payment to the lawyer for Woman-2 in coordination with and at the direction of Client-1, and others within the Company. Michael was assured by Client-1 that he would be repaid for his advance of funds, and, later, again with the approval of Client-1, agreed to an arrangement conceived by an executive of the Company whereby Michael would receive reimbursement during 2017 in the form of monthly payments by the Company for invoiced legal fees. With respect to the conduct charged in these Counts, Michael kept his client contemporaneously informed and acted on his client's instructions.... [A]s personal counsel to Client-1, Michael felt obligated to assist Client-1, on Client-1's instruction, to attempt to prevent Woman-1 and Woman-2 from disseminating narratives that would adversely affect the Campaign and cause personal embarrassment to Client-1 and his family.*[ccclxviii]

If these payments were felonies for Cohen then, obviously, they were felonies for "Individual-1" as well. Trump, like President Nixon, is an unindicted co-conspirator.[ccclxix]

William Sulzer and Thomas Porteous were impeached, convicted and removed from office for dishonest misconduct when they were seeking high office. Should Donald Trump be impeached, convicted and removed from office for the same reason?

$\mathcal{P}$ART III –

<u>MISDEMEANORS</u>

CHAPTER VII:
CONDUCT UNBECOMING

The Constitution authorizes impeachment for treason, bribery, high crimes and misdemeanors. A number of public officials have been impeached and convicted for misconduct that was not treason, not bribery, and perhaps a crime, but difficult to characterize as a 'high' crime — just as the Three Stooges are perhaps comedy, but difficult to characterize as 'high' comedy. (Deadpool? High concept, but low comedy.) These officials were tried, often explicitly, under the provision in the Constitution authorizing impeachment for "Misdemeanors." So, then, what is a "misdemeanor," in the Constitutional sense?

In an English impeachment case dating from the 1300's, breaking a promise to Parliament was deemed to be an impeachable "misdemeanor." It was not a crime.[ccclxx] Similarly, Founder James Iredell said that under the Constitution, providing misinformation to the Senate would be an impeachable offense.[ccclxxi] James Madison said that the President could be impeached for "wantonly" dismissing "meritorious" members of the Cabinet.[ccclxxii]

In modern usage, the term "misdemeanor" means a crime punishable by less than one year in prison. Some modern misdemeanors are, in fact, impeachable offenses. For instance, disorderly intoxication is a misdemeanor,[ccclxxiii] and an official's disorderly intoxication on the job has resulted in impeachment (Judges Pickering and Delahay, discussed below).

But as the Nixon-era House Judiciary Committee observed, "the phrase 'high Crimes and Misdemeanors' was confined [in English law] to parliamentary impeachments; it had no roots in the ordinary criminal law, and the particular allegations of misconduct under that heading were not necessarily limited to common law or statutory derelictions or crimes."[ccclxxiv] Generally, therefore, impeachment proceedings call upon the traditional usage of the term "misdemeanor": "mis-" meaning bad and "-demeanor" meaning your comportment, or your behavior as seen by others. "Misdemeanor" = bad behavior. In that light, the term "Misdemeanors" in Article II of the U.S. Constitution is the flip side of the term "good behaviour" as used in Article III, Section 1, delimiting the service of federal judges. (Judges "shall hold their Offices during good Behaviour.") Engage in "good behaviour" and you stay in; indulge in any "mis-" in your "-demeanor" and you're out.

An impeachment charge of misdemeanors against an official often coincides with a general sense that he or she[ccclxxv] is unfit for office. The U.S. Constitution, however, requires a trial of specific acts of misconduct, not a weighing of one's spirit or a judgment of one's soul. So the test is something like the military one: "conduct unbecoming an officer."[ccclxxvi]

John Pickering

Federal Judge. Charge: Conduct Unbecoming a Judge. On March 2, 1803, the U.S. House voted 45 to 8 in favor of four articles of impeachment. On Jan. 4, 1804, the Senate convicted Pickering on all counts, by a vote of 19 to 7.

John Pickering

The Pickering situation is well-summarized by this commenting legal scholar:

"The unfortunate old man had been an insane drunkard for some time and was clearly unable to perform his duties as a federal judge."[cclxxvii]

What was wrong with Pickering? This was how his condition was described by a sympathetic observer: "[A]t the turn of the century, the sixty-three-year-old jurist, who had for some time been increasingly hypochondriac and subject to such eccentricities as an unreasoning fear of water travel, showed evidence of definite mental derangement...a helpless lunatic...a psychopath who was afraid of ferries!"[ccclxxviii] (This, from a friend, gives you an idea of what Pickering's critics might say.) The practical problem with this, for a federal judge in New Hampshire in 1800, was that you had to travel around your district to hear cases, and New Hampshire then had a river or two. Since Pickering wouldn't travel, on April 25, 1801, with the acknowledgement that Pickering had been "incapacitated," the U.S. Court of Appeals for the First Circuit appointed Jeremiah Smith to relieve Pickering of his case load.[ccclxxix] But a year later, on April 29, 1802, the Judiciary Act of 1802 wiped out the circuit courts, eliminating that finesse for dealing with Pickering's immobility.

There followed the trial of *The Eliza,* a ship owned by a Pickering political ally that allegedly was offloaded without going through customs, and paying proper duties:

"On the opening day of the trial, Pickering came to the courtroom thoroughly intoxicated. He staggered to the bench and ordered the court to open; then, feeling lonely, commanded the Republican deputy-marshal to sit beside him. That startled officer demurred, whereupon Pickering cursed him roundly and frightened him into hasty compliance. At this moment, a young lawyer named John Wentworth, who had been educated in England, entered the bar and Pickering, with the drunken notion that the [English] Inns of Court might throw some direct light on the case, demanded his assistance on the bench. Wentworth refused; the judge started down to cane him, but, seeing a former British naval officer among the spectators, decided that he [the naval officer] would be an acceptable substitute for the position at his left hand. Thus fortified against Jacobins, Pickering roared, "Now damn them, we will fight them," and ordered the parties to proceed.

The unctuous district attorney, John Samuel Sherburne, reminded Pickering that the libels [charges] had not been read; the judge replied that he had heard enough about the damned libels and would decide the case in four minutes. Livermore, seeing that no trial could be held under these conditions, obtained Sherburne's consent to a motion for postponement. Judge Pickering instantly brightened. "My dear, I will give you all eternity," he said to the Federalist lawyer, and ordered the trial postponed until the next day, remarking that he would then be sober.

Unfortunately, he was not. When the court reconvened, Pickering was even more inebriated. After hearing Livermore's case and a few minutes of an argument between the attorneys as to the competence of Sherburne's witnesses, Pickering suddenly decreed restoration of property to the claimant [i.e., Pickering's ally].

"We will not sit here to eternity to decide on such damn'd paltry matters," he declared.

Sherburne remonstrated and begged that his witnesses be heard.

"Very well," said Pickering amiably. "We will hear everything – swear every damn scoundrel that can be produced – but if we sit here four thousand years[,] the ship will still be restored."

A few minutes later, however, he shut off the witnesses and again ordered the case dismissed. Sherburne protested that this decision would injure the revenue [i.e., the duties collected by the government at the port].

"Damn the revenue," shouted Pickering. "I get but a thousand dollars of it."[ccclxxx]

Pickering then summarily denied an appeal.

Witnesses in the courtroom submitted affidavits of the proceedings, ascribing Pickering's conduct to habitual drunkenness. The U.S. House of Representatives voted 45 to 8 to impeach Pickering.[ccclxxxi]

And that should have been the end of it, right? But anyone who thinks that we live in an era of unprecedented political party pugilism should take a look at how matters stood in 18-ought-4.[ccclxxxii] Which grasshopper lies heavier, Mitch McConnell's refusal to provide advice or consent on President Obama's Supreme Court pick Merrick Garland, or the Federalists' creation of an entire judicial tier, the circuit judges, who lorded it over on all the existing district judges? The 67 impotent, feckless – no, feck-free — attempts by the GOP to repeal Obamacare, or the guillotine beheading of the Federalists' Judiciary Act of 1801 by the Democratic-Republicans' Judiciary Act of 1802? (Guillotines being so popular at that time.)

In fact, the strident and emphatic talking points of Demopublican talking heads today are little or nothing, when measured against the endless whinery in 1804 over the obvious need to repeal and replace Pickering, that cartoon version of a judge. Whine #1: "The Democratic-Republicans, not the Federalists, will choose his replacement." Yes, and so it goes. Whine #2: "The judge cannot be tried in absentia." But imagine the outraged cries if a writ of *capias ad respondendum* had been issued, and the poor fool dragged in shackles on the fourteen-day ride from New Hampshire to Our Nation's Capital, river crossings included. Whine #3: "The judge has no lawyer at the trial." Yes, but one magically appeared at trial for *his son,* to make all of the arguments that a lawyer for Pickering would have made.

And oh!, the gnashing of teeth, the clutching of pearls and the rending of garments, the consternation and the indignation over a comment made *in jest* by a Pickering critic — that a true friend of Pickering would have forged Pickering's signature on a resignation letter. Oh, the horror! The horror! (as Joseph Conrad's fictional Col. Kurtz would say a century later, or actually as he wouldn't say, since Kurtz was fictitious).

Pickering's critics in the House of Representatives laid out four straightforward articles of impeachment against Pickering. The first simply alleged that Pickering had decided the *Eliza* case incorrectly, "contrary to his trust and duty as judge of the said district court, against the laws of the United States, and to his manifest injury of their revenue." The second alleged that Pickering had refused to hear the testimony offered by the government attorney, "contrary to his trust and duty as judge of the said district court, against the laws of the United States, and to his manifest injury of their revenue." The third alleged that Pickering had refused to allow an appeal from his decision, "disregarding the authority of the laws, and wickedly meaning and intending to injure the revenues of the United States, and thereby to impair their public credit … contrary to his trust and duty as judge of the said district court, against the laws of the United States, to the great injury of the public revenue, and in violation of the solemn oath which he had taken to administer equal and impartial justice." The fourth article alleged "for the due, faithful, and impartial administration of justice, temperance and sobriety are essential qualities in the character of a judge, yet the said John Pickering, being a man of loose morals and intemperate habits," appeared in court on Nov. 11 & 12,

1802 "in a state of total intoxication, produced by the free and intemperate use of inebriating liquors, and did then and there frequently, in a most prophane [sic] and indecent manner, invoke the name of the Supreme Being, to the evil example of all good citizens of the United States; and was then and there guilty of other high misdemeanors, disgraceful to his own character as a judge and degrading to the honor and dignity of the United States."[ccclxxxiii] In other words, Judge Pickering had had not just one very bad day in court, but two very bad days in court. And as for Pickering's "free and intemperate use of inebriating liquors," one doubts that the liquor was free.

Given the open warfare between the Federalists and the Democratic-Republicans at the time, the Democratic-Republican move to impeach Pickering meant that Federalist Pickering had his staunch Federalist defenders. They took a very extreme approach: they argued that Pickering should remain on the federal bench because he was nuts. (This calls to mind the gentleman who arrived at immigration in Australia and noted that the immigration form asked whether he had ever committed a felony. "Is that still required?" he asked.) As one observer later put it: "He [Pickering] was charged with habitual drunkenness, although his friends claimed that he was insane [instead]."[ccclxxxiv] (With friends like that ... .) Pickering's own son submitted a petition declaring Pickering insane, as did three doctors. To prove this point, Pickering's court clerk testified that he had seen Pickering sober and, at the same time, demented. Other witnesses confused this "issue" even further by testifying that abuse of alcohol had made Pickering crazy. A Senator who had previously served as a judge with Pickering testified that Pickering had become a drunkard only after he was elevated to the federal bench – being a judge drove him to drink.[ccclxxxv]

What was the point of Pickering's allies tagging him with mental infirmity? William Plumer, U.S. Senator from Pickering's State of New Hampshire and, like Pickering, a Federalist, maintained that insanity is not a ground for impeachment. Plumer also argued in Pickering's defense that Pickering's insanity had made him a drunk, not *vice versa*. In fact, a motion was made to *stay* the impeachment trial, and let Pickering return to duty as a federal judge, because Pickering "for some time before, and ever since, has been, and still is, insane, his mind wholly deranged, deprived of the exercise of judgment and the faculties of reason; and as such ... not amenable for his actions to any judicial tribunal," including the Senate. (These were Pickering's supporters, mind you, praising Pickering with what they thought were faint damns.) Perhaps the only conceivable defense of Pickering that was never asserted was the Brett Kavanaugh defense: "I like beer."

Senator Logan of Pennsylvania betrayed an unusual degree of sanity himself when he observed: "if the Judge is insane… he is incapable of discharging the duties of a Judge… & a complaint being made to us, it is our duty to remove him."[ccclxxxvi] John Quincy Adams recounted in his memoirs that "Mr. Jackson was for hearing none of these pretenses [sic] of insanity; because they might prevent us from getting rid of the man."[ccclxxxvii] President Thomas Jefferson concurred that sanity seemed to be sort of a baseline requirement for being a federal judge. Jefferson said: "If the facts of his denying an appeal & of his intoxication, as stated in the impeachment[,] are proven, that will be sufficient cause of removal without further enquiry."[ccclxxxviii]

Following Jefferson's lead, 19 Republican Senators found Pickering guilty on all four articles of impeachment "as charged." (This included both Senators John Smith, i.e., John Smith of New York and John Smith of Ohio. Senator Israel Smith of Vermont provided the third and unanimous Smith vote for Pickering's conviction. There were no Senator Joneses at the time.) Seven Federalist Senators found him innocent. Pickering then was removed from office by a separate vote of 20 to 6.

When the choices are just yea, nay or present, it's difficult to do anything truly interesting with your ballot, but every once in a while, someone earns an Academy Award in voting. The Academy Award for Most Interesting Votes of 1804 goes to Senator Wells of Delaware, the only Federalist Senator from outside New England. Wells voted that Pickering was not guilty on any charge, but that he should be removed from office anyway.[ccclxxxix]

The impeachment and conviction of John Pickering provides an important perspective on impeachment — directly from Thomas Jefferson, a Founding Parent. Pickering what not guilty of any high crime or any low crime, and Pickering was guilty of a misdemeanor only in the sense that, for sure, his demeanor was amiss. Nevertheless, President Jefferson made it quite clear that Pickering could be, and should be, impeached and removed from office, as long as Pickering's misconduct was proven. Or, to put it as scholar Lynn Turner did, "the wise creators of our Constitution would not deliberately have subjected their descendants to the monstrous misgovernment of courts presided over by irremovable lunatics."[cccxc] (Nor monstrous misgovernment by a lunatic President, *a fortiori*.)

John Quincy Adams, a subsequent President and the offspring of a Founding Parent, was queasy about this, though:

"On the impeachment of Mr. Pickering there are two remarks which have impressed themselves on my mind with peculiar force – the subserviency of the Senate, even when acting as a Judicial Court, to a few leading members of the House of Representatives, and the principle assumed, though not yet openly avowed, that by the tenure of good behavior is meant an active, continual, and unerring execution of office. So that insanity, sickness, any trivial error of conduct by a Judge, must be construed into misdemeanors, punishable by impeachment."

Mark Delahay

Federal Judge. Charge: Conduct Unbecoming a Judge. On Feb. 28, 1873, the U.S. House of Representatives voted "without division" in favor of impeachment. Delahay resigned, avoiding a Senate trial.

Mark Delahay

On March 19, 1872, the U.S. House of Representatives opened an investigation into the conduct of Mark Delahay, a federal judge in Kansas. After an investigation, on Feb. 28, 1873, Delahay was unanimously impeached by the House for "improper personal habits." As Rep. Ben Butler explained about Delahay in the official proceedings against Delahay:

"The most grievous charge, and that which is beyond all question, was that his personal habits unfitted him for the judicial office; that he was intoxicated off the bench as well as on the bench. This question has also been decided by precedent. That was the exact charge against Judge Pickering, of New Hampshire, who, with one exception, is the only judge who has been impeached."[ccxci]

Butler then read testimony showing that the judge had sentenced prisoners when intoxicated, "to the great detriment of judicial dignity." Robert Crozier, a Senator from Delahay's home state, had testified: "I am compelled to say that Judge Delahay frequently becomes inebriated. I have seen him in that condition very frequently off the bench, and several times on it."[ccxcii]

There also was concern that Delahay was corrupt, since the House had taken testimony that the U.S. Treasury had not received any court forfeitures from Delahay's district of Kansas since 1860. The House decided to proceed on the basis of intoxication alone, however.[ccxciii] Rather than face a trial in the Senate, Delahay resigned.

Another federal judge more recently left the bench because of substance abuse, but resigned before he could be impeached. In 2008, Jack Camp, 67 years old and married, was charged for purchasing cocaine, marijuana, oxycodone and hydrocodone and then offering it to an exotic dancer who happened to be an undercover FBI agent. He was indicted on five charges, pled guilty to three, and retired as a federal judge as part of his plea agreement. The charges did not involve any misconduct on the bench. Camp was sentenced to 30 days in prison.[ccxciv]

Note that in the cases of both Pickering and Delahay, unlike Camp, neither one committed a crime of any sort. Consuming alcoholic beverages was not a crime in New Hampshire in 1802, nor in Kansas in 1873. In 1830, the average American consumed more than seven gallons of pure alcohol each year, morning, noon and night. (That's equivalent to five bottles of wine each week. Today, average consumption is two gallons, the equivalent of 1½ bottles each week.)[ccxcv] Being an "insane drunkard" was perfectly legal for both Pickering and Delahay – just a "misdemeanor" incompatible with the responsibilities of federal office.

Donald Trump

Trump Fun Fact: When Trump's Castle Casino in Atlantic City was about to miss a bond payment in 1990, Trump's father sent his lawyer to the rescue with a $3,350,000 cashier's check to buy casino chips, which were never used to place bets. This illegal loan resulted in a $60,000 fine. The casino went bankrupt a year later, anyway. Impeachment Charges: Conduct Unbecoming the Office.

Donald Trump [cccxcvi]

Donald Trump is not an alcoholic. His older brother, Fred Trump, Jr., was an alcoholic, and Fred died at the age of 43. Donald Trump says that, as a result of that, he does not drink alcoholic beverages. Trump may have many flaws, but alcoholism does not appear to be one of them.

However . . . .

Performers Tom Arnold and Noel Casler have reported witnessing Donald Trump snort Adderall on the set of the TV show _Celebrity Apprentice_. "He's a speed freak. He crushes up his Adderall and he sniffs it, because he can't read, so he gets really nervous when he has to read cue cards . . . . So he gets nervous and he crushes up these pills, and that's why he's sniffing when you see him in debates and when you see him reading," said Casler. (Casler worked for Trump's show _Celebrity Apprentice_ for six years.) [cccxcvii] Progressive Blogger Howie Klein has reported that there are medical records indicating the source of Trump's Adderall: a Florida cosmetic doctor who prescribed it for Trump.[cccxcviii]

Adderall is a drug that combines four amphetamines. It is used to treat attention deficit disorder. Addiction is a serious risk. Side effects of Adderall include delusions, megalomania, paranoia, mood swings and psychosis.[cccxcix] Adderall is prescribed in the form of a pill; snorting it in order to have it take effect more quickly is dangerous.[cd]

It should be noted that Adderall is a controlled substance. Doctors are not allowed to send prescriptions for it electronically; there has to be a paper trail. Patients who fill prescriptions for it have to provide identification. Prescription records must be kept for five years.[cdi] There probably is no practical way for the President of the United States to obtain a regular supply of Adderall unless it is being prescribed for him or a family member. Therefore, it should be relatively easy to investigate this allegation and determine whether or not it is true.

If Trump is illegal abusing an addictive drug, should he be impeached and removed from office? The Pickering and Delahay precedents indicate that the answer is "yes." Frankly, the notion that the person who controls our nuclear arsenal might be a "speed freak," subject to delusions and psychosis, is far more disturbing than anything that Pickering and Delahay could possibly have perpetrated on their worst days in office.

Moreover, the question on impeachment is not whether Trump shares the specific condition (alcoholism) that bedeviled Pickering and Delahay, but whether Trump exhibits the same kind of misconduct in office that they did. Here are some of the indicators of alcohol abuse and substance abuse, according to the professionals:

- Emotional or mental crises;
- Dishonesty, deceit or denial;
- Emotional outbursts;
- Unexplained absences;
- Extramarital affairs;
- Observable decline in emotional or mental health;
- Inability to focus mentally;
- Slurred speech;

- Face flushed or bloated;
- Runny nose and constant sniffling;
- Unsteady gait;
- Embarrassing social behavior;
- Disorganized schedule;
- Unpredictable workplace behavior;
- Sporadic punctuality; and
- Defensive if questioned or confronted about job performance or conduct.[cdii]

Do any of these, any of them at all, ring a bell?

On the more general subject of whether Donald Trump is guilty of conduct unbecoming a President, that subject cannot be covered in any single missive, but only, perhaps, in a 12-volume set. The pathological lies, the insults, the bullying, the incessant factual errors, the terminal narcissism, the bigotry, the gross incompetence, the pettiness, the attention deficit (treated or untreated), the buffoonery, the callousness (tossing paper towels at hurricane victims!!!), the egomaniacal sociopathy, they all shriek for themselves. I wasn't alive at the time to witness it myself, but I sincerely doubt that Judge Pickering or Judge Delahay was any worse.

If John Pickering and Mark Delahay were impeached and removed from office because of their conduct unbecoming their office, then if Donald Trump exhibits conduct unbecoming his office, shouldn't he be impeached and removed from office?

CHAPTER VIII:

SEXUAL MISCONDUCT

Eric Greitens

Governor of Missouri. Charge: Sexual Abuse (before office). In May 2018, the Missouri Legislature issued a report on Greitens' misconduct, and called itself into special session to impeach Greitens. Greitens resigned, effective on June 1, 2018, as part of a plea agreement.

Eric Greitens[cdiii]

Eric Greitens (R-MO), Governor of Missouri, resigned in May 2018 after the Missouri Legislature called itself into session to impeach him. He had been indicted by local prosecutors twice: once for allegedly blackmailing an ex-girlfriend with a nude photo of her that he had taken on his cell phone, and once for allegedly taking a contribution list from a charity he founded to use it for fundraising for his campaign. In both cases, the alleged misconduct occurred before he took office.

Greitens ran for Governor in 2016. He did not report a $2 million anonymous campaign contribution to his primary, the largest in the history of Missouri, until after the election. That was not an impeachable offense, however; in fact, it wasn't an offense at all. Greitens wasn't required to report it until after the election. In the strange world that we live in, that was perfectly legal.

In 2007, Greitens started a nonprofit group he called "The Mission Continues," which helps veterans volunteer for community service. In October 2016, AP reported that Greitens took e-mail and donor lists from "The Mission Continues" and used them in his campaign. Greitens first denied it, then admitted it, but only after the election. On May 14, 2018, Greitens was charged with a felony, "tampering with a computer," for taking the lists.

On January 10, 2018, the CBS station in St. Louis reported that Greitens had had extramarital encounters in 2015 (*i.e.,* during his gubernatorial campaign, and while his wife was pregnant) with his hair stylist. Greitens appears to have intended to engage with the hair stylist in what might politely be described as S&M for beginners, but he neglected to inform her of that. Since we are hoping for a PG rating for this book, we will not enumerate the 50-Shades-of-Greitens, icky particulars. Of legal consequence, however, is that Greitens allegedly took pictures of the hair stylist *au naturel,* and he then told her that if she talked about the affair to anyone, he would disseminate the picture, no pun intended. Specifically, the hair stylist testified that Greitens said this to her:

"You're not going to mention my name. Don't even mention my name to anybody at all, because if you do, I'm going to take these pictures, and I'm going to put them everywhere I can. They are going to be everywhere, and then everyone will know what a little whore you are."[cdiv]

Notably, Greitens issued this threat in Missouri, the "Show Me" State.

Further tawdry, coercive events ensued between Greitens and the hair stylist. "Witness 3," evidently the hair stylist's husband, described her experience as her being "half-raped and blackmailed," and she agreed with that characterization.[cdv]

On Jan. 22, 2018, at a news conference, Greitens declared the encounters a private matter, denied any wrongdoing, and added that he was "grateful to God for His forgiveness."[cdvi] (The media was unable to confirm this forgiveness; God declined to comment.) Someone, a very generous "unidentified third-party," gave the hair stylist $15,000 – not for hush money, but rather, as she explained, "to cover lawyer fees and all of the things that were about to happen to me financially because of the fallout."[cdvii] (It would have been poetic injustice if this money came from the same good Samaritan who gave the Greitens campaign $2 million, but we'll never know.) On Feb. 22, 2018, Greitens was charged with a felony: invasion of privacy. On April 11, 2018, the Missouri House released a detailed report on *L'Affaire Greitens.*

In Greitens's case, the Missouri Legislature was rather less forgiving than God. It called itself into session, to consider impeachment.

While this was happening, prosecutors dismissed the invasion of privacy charge against Greitens at the last possible moment – in the midst of jury selection —*because investigators could not find the photo.* The second charge, computer tampering, was dismissed in exchange for Greitens's resignation effective on June 1, 2018, as the Missouri House was considering impeachment.[cdviii]

The Missouri House never had the opportunity to vote on Gov. Greitens's impeachment, but the Missouri Legislature did not hesitate to convene a special session for that purpose, even though the misconduct at issue:

- Predated Greitens's term in office;
- Was not connected with any official abuse of power;
- Was only tangentially related to his campaign; and
- Involved only personal misconduct, not any political or official misconduct.

IMPEACHMENT INSIGHT—

AS IN THE *GREITENS* CASE, IT'S POSSIBLE TO FACE IMPEACHMENT FOR SERIOUS PERSONAL MISCONDUCT THAT IS NOT POLITICAL OR OFFICIAL.

There appeared to be a strong sense on the part of many that Greitens had fooled the voters, and that they would not have voted for him if they had known the details of his misconduct with the hair stylist. Admittedly, Greitens' gubernatorial campaign had not focused on his "love" affair with his hair stylist, but rather, on his love affair with semi-automatic weapons, and also his pecs.[cdix] On the other hand, if we knew every candidate's darkest secrets, then for whom would we vote, Peewee Herman? (Bad example.)

For whatever reason, Greitens evidently still held onto his "base," even at the bitter end. A poll in late April 2018, weeks after the wall-to-wall media coverage and the Missouri House report, and just days before Greitens resigned, showed that 33% of the votes still somehow approved of Greitens (the S&M vote, perhaps?), and 46% did not.[cdx]

The case of Eric Greitens illustrates how dark American politics has become. In the early 20th century, an impeachment sex controversy involved modeling, love letters, a woman named after a steak and "will you marry me?" In the late 20th century, an impeachment sex controversy involved a stained blue dress, an intern doing something internal with a damp cigar, and a heated debate over whether oral sex is sex. In the early 21st century, an impeachment sex controversy involves sex, lies and photography; hands taped to exercise rings above one's head; spanking; blackmail; a heated debate over whether oral sex was consensual; and 50 shades of weird. The way things are going, by the end of the 21st century, an impeachment sex controversy will involve forceps, biceps, tongs, thongs, lipstick on a pig, ben wa balls, fava beans, and a robot with long eyelashes.

And by the next century, no one will have any idea what sex is, or rather, what it used to be.

Samuel Kent

Federal Judge. Charges: Sexual Assault, Lying Under Oath. On June 19, 2009, the U.S. House of Representatives voted unanimously in favor of four article of impeachment. Kent resigned in order to avoid a Senate trial.

Samuel Kent

Samuel Kent began his service as a federal judge on Oct. 1, 1990. For the first 17 years of his time on the bench, he rendered a number of somewhat injudicious judicial opinions, which may have caused Kent to get notoriety all confused with fame.[cdxi] Here's one:

"Before proceeding further, the Court notes that this case involves two extremely likable lawyers, who have together delivered some of the most amateurish pleadings ever to cross the hallowed causeway into Galveston, an effort which leads the Court to surmise but one plausible explanation. Both attorneys have obviously entered into a secret pact – complete with hats, handshakes, and cryptic words – to draft their pleadings entirely in crayon on the back sides of gravy-stained paper place mats, in the hope that the Court would be so charmed by their child-like efforts that their utter dearth of legal authorities in their briefing would go unnoticed."[cdxii]

In 2007, a sexual misconduct complaint regarding Kent was made to the Judicial Council of the Fifth Circuit, a panel of federal judges responsible for federal judicial administration in Texas, Louisiana and Mississippi. This led to Kent's indictment on August 28, 2008. The indictment, as amended, charged Kent with five counts of sexual assault on two different court staffers between 2003 and 2007, and one count of obstruction of justice for lying to the Fifth Circuit's Special Investigative Committee when Kent testified that "the extent of his unwanted sexual contact with Person B was one kiss."[cdxiii] On Feb. 23, 2009, after jury selection at his trial had begun, Kent agreed to plead guilty to the obstruction of justice count only, and retire as a judge. Kent was sentenced to 33 months in prison, and he began to serve that sentence on June 15, 2009. (Kent spent most of that time in solitary confinement for his own safety;[cdxiv] judges apparently do not enjoy a warm welcome when they join the company of those whom they have sentenced.)

As for the disposition of Kent's gavel, it wasn't that simple. Judge Kent was too young to retire, absent a disability. The Chief Judge understandably refused to certify that Kent had a disability. That meant that the only ways to end Kent's judicial service were (a) impeachment and conviction, (b) resignation, or (c) death. Since resignation was not on the table, the Chief Judge prudently recommended impeachment and conviction, [cdxv] although she may have secretly preferred death.

On June 2, 2009, shortly before Kent exchanged his black robe for an orange jumpsuit, he submitted his resignation effective *one year later,* hoping to continue to draw his salary as a judge from behind bars. In response, the U.S. House of Representatives unanimously (except for one Member on one Article voting "present") issued four Articles of Impeachment, on June 19, 2009.[cdxvi]

The four succinct Articles read as follows: Articles I and II charged Kent with sexual assault against two court staffers, who were named. Article III charged Kent with lying to the Special Investigative Committee, a charge to which Kent already had pled guilty criminally. Article IV charged Kent with lying to the FBI during its investigation.[cdxvii]

On June 25, 2009, Senate officials traveled to Kent's prison to serve him with a summons to the Senate trial. He greeted them with a resignation letter, effective five days later. This letter was accepted, and the impeachment proceedings against Kent closed.[cdxviii]

Kent's impeachment, like those of Judges Claiborne and Nixon, did not accuse him of misconduct acting within the scope of his duties as a judge. Here again, however, neither the House nor the Senate hesitated to employ impeachment and removal following criminal conviction. Nor did they hesitate to employ impeachment and removal for misconduct off the bench, as discussed separately regarding Judge Thomas Porteous.

Donald Trump

Trump Fun Fact: Won the 1990 *Razzie Award* for "Worst Supporting Actor" in the film *Ghosts Can't Do It,* starring Bo Derek. Impeachment Charge: Sexual Misconduct, as accused by 24 women.

Donald Trump

Twenty-four women have accused Donald Trump of sexual misconduct. In fact, Donald Trump is the sperm whale of sexual misconduct. *Business Insider* has compiled a comprehensive list,[cdxix] to which we add the recently reported case of E. Jean Carroll:

- Jessica Leeds says that Trump groped her on a flight in the late 1970s and then, when she saw him at a gala three years later, he called her the c-word.
- Ivana Trump, Trump's first wife, testified in 1990 that he had violently raped her in 1989.
- Kristin Anderson, a photographer, says that Trump reached under her skirt and groped her at a nightclub in the early 1990s.
- Jill Harth, who worked with Trump, says that Trump pushed her up against a wall and put his hand up her skirt at Mar-a-Lago in the early 1990s.
- E. Jean Carroll, an *Elle* columnist, says that Trump sexually assaulted her in a Bergdorf Goodman dressing room in late 1995 or early 1996, and she reported this to two friends.[cdxx]
- Lisa Boyne, a businesswoman, says that when she had dinner with Trump and others in 1996, she had to get up and walk on top of and across the table in order to leave, and that as she did so, Trump looked up her skirt and commented on her genitals.
- Mariah Billado and Victoria Hughes, two Miss Teen USA contestants in 1997, say that Trump walked in on them as they were changing clothes in their dressing room. Trump more-or-less admitted this on the Howard Stern Show in 2005.
- Temple Taggert, formerly Miss Utah and a Miss USA contestant in 1997, says that Trump kissed her on the lips twice without her permission, and offered to aid her modeling career.
- Cathy Heller says that at Mar-a-Lago in the 1990s, Trump "forcibly kissed" her without her permission, in front of her family (including her husband).
- Karena Virginia says that Trump groped her while she waited for her car at the U.S. Open in 1998, as he imparted the very Trumpian phrase, "don't you know who I am?"
- Tasha Dixon and Bridget Sullivan say that at the 2001 Miss USA pageant, Trump walked into their dressing room when they were not fully clothed, and "ogled" them. Sullivan says that Trump hugged her without permission, when she was naked.

- Melinda McGillivray says that Trump grabbed her buttocks at a Mar-a-Lago concert in 2003.
- Natasha Stoynoff, a *People* magazine reporter, says that Trump forced his tongue down her throat and told her that they were going to have an affair during an interview in 2005, at Mar-a-Lago. She had been sent to Mar-a-Lago to report on Trump and his then-new wife, Melania.
- Jennifer Murphy, a contestant on "The Apprentice," and Juliet Huddy, a former Fox News anchor, say that Trump kissed them on the lips without their consent in 2005 or 2006, although they say that they were not offended by this.
- Rachel Crooks, a receptionist at Trump Tower, says that Trump kissed her on the mouth, without her consent, in 2005.
- Samantha Holvey, a 2006 Miss USA contestant, says that Trump looked over the contestants "from head to toe like we were just meat, we were just sexual objects."
- Ninni Laaksonen, former Miss Finland, says that Trump groped her, grabbing her buttocks, backstage at the "Late Show with David Letterman" in 2006.
- Jessica Drake, an adult-film actress, says that Trump grabber her and kissed her without permission, and offered her money for sex, in Lake Tahoe in 2006.
- Summer Zervos, a contestant on "The Apprentice," says that at the Beverly Hills Hotel in 2007, Trump grabbed her shoulder, put his hand on her breast, grabbed her hand and "thrust himself on her," before she fled. Trump said that he never met her at a hotel, or "greeted her inappropriately." After Trump denied the misconduct, Zervos sued him for defamation, in New York State court. As this is written, the lawsuit is pending.
- Cassandra Searles, a 2013 Miss USA contestant, says that Trump repeatedly grabbed her buttocks, and invited her to his hotel room. She adds that Trump treated the contestants "like cattle."
- Alva Johnson, a Trump campaign staffer, says that Trump grabbed her hand and kissed her without her consent at a campaign rally on Aug. 24, 2016.

The Oaf of Office's attitude toward women was inadvertently exposed in a 1992 letter that *New York* magazine received, signed by "Carolin Gallego," who claimed to be Trump's secretary. The letter stated, in part, "I do not believe any man in America gets more calls from women wanting to see him, meet him, or go out with him. The most beautiful women, the most successful women—all women love Donald Trump." The *Washingtonian* magazine later concluded that the letter was written by Trump himself.[cdxxi]

Are these allegations of sexual harassment and sexual assault true? Well, listen to what Trump himself has to say. Trump admitted to the beauty pageant allegations on the *Howard Stern Show,* as noted above. And Trump boasted about his *modus operandi* on the *Access Hollywood* recording:

> **Trump**: You know, I'm automatically attracted to beautiful [women] — I just start kissing them. It's like a magnet. Just kiss. I don't even wait. And when you're a star, they let you do it. You can do anything.
> **Billy Bush**: Whatever you want.
> **Trump**: Grab 'em by the pussy. You can do anything.[cdxxii]

Since Trump took office, the "familiar refrain" (as the media has called it) from Trump's staff on this has been as follows:

"The president has addressed these accusations directly and denied all of these allegations and this took place long before he was elected to be president, and the people of this country had a decisive election, supported President Trump, and we feel like these allegations have been answered through that process."[cdxxiii]

Of course, Governor Eric Greitens' Press Secretary could have said the same thing, before he was swept from office.

So, are these impeachable offenses? The public has heard the arguments in Trump's defense: Trump's sexual misconduct took place before he took office. Although he misused his then-"office" (for instance, as the host of *The Apprentice* and the Miss USA contest) to force himself on women, he didn't misuse the office of the President the same way (as far as we know, and not yet). Most of these incidents were publicly known before Trump was elected, and as Trump defenders frequently assert, they were "litigated" in the "court of public opinion."

And, having heard the arguments in Trump's defense, what does that court of public opinion have to say? In December 2017, one year *after* the election, Americans said (50 percent to 46 percent) that Trump should *resign* because of the sexual harassment allegations against him:

> *"37. As you may know, President Trump has been accused of sexual harassment and sexual assault by multiple women. Do you think President Trump should resign, or not?*

> | | |
> |---|---|
> | *Yes/Resign* | *50%* |
> | *No* | *46%* |
> | *Don't Know/No Answer* | *4%" cdxxiv* |

Independent voters said, 52% to 44%, that Trump should resign because of the sexual harassment accusations against him.

Maybe the voters have the sense that in Trump's case, we've seen only the tip of the iceberg. Only 23 percent of sexual assaults are reported *to the police.* cdxxv Trump's 24 reported victims could represent 100 actual victims, or more. In other words, a lifelong pattern of serial and serious sexual misconduct.

Moreover, this pattern of misconduct opens Trump to undue influence or even blackmail, not a good thing for a President of the United States. How do we know that? Because Trump did actually authorize hush money to at least two women, Stormy Daniels and Karen MacDougal, during the 2016 Presidential campaign. cdxxvi If someone does have a "peepee tape" of Trump, who knows what concessions he or she might be able to extract from POTUS?

As the Greitens and Kent cases demonstrate, sexual misconduct is an impeachable offense, a "misdemeanor" in the Constitutional sense. Sexual misconduct *before taking office* is an impeachable offense, as Gov. Greitens learned. Virtually every one of these Trump sexual misconduct incidents would qualify as a crime, under state law. They are confirmed by Trump's own words, on the *Access Hollywood* recording.

If Eric Greitens was going to be impeached because of sexual misconduct against one woman, and Samuel Kent was impeached because of sexual misconduct against two women, then shouldn't Trump be impeached because of sexual misconduct against at least 24?

$\mathcal{C}$HAPTER IX:
TAX EVASION

Harry Claiborne

Federal Judge. Charge: Tax Evasion (before office). On July 22, 1986, the U.S. House of Representatives voted unanimously (406-0) in favor of four articles of impeachment. On Oct. 9, 1986, the Senate voted in favor of three of them (87 to 10, 90 to 7 and 89 to 8), but not in favor of one article based solely on Kent's criminal conviction (46 in favor, 35 "present," 17 against).

Harry Claiborne

Harry Claiborne was a federal judge in Nevada. On Dec. 9, 1983, Claiborne was indicted in a seven-count indictment. (Although DOJ is currently of the opinion that a sitting *President* cannot be federally indicted, the courts have held repeatedly that a federal judge can be both indicted and impeached.[cdxxvii])

The first three counts against Claiborne alleged bribery and obstruction of justice between Claiborne and Joseph Conforte, a brothel owner. (The bribes started in 1978, four years after *The Godfather, Part II,* which portrayed bribery and obstruction of justice between a Nevada public official and brothel owner Fredo Corleone, Michael Corleone's brother. See that? Life does imitate art.) The next three counts in the Claiborne indictment alleged that Claiborne had filed false tax returns in 1978, 1979 and 1980. The last count alleged that Claiborne had filed a false financial statement, not disclosing a $75,000 loan.[cdxxviii] A jury deadlocked on all seven charges against Claiborne.

At the retrial, the prosecution limited itself to the 1979 and 1980 tax charges and the non-disclosure charge, dismissing the rest. The second jury convicted Claiborne on the two tax charges, and acquitted him on the non-disclosure charge.[cdxxix]

The background here was that Claiborne had become a judge on Aug. 11, 1978.[cdxxx] In 1979 and 1980, there were "legal fees he received from his prior law firm for work he had performed before becoming a judge." Claiborne had received around $41,000 in 1979, and reported only $22,000 of it. As it turned out, Claiborne reported as income the checks he had deposited at a bank, but not the checks that he had cashed at casinos. (A decade later, as noted above, Donald Trump's father would perform a similar maneuver, giving Trump a $3.35 million casino bailout by buying that much in unused casino chips.[cdxxxi])

As for the 1980 tax charge, Claiborne had received around $88,000 in pre-judge income in 1980, and didn't report any of it. He asserted that he had included that income in the $150,000 sale price of his interest in his former law firm. Claiborne also claimed that he had relied on the advice of his tax accountants, but there was evidence that he had misinformed them.

Claiborne appealed from the conviction at his second trial. On July 8, 1985, Claiborne's criminal conviction was affirmed on appeal.[cdxxxii]

Claiborne went to prison on March 16, 1986, but like Samuel Kent, Claiborne did not resign his position as a federal judge. This led the House Judiciary Committee to approve articles of impeachment on June 26, 1986.

There were four Articles. The first two alleged that Claiborne had "willfully and knowingly" filed tax returns that failed to report substantial income. The third noted that a jury had found Claiborne guilty of this. The fourth alleged that Claiborne, in filing these returns, had "betrayed the trust of the people of the United States, and reduced confidence in the integrity and impartiality of the judiciary, thereby bringing disrepute on the Federal courts and the administration of justice by the courts."[cdxxxiii] All of the Articles of Impeachment were ringing the same chime, *i.e.,* Claiborne knowingly filing false tax returns. All of them characterized this as both a "high crime" and a misdemeanor, although in Constitutional terms, filing false tax returns regarding pre-office income seems to be more of a misdemeanor than a high crime.

The Senate appointed a committee of 12 Senators to hear impeachment testimony. Claiborne argued to the courts that this procedure (having less than the full Senate hear his defense) denied him due process. The courts refused to interfere in the Senate proceedings, however. Later, the U.S. Supreme Court took the same "leave-us-out-of-this" position in another judicial impeachment case.[cdxxxiv]

The Senate showed no concern whatever for Claiborne's argument against impeachment that his conviction related to the misreporting of income he had earned before he had assumed office. Nor was the Senate concerned that the misreporting had nothing to do with Claiborne's official duties as a judge. The focus of the Senate testimony was on: (1) whether Claiborne's errors were honest mistakes, and (2) whether he had been selectively prosecuted because the FBI was angered by his pro-defendant judicial decisions, when for anyone else this would have been treated as a civil matter. (The IRS did not participate in the criminal case against Claiborne.)

The Senate voted overwhelmingly against Claiborne. He drew only 10 votes to acquit on Article I, 7 votes to acquit on Article II, and 8 votes to acquit on Article IV. He fared better on Article III only because 35 of the 98 Senators voted "present," believing that the Senate should not rubber-stamp a criminal jury verdict. But five of the ten Senators who had voted with

Claiborne on Article I abandoned him on Article III. This meant that when the impeachment proceedings and Claiborne's career reached their simultaneous *denouement,* only five of the 98 Senators had voted with Claiborne on every count.[cdxxxv]

The Claiborne case was something of a worst-case scenario for someone facing impeachment: a federal judge *in prison for tax evasion,* drawing a full salary, and planning to put the black robe back on as soon as he took off the prison stripes. Nevertheless, it puts to rest the argument that a federal official can be impeached and convicted only for his official acts.

Donald Trump

Trump Fun Fact: Trump negotiated to buy the New England Patriots in 1988, but walked away because he thought it was a bad investment. The Patriots were sold later that year for $85 million. They are now worth $4 billion. Impeachment Charge: Tax Evasion.

Donald Trump[cdxxxvi]

Inheritance Tax Fraud. The "bible" on Trump inheritance tax fraud, as publicly reported, is the Oct. 2, 2018, *New York Times* exposé on the subject, running 15,000 words. The *Times* report is based on its review of more than 100,000 pages of documents. The *Times* concluded that "Trump participated in dubious tax schemes during the 1990s, including instances of outright fraud...."[cdxxxvii] The *Times* noted that Trump could face civil fines for that, even today.

Trump's inheritance tax fraud included: (a) draining the value of Trump's father's estate by inflating expenses charged to his properties (through a pass-through mark-up imposed by 'All County Building Supply and Maintenance'); (b) giving them a low value for tax purposes while giving them a high value for investment purposes; (c) Trump taking interests in his father's properties at bargain values (even as a child); and (d) borrowing money from his father that may or may not have been paid back, with or without interest.

Regarding Trump's loan fraud, as early as 1979, "Trump [took] out several large loans from his father to help maintain his businesses. Many of these loans came with no set interest or payment plan, making them glorified gifts."[cdxxxviii] Adjusted for inflation, these fake loans to Trump grew to total $413 million.[cdxxxix] Regarding the valuation fraud, in 1981, Trump inherited $90 million in property, and claimed that was worth only $13 million, in order to avoid inheritance taxes. In 1989, Trump gave his father a 7.5% interest in a condominium in return for releasing Trump from $11 million in debt. Two years later, his father sold this interest back to Trump for $10,000. [cdxl]

Trump cannot disclaim responsibility, because he signed many of the documents in question personally. As the *Washington Post* put it, "we now have *hard evidence* — not allegations, not hearsay, not suspicion, but hard evidence — that Donald Trump and his family committed tax fraud on a massive scale." In response, Trump and his Press Secretary dismissed the *New York Times* article as "very boring."[cdxli] But Trump's sister, a federal judge, retired shortly thereafter, quite possibly to avoid the ensuing investigation into her part in the scheme.[cdxlii]

Property Tax Fraud. At a hearing before the House Oversight Committee on Feb. 27, 2019, in response to questions by Rep. Alexandria Ocasio-Cortez, Trump's personal attorney Michael Cohen confessed to Trump's property tax fraud:

> ***Ocasio-Cortez:*** *Mr. Cohen, I want to ask you about your assertion that the president may have improperly devalued his assets to avoid*

paying taxes. According to an Aug. 24-Aug. 21, 2016, report by
The Washington Post, while the president claimed in financial dis-
closure forms that Trump National Golf Club in Jupiter, Florida,
was worth more than $50 million, he had reported otherwise to
local tax authorities that the course was worth "no more than $5
million." Mr. Cohen, do you know whether this specific report is
accurate?

Cohen: *It's identical to what he did at Trump National Golf Club at*
Briarcliff Manor.

Ocasio-Cortez: *Do you know, to your knowledge, was the president*
interested in reducing his local real estate bills? Tax bills?

Cohen: *Yes.*

Ocasio-Cortez: *And how did he do that?*

Cohen: *What you do is you deflate the value of the asset, and then you*
put in a request to the tax department for a deduction.

Ocasio-Cortez: *Thank you.*[cdxliii]

The *Washington Post* documented the same scam in eight of the ten
golf courses on which Trump pays taxes, showing gross disparities between
Trump election filings and property tax filings:

"He will tell everyone his courses are worth $50 million or whatever,
that they're the greatest courses in the world, but then go to the county
assessor and, under threat of perjury, sign documents that the mar-
ket value is under $10 million," said Arthur E. Gimmy, a veteran
California appraiser who has assessed golf courses in 20 states. "It's total
nonsense."[cdxliv]

Income Tax Fraud. As for Trump's income tax, the investigative journalist David Cay Johnson noted on *Democracy Now* that Trump was tried
twice for income tax fraud (civilly, not criminally). Trump lost both cases,
facing harsh criticism from the judges. Johnson also observed that Trump
has claimed the STAR tax credit on his New York residence four times. That
tax credit that is available only to persons making less than $500,000 per
year, making Trump's claim for it likely fraudulent.[cdxlv]

The subject of Trump's tax evasion came up, pointedly, in the Sept. 26, 2016 Trump-Clinton Presidential Debate:

> *Hillary Clinton: You've got to ask yourself, why won't he release his tax*
> *returns?... Maybe he doesn't want the American people, all of you*
> *watching tonight, to know that he's paid nothing in federal taxes.*
> *Because the only years that anybody has ever seen were a couple of*
> *years when he had to turn them over to state authorities, when he*
> *was trying to get a casino license, and they showed that he didn't pay*
> *any federal income tax.*
> *Donald Trump: That makes me smart!*
> *Hillary Clinton: So if he's paid zero, that's zero for troops, zero for vets,*
> *zeros for schools or health.*[cdxlvi]

Trump is the only Presidential nominee in modern times to refuse to release his tax returns. The Internal Revenue Service (IRS) has automatically audited the President's tax return for almost half a century, but there has been no word on what happened when (or if) the IRS has audited Trump's.[cdxlvii] When the Chairman of the House Ways and Means Committee invoked a law *requiring* Trump to turn them over to Congress, Trump's Chief of Staff said on national TV that Congress would "never" get them.[cdxlviii]

The Trump tax fraud documented by the *New York Times,* the *Washington Post* and Michael Cohen's Congressional testimony may have started thirty years ago, but it evidently continues to this day, during Trump's Presidency. The Judge Claiborne impeachment case shows that a federal official can be impeached for misreporting income for work done before becoming a federal official — on merely two tax returns, not a lifetime's worth.

If Harry Claiborne could be impeached and removed from office for tax evasion regarding pre-office income on two of his income tax returns, shouldn't Trump be impeached for inheritance tax, property tax and income tax evasion spanning three decades?

$\mathcal{C}$HAPTER X:

OUTSIDE INTERESTS

Kenesaw Mountain Landis

Federal Judge. Charge: Outside Interests. On Feb. 14, 1921, the House Judiciary Committee voted 24 to 1 to investigate Landis for remaining a federal judge while serving as Commissioner of Baseball. On Feb. 21, 1922, Landis resigned as a judge.

Kenesaw Mountain Landis

Judge Landis was appointed a federal judge in 1905. He was, very likely, the most well-known federal judge of his time. In 1907, he fined Standard Oil $29 million, then the largest fine in history, for taking illegal rebates from railroad companies. He ordered John D. Rockefeller, the richest man in America, to testify, even though Rockefeller had evaded testimony in any court for almost 20 years.

During World War I, Landis tried 120 draft evaders. He gave 83 of them the maximum sentence, and ordered them to submit to the draft upon their release. As for the other 37, he deported them. Landis sentenced 'Big Bill' Haywood, the head of the Industrial Workers of the World (the 'Wobblies'), to twenty years in prison for opposing the war. (Haywood fled to the Soviet Union to avoid serving the sentence.) Landis also sentenced seven members of the Socialist Party (including one who had been elected to Congress) to twenty years in prison under the Espionage Act; the convictions were over-turned and the charges dropped after the U.S. Supreme Court concluded that Landis was biased and should not have tried the case. Landis also called for Kaiser Wilhelm, the German leader, and his six sons to be "lined up against a wall and shot."

After the war, Landis imposed a 12.5 percent pay cut on union con-struction workers in an arbitration case. (The employers had asked for a 20 percent cut.)[cdxlix] Aside from his famous, or infamous, rulings, Judge Landis also was known for his wicked sense of humor. When an older defendant claimed that he would not survive a five-year prison sentence, Landis said, "well, you can try, can't you?"[cdl]

In 1920, Landis was appointed as the first Commissioner of Baseball – without stepping down as a judge. This was, arguably, payback for Landis refus-ing to issue a decision in a 1915 antitrust case against the major leagues, forcing a settlement. Although Landis's crackdown on baseball corruption in the wake of the Black Sox scandal was extremely popular with the public, Landis's wear-ing two hats nevertheless elicited a collective "huh-uh" from the U.S. House Judiciary Committee. On Feb. 14, 1921, it voted 24 to 1 to investigate Landis for this moonlighting, to determine whether he should be impeached.

The Attorney General, however, issued a legal opinion that Landis could hold both jobs.[cdli] On Feb. 28, 1922, Landis, perhaps not wanting to put this to the test, reached the startling conclusion that he would rather be Commissioner of Baseball than a federal judge, so he hung up the black robe.[cdlii] Landis then served as Commissioner of Baseball for 24 years.

The House never had to rule on Landis's switch-hitting, but the experience does demonstrate that outside interests, and potential conflicts of interest, can create grounds for impeachment.

Donald Trump

Trump Fun Fact: Trump owned the New York team in the United States Football League, and is credited with the destruction of the league by insisting that it go head-to-head against the NFL. He was so rude that one co-owner threatened to punch him in the mouth. Impeachment Charge: Outside Interests

Donald Trump[cdliii]

In the Complaint filed by Members of Congress against Trump under the Foreign Emoluments Clause, there is one anecdote that stands out. After the 2016 Presidential election, Mauricio Macri, the President of Argentina, called Trump to congratulate Trump on his victory. Trump took the call, and told the President of Argentina to "deal with" the permit issues that were holding up the development of a Trump office building in Buenos Aires. The Trump project got the go-ahead three days later.[cdliv] And the Trump Administration has doubled foreign aid to Argentina.[cdlv]

Is that how a President-Elect should deal with a foreign leader?

Trump also personally asked Nigel Farage, a United Kingdom representative to the European Parliament and the Brexit Party leader, to oppose the construction of wind farms off the coast of Trump's two Scottish golf courses.[cdlvi] (Shortly afterward, Farage was fatally struck down with wind farm cancer, a malady that Trump had warned him about. No, actually, that never happened, although Trump certainly has warned that wind farms can cause cancer — a Trump statement that Politifact rated "Pants on Fire."[cdlvii])

If Trump can't think of anything to talk about to the President of Argentina other than getting permits for his property in Buenos Aires, then maybe he shouldn't be President of the United States. He doesn't seem to have the time.

If Kenesaw Mountain Landis was threatened with impeachment, and forced to resign, because of his outside interests, then shouldn't Donald Trump be impeached and removed from office because of his?

CHAPTER XI: "THEY HAD THE VOTES. NOTHING ELSE MATTERED."

Henry Johnston

Governor of Oklahoma. Charge: "General Incompetence." On Jan. 21, 1929, the Oklahoma House of Representatives impeached Johnston on 13 charges. On March 20, 1929, the Oklahoma Senate voted 35 to 9 to convict him on just one: "general incompetence."

Henry Johnston

Governor Henry Johnston (D-OK) was impeached and removed from office on what may be the most insulting basis for impeachment in history: "general incompetence."

Johnston was pretty nutty. He was a Rosicrucian, a secret society of mystics and believers in magic and witchcraft. Johnston believed that he was reincarnated, and in prior lives, he had been Patrick Henry and Julius Caesar. (Which raises the not-so-fascinating question of whether Patrick Henry was the reincarnation of Julius Caesar – is reincarnation transitive? Ask a Rosicrucian.)

Johnston also had the misfortune of succeeding Governor J.C. Walton (D-OK), whom the Oklahoma Legislature had impeached and removed from office in less than a year. The Oklahoma Legislature was in an impeaching mood.

From the time Johnston took office, he was under attack for not doing the job. Legislators claimed that Johnston's private secretary, Mayme O. Hammonds, was making all the decisions. Johnston staved off impeachment in his first year in office by the rather extreme expedient of ordering the Oklahoma National Guard to prevent the Legislature from meeting in special session in the Capitol to impeach him.

That dog didn't hunt when it came time for the regular session of the Oklahoma Legislature, in 1929. The Oklahoma House promptly issued 13 articles of impeachment, and the Oklahoma Senate accepted 11 of them for trial. After a six-week trial, the Oklahoma Senate dismissed ten of the charges, but the Senate convicted Johnston on the charge of "general incompetence," by a vote of 35 to 9.

Much, much later, the *Tulsa Tribune* interviewed Johnston when he was 96 years old, a few weeks before he died. Demonstrating a perspicacity that he may have lacked as Governor, Johnston had this to say about his impeachment:

"I didn't suit them. There were 25 or 30 and they said 'Let's get him out of here. We don't have to be bothered with him.'"

Said the *Tribune:* "It was an excellent summation of the basis for his removal from office. His opponents had the votes. Nothing else mattered."

Donald Trump

Trump Fun Fact: Trump frequently telephoned reporters posing as his own publicist, using the names John Barron and John Miller, and praised himself profusely. The *Washington Post* posted a "John Miller" recording. Impeachment Charge: "They Have the Votes".

Donald Trump[cdlviii]

It is tempting to look at the precedent of Governor Johnston and resolve that Donald Trump should, like Johnston, be impeached and removed from office for General Incompetence. Why not? Trump ranks as a Major Disaster. For America, his Presidency constitutes Corporal Punishment. And for sure, we've learned more than enough – TMI – about his Private Parts.

But the Governor Johnston precedent has another meaning. Some observers look at the party composition of the U.S. Senate today – 48 Democrats and Independents, 52 Republicans — and measure that against the requirement of for a 2/3 votes to convict on impeachment – 67 votes. The same fear, however, could have overcome virtually any impeachment effort in history, including Johnston's. (Johnston was a Democrat, and the Democrats controlled the Oklahoma Senate from 1907 to 2006.)

In the first 40 years after the Senate convened, it was common for one party (or "faction") to have a 2/3 majority, but since the administration of

John Quincy Adams beginning in 1825, the 6th President, that has been very rare. Since then, one party in the Senate has had a 2/3 majority only during 1837-1839, 1861-1875, 1907-1909, 19351943 and 1963-1967.[cdlix] That's 28 years out of 194, *i.e.,* only 14 percent of the time. Of the 16 impeachments by the U.S. House of Representatives since 1825, *only three* took place when one party had a 2/3 Senate majority, all three during the Civil War/Reconstruction period (President Andrew Johnson, and Judges Humphreys and Delahay). And in one of those three cases, Judge Delahay's, the judge's *own party* held the 2/3 Senate majority. Hence among the 16 federal impeachments during the last 40 Presidential Administrations, only two (Johnson and Humphreys) were launched when one party enjoyed a 2/3 majority in the Senate, and a federal official of the other party was being impeached.

The record on impeachment in those two cases (when the impeachment effort was supported by the fact that one party had a 2/3 majority in the Senate, and the official facing impeachment belonged to the other party) was 1 to 1 (one removal, one acquittal). The record in the other cases was 9 to 5 (nine removals or resignations, five acquittals). In other words, impeachment was *more* successful when the impeached official *did not* face a 2/3 partisan majority against him in the Senate.

But as the President Johnson impeachment illustrates, numbers do matter – to get the ball rolling, in the House. Rather than focusing on the partisan split in the Senate, where history so rarely has provided a 2/3 majority against the "impeachee," it would make more sense to focus on the partisan split in the House, which has *always* had the requisite Constitutional majority for one party or the other. In the House, Trump's Democratic opponents currently have the votes.

And as the President Johnson impeachment also illustrates, if a President does survive a Senate conviction vote, impeachment by the House and acquittal by the Senate does not qualify as a ringing endorsement. Andrew Johnson was acquitted by the Senate on May 26, 1868. On July 4, 1868, just five weeks later, this incumbent President won only 65 out of 317 votes at the national convention of his own party, which nominated the former Governor of New York instead.[cdlx] Similarly, in President Nixon's case, polling shows that the impeachment proceedings dramatically eroded his public support.[cdlxi]

In other words, when you have the numbers, in the House, it matters.

$\mathscr{C}$HAPTER XII

IMPEACHMAGGEDON

Donald Trump

Trump Fun Fact: The *Washington Post*'s running count of Trump's lies in office surged over 13,000. That's more than a dozen times a day – Trump may lie more often than he urinates.

Impeachment charges:

Assuming that there is anyone left to look back at us, future historians will look back at April 18, 2019 as the beginning of Impeachmaggedon, the inception of the Trumpocalypse. On that date, the Mueller Report, minus its 900 redactions, was released.[cdlxii]

And then, to Trump's own surprise, nothing really bad happened. Mueller had swallowed the bunkum, spun out by politically ambitious DOJ climbers and wannabees, that the President could not be indicted. (Or, to quote inadvertent impeachment expert Richard Nixon, "when the President does it, that means that that is not illegal.")[cdlxiii] In Trump's mind, that made him bulletproof, impregnable, unbeatable and indestructible – except, of course, destructible by Trump himself. (What happens if Superman scratches himself really hard? He bleeds, right?) Trump even felt safe to confess to Russia "helping me to get elected."[cdlxiv]

So after the Mueller Report was released, Donald Trump's id raised a mighty sword, and cleanly lopped off the always-flaccid head of Donald Trump's superego. Starting on April 18, 2019, Donald Trump was not only unbrained, but also unchained. And impeachable offenses then rained down from the heavens, like hail the size of baseballs, made wholly of excrement. The Mueller Report should have been disseminated (note to Trump: "disseminated" is not a bad word) with a yellow Post-It note on the front that said, "*Apres moi, le deluge.*"[cdlxv]

Speaking of bullets and bulletproof, in 2016, Trump had said – maybe rhetorically, maybe not -- "I could stand in the middle of Fifth Avenue and shoot somebody and wouldn't lose any voters, okay?"[cdlxvi] After the Mueller Report was released, one of Trump's belligerent and numerous[cdlxvii] enablers, who could not have possibly passed the Constitutional Law class in law school, told a federal appeals court that while in office, Trump could not be prosecuted – or even investigated – if he shot someone on Fifth Avenue. [cdlxviii] (The legal disposition of a shooting on Sixth Avenue, the Avenue of the Americas, was not addressed. Trump may build a wall down the median strip.)

Anyway, April 18, 2019, marked the End of Days for all restraint. Much like the Ten Plagues of Egypt, each dawn thereafter yielded a new impeachable offense.

<u>Syria.</u> On October 6, 2019, the Commander-in-Thief ordered U.S. troops out of Syria, in order to facilitate an invasion by Turkey (and thereby abandoning the Kurds, who had lost 11,000 soldiers taking the area from ISIS at America's behest).[cdlxix] Was Trump simply being a peacenik, tree-hugging flower child, seeking to heal this war-torn country? Uh, no. When it

comes to Turkey and Syria, here is what Trump himself told Breitbart News, in 2015: "I have a little conflict of interest 'cause I have a major, major building in Istanbul. It's a tremendously successful job. It's called Trump Towers — two towers, instead of one, not the usual one; it's two."[cdlxx]

This proves two things. First, when pressed, Trump can count all the way up to two. Second, Trump has *divided loyalty* on issues of war and peace – divided between loyalty to American interests and loyalty to his property interests. And divided loyalty is an impeachable offense. (Trump also opened the door to Russia and Syria then taking back a large part of eastern Syria from the Kurdish alliance[cdlxxi] – Trump helping Russia yet again.)

Divided loyalties. Impeachable offense.

Sharpiegate. On August 25, *Axios* reported that Trump had suggest nuking hurricanes[cdlxxii] – and with them, the entire food chain. "I got it! I got it! Why don't we nuke them?" the Fascist Carnival Barker[cdlxxiii] suggested. Well, that is really thinking outside the box, if "the box" is sanity. You know, it's been quite a while since we had strontium-90 in our milk. I guess that Trump kind of misses it. Nevertheless, it might be better if he just stuck to pummeling the hurricane victims with paper towels, while urging them to have a good time.

Wait. Wait. The Master of Disaster was just getting warmed up.

On August 30, 2019, the National Weather Service issued an advisory that the city of Montgomery, Alabama had *an 11 percent chance* of seeing winds from Hurricane Dorian that exceeded *39 miles an hour*.[cdlxxiv] (That's not a hurricane -- by definition, hurricanes have sustained winds of 75+ miles an hour.[cdlxxv]) Those of us who were actually paying attention then quickly learned that the 89% thing was going to happen, instead of the 11% thing. Hurricane Dorian turned northward, not westward, eventually making U.S. landfall much later in North Carolina, three states to the right of Alabama.[cdlxxvi]

Two days following the National Weather Service's 11%/39 mph advisory, however, after the storm already had turned north, Donald Trump tweeted that Alabama "will most likely be hit (much) harder than anticipated. Looking like one of the largest hurricanes ever. Already category 5. BE CAREFUL! GOD BLESS EVERYONE!"[cdlxxvii] The White House Weatherman then, in the midst of two hardworking days of golf at the Trump

National Golf Club,[cdlxxviii] made this statement at a Dorian briefing: "It may get a little piece of a great place — it's called Alabama," Trump said, clarifying this important point for those of us who have never heard of Alabama, or have heard of it, but just don't what it is called. ("Martha, what is that thing shaped like a shovel with a broken handle, west of Georgia?" "Why, Fred, that's Alabama, you silly goose!") "And Alabama could even be in for at least some very strong winds and something more than that, it could be," the Oaf of Office continued. "This just came up, unfortunately."[cdlxxix] That was a very bad 'Dewey Beats Truman' type of mistake, probably on par with, like, no one else in public office, ever, but ... that should have been the end of it. Everyone make a mistake or two, or two million, right? *Mais non!* Twitter's NiTwit just had to prove that he had retroactive command of the winds, the sun, the moon and the stars. On Sept. 4, *with Dorian not even having made U.S. landfall yet,* the actual President of the United States, not some satirical doppelganger, held up a National Hurricane Center map of the Southeastern United States, altered with a black Sharpie to make it look as if Hurricane Dorian had been projected to hit Alabama. The world responded with palms on forehead, eyes closed, shaking its collective head, feeling like crying.[cdlxxx] When Trump was asked who had despoiled the hurricane map with the Sharpie, he replied "I don't know. I don't know. I don't know." Which happens to be the same number of denials as Judas's.

Here was a Trump high crime or misdemeanor that actually is, indisputably, a misdemeanor. Section 2074 of the U.S. Criminal Code reads as follows: *"Whoever knowingly issues or publishes any counterfeit weather forecast or warning of weather conditions falsely representing such forecast or warning to have been issued or published by the Weather Bureau ... shall be fined under this title or imprisoned not more than ninety days, or both."* Question: In all of human history, has there ever been an elected official, anywhere, anywhen, who did anything as STUPID as this? Trump has sunk way below "inept"[cdlxxxi] and has established himself as no ept at all.

Conduct Unbecoming a President. Impeachable offense.

But before anyone could wrap their heads around profane absurdity of this, it was Onward! Onward! to the next impeachable offense.

The Cover-Up of the Cover-Up of the Cover-Up – After Trump asserted "executive privilege" over the entire Mueller Report on May 8, 2019 (or at least his attorneys mouthed some syllables that correspond to such words, since the privilege itself has virtually no conceivable application to the Mueller Report),[cdlxxxii] Trump ordered everyone and anyone who has even looked at the White House – everyone who has ever seen the color white -- not to testify to Congress, starting with former White House counsel Don McGahn.[cdlxxxiii] On July 17, 2019, the House voted to hold Attorney General William Barr and Commerce Secretary Wilbur Ross in criminal contempt, in connection with a Census Bureau cover-up.[cdlxxxiv] Follow-up battles continue in the courts, every day.

Obstruction of justice. Impeachable offense.

"All the President's Women" – On Oct. 22, 2019, in the book entitled "All the President's Women," Barry Levine and Monique El-Faizy uncovered 43 *new* allegations of sexual misconduct by Donald Trump, bringing the official count to eleventy-eight.

Sexual improprieties. Impeachable offense.

Seepage – As it turns out, there are even more impeachable offenses from those halcyon "covfefe" days of the Trump Maladministration, impeachable offenses we didn't know about that are being transuded outward only now. Back when Putin errand-boy Rex Tillerson was Secretary of State, Trump pressed Tillerson to get the Department of Justice to drop charges against a Rudy Giuliani client.[cdlxxxv] Funny – that's a lot like what got Gov. Evan Mecham (R-AZ) impeached and removed from office.

In the summer of 2018, Trump extended his vendetta against Jeff Bezos, the owner of the Washington Post and the largest shareholder in Amazon, by directing his then-Chief of Staff to "screw Amazon" out of a $10 billion cloud-networking government contract.[cdlxxxvi] Funny – that's a lot like what got Gov. 'Pa' Ferguson (D-TX) impeached and removed from office.

And ProPublica has reported on irreconcilable differences between what Trump has said to bankers (to get loans) and what Trump has said to government officials (to avoid taxes),[cdlxxxvii] differences so large that you could almost drive Trump's ego through them. Furthermore, a whistleblower complaint has been filed regarding undue pressure exerted on the Internal Revenue Service regarding the automatic audit of Trump's tax returns.[cdlxxxviii] Funny – that's a lot like what got Judge Harry Claiborne impeached and removed from office.

Vanity Fair points out *big-league* insider trading and securities fraud front-running Trump news announcements; one trade alone had a potential profit of more than $1,000,000,000.00, made shortly before Trump lied about Chinese leaders calling him and asking to re-start trade talks.[cdlxxxix] Funny – that's a lot like what almost got Vice President Schuyler Colfax impeached and removed from office, until he ran out the clock.

G7/Doral – Oh, the impeachable offenses are flying thick and fast. On Oct. 17, 2019, the White House Chief of Staff announced that next year's G7 Summit of world leaders would be held at Donald Trump's failing Doral golf resort.[cdxc] And then on Oct. 19, 2019, two days later, Trump announced that it wouldn't.[cdxci] Trump, of course, had to take a tweet-swipe at the "phony" Emoluments Clause in the Constitution, which prohibits this self-bribery and corruption[cdxcii] (as would any bare thread of integrity, but that, of course, is truly beside the point). Maybe Trump muttered "stupid Constitution!" as he tweeted this out. Notably, this is the only case on record of Trump *not* committing an impeachable offense.

What the Doral dopery demonstrates is that now, during Phase Last of the Trump Regime, Donald Trump is completely surrounded by yes-men, toadies and enablers. "I want to buy Yellowstone Park for a dollar," Trump could say. "Make sure that you put a Trump Hotel next to Old Faithful," his Secretary of the Interior would reply. "I want to copyright the American flag, and charge royalties on it," Trump could say. "Since no one else has copyrighted it already, that would be fine," his Secretary of Commerce would reply. "I want to carve my rear end into Mt. Rushmore, and moon FDR every night when there is a full moon. Here, take a picture of my backside!" Trump could command. "Just a minute while I load the photo app on my phone. We will reprogram defense funding for this," his Chief of Stuff would reply, as the gofer tapped in his Notes app "replace Teddy with Franklin D."

Unfit for Office. And then all the *miscellaneous* stupid, crazy stuff after the Mueller Report was published: Trump directing air strikes against Iran for shooting down a drone and then turning the strikes back in mid-air (invoking the unique insight that airstrikes might kill people).[cdxciii] Trump saying on July 4th that George Washington's Revolutionary War troops "took over the airports" (and then blaming his teleprompter, rather than his first-grade reading skills).[cdxciv] Trump saying that he was building a border wall in Colorado[cdxcv] (there's a whole lot of New Mexico between Colorado and the Mexican border). Trump ignoring the GOP-controlled U.S. Senate when it voted twice to disapprove of Trump's diversion of military funds to build said border wall.[cdxcvi] Trump sending a typed letter to Turkish President Erdogan threatening to destroy Turkey (it looked like the original was written in single letters cut from magazines), and then promptly adopting Erdogan's talking point that some Kurds are "worse" than ISIS.[cdxcvii] Trump pressuring DHS officials to the point where they have migrants drinking out of toilets.[cdxcviii] Trump, that "very stable genius," saying that he is "the chosen one"[cdxcix] (where does that leave Anakin Skywalker?), quoting a supporter who called Trump "the second coming of God"[d] and lauding himself for his own "great and unmatched wisdom"[di] (patting himself on the back so hard that he probably dislocated his shoulder). Trump mischaracterizing the Mueller investigation as an "attempted overthrow" of the government,[dii] and the impeachment investigation as a "lynching."[diii] Trump telling three American-born women of color in Congress to "go back" to the countries they came from,[div] Trump dismissing Republican critics as "human scum,"[dv] and on, and on, and on .... What was it that Trump said during his campaign? "We're going to lie so much, you're going to be so sick of lying"? Something like that.

It's enough to make the Statute of Liberty cry. But the big enchilada since the publication of the Mueller Report, the enchilada that Trump just can't wall off, is:

DNEIPERGATE! – And as soon as the Mueller harness was off, Trump set in motion a high crime so high, so heinous, so hideous, so horrible and so horrifying, that even the most feck-free of feckless Congressional Democrats could not ignore it. Call it ... Dneipergate!

Three weeks after the Mueller Report was published, Rudy Giuliani announced – in the New York Times! – that he was going to Ukraine to get the Ukrainian Government to investigate Democratic Presidential candidate Joe Biden and Biden's son, Hunter Biden (Hunter having served on the Board of Burisma, a Ukrainian company). Why? For whom? "My only client is the President of the United States," said Giuliani, for those who find it difficult to add two plus two.[dvi]

See what happens when Rudy Giuliani goes for three weeks without a camera in his face?

On the next day, Sen. Murphy (D-CT) tweeted: "The President is openly asking a foreign government to investigate his rival. This is the next level." The day after that, Giuliani canceled his trip. But... Giuliani did meet with a top Ukrainian prosecutor in Paris that same month, who then announced that the investigation of Joe Biden's son should be reopened.[dvii]

Giuliani continued to pressure Ukraine with this tweet, on June 21: "New Pres of Ukraine still silent on investigation of Ukrainian interference in 2016 election and alleged Biden bribery of Pres Poroshenko."[dviii] Except that the only one who ever alleged Biden bribery of Pres. Poroshenko was... Rudy Giuliani.

Giuliani, a desperately shy introvert with a deep aversion to any public attention whatsoever, later (on Sept. 20, 2019) explained, unexplained, re-explained and then dis-explained his un-, under-, non-, contra- and mis-conduct, on national TV. Chris Cuomo asked Giuliani whether Giuliani had requested any Ukrainian officials to investigate Joe Biden:

> Giuliani: *"No, actually I didn't. I asked Ukraine to investigate the allegations that there was interference in the election of 2016 by the Ukrainians for the benefit of Hillary Clinton."*
> Cuomo: *"You never asked anything about Hunter Biden? You never asked anything about Joe Biden and the prosecutor?"*
> Giuliani said the "only thing" he asked was how the prosecutor got dismissed.
> Cuomo: *"So you did ask Ukraine to look into Joe Biden."*
> Giuliani: *"Of course I did."*
> Cuomo: *"You just said you didn't!"*[dix]
> Giuliani clearly has an *idée fixe* here; he continued trashing Biden in a butt-dialed phone call to an NBC reporter.[dx]

But Giuliani was not the lone gunman in this particular book depository. Far from it. In mid-July, Trump ordered Trump's Chief of Staff, Mick Mulvaney, to hold back $400 million in aid to Ukraine, and on July 18th, Mulvaney did so.[dxi] Mulvaney later admitted that this was to pressure

Ukrainian officials into "cooperating in an ongoing investigation with our Department of Justice,"[dxii] the term "our Department of Justice" evidently being inside-the-Beltway slang for "Rudy Giuliani." An ABC White House reporter said to Mulvaney: "What you just described is a *quid pro quo*. It is [that] funding will not flow unless the investigation into the Democratic server happens as well." Mulvaney agreed.[dxiii]

Bingo – high crime. A high crime ordered by the Cheeto Bandito himself. We're not done yet. The worst is yet to come. The plot sickens.

A call was scheduled between Donald Trump and Volodymyr Zelensky, the President of Ukraine. On July 19, 2019, the day after U.S. aid to Ukraine was cut, Kurt Volker, the U.S. "Special Representative for Ukraine Negotiations," helpfully suggested: "Most impt is for Zelensky to say that he will help investigation." On July 25, just before the call, Volker dangled a Trump meeting (and oh! what a joy that must be) in front of Zelensky – if Zelensky cooperated: "Heard from White House-assuming President Z convinces trump he will investigate / 'get to the bottom of what happened' in 2016, we will nail down date for visit to Washington."[dxiv]

And in the call itself? The grand finale? The final curtain? The *denouement?* Zelensky and Trump must have hit it off immediately, because Zelensky is a former comedian who tells jokes, and Trump is a joke. Here is what Trump said to Zelensky, according to a rough, ellipsis-strewn transcript released by the White House:

"I would like you to do us a favor though because our country has been through a lot and Ukraine knows a lot about it," Trump says before floating the CrowdStrike investigation.... *"The other thing, there's a lot of talk about Biden's son, that Biden stopped the prosecution and a lot of people want to find out about that so whatever you can do with the Attorney General would be great. Biden went around bragging that he stopped the prosecution so if you can look into it.... It sounds horrible to me."*[dxv]

Now, there's a beseechment that will end in impeachment.

In the following weeks, intermediaries sent some positive signals on cooperation to the Trump Administration. Vice President Pence met with Zelensky on Sept. 1, 2019, deemed him "receptive," and reported this to Trump – although, Pence claims, he had absolutely no idea whatsoever, certainly not, nuh-huh, that Trump had asked Zelensky to investigate the

Bidens.[dxvi] The U.S. aid to Ukraine was released on Sept. 11, 2019, a week before the whistleblower complaint about Dneipergate became public.[dxvii]

Trump publicly asked China to investigate the Bidens, as well,[dxviii] demonstrating that two wrongs don't make a right, but they do make quite a sight. "By the way, likewise, China should start an investigation into the Bidens,"[dxix] said Benedict Donald. This polite request came after Trump slapped $550 billion in U.S. tariffs exclusively on Chinese exports to the United States.[dxx]

On Sept. 24, 2019, Speaker Nancy Pelosi announced an impeachment inquiry into Dneipergate. Two weeks later, a Fox News poll showed that *51% of Americans are in favor of impeaching Trump and removing him from office*.[dxxi] On the day after that, Trump condemned Fox News -- for reporting the poll.[dxxii] (A Gallup Poll put support for impeachment and removal at 52%, versus 58% when Nixon left office.[dxxiii])

Trump has directed Administration officials to refuse to provide information on Dneipergate to Congressional investigating committees.[dxxiv] O-b-s-t-r-u-c-t-i-o-n—o-f—j-u-s-t-i-c-e. Trump complains that the House of Representatives has always voted to authorize an impeachment investigation before one gets underway, but – surprise! – Trump is lying. Three of the last five House impeachments were not preceded by an authorizing vote.[dxxv]

Meanwhile, Attorney General William Barr evidently has happily acceded to the Demander in Chief's very public demands for investigation and prosecution of Trump's political opponents and other mental demons, starting with former CIA Director John Brennan.[dxxvi] The State Department is flagellating a deceased equine by "intensifying" its investigation of… Hillary Clinton's e-mails.[dxxvii]

Speaker Nancy Pelosi got it exactly right: Trump is "self-impeaching."[dxxviii] Q.E.D. Mic drop. Case closed. Here is the article of impeachment:

Article of Impeachment –
Abuse of Power/Malicious Prosecution

WHEREAS Donald Trump personally, and through others at his direction including Chief of Staff Mick Mulvaney and Trump counsel Rudy Giuliani, employed the powers of the Presidency to suspend $400 million in military aid to Ukraine and otherwise to pressure, entice and influence Ukraine to investigate former Vice President Joe Biden and his son Hunter Biden;

WHEREAS Donald Trump attempted to extend this scheme to an investigation by China, in the midst of what Trump as described as his "trade war" with China as leverage;

WHEREAS Donald Trump has repeatedly, both publicly and privately, demanded that the U.S. Department of Justice investigate and prosecute Trump's critics, some of whom Trump has accused of "treason";

WHEREAS there is evidence that his Attorney General, William Barr, is carrying out such investigations: Now, therefore, be it

RESOLVED, That the House of Representatives—

<u>impeaches</u> President Donald Trump for abuse of power and malicious prosecution, and for such high crimes and misdemeanors, and asks the U.S. Senate to try him on his removal from office and barring him for any office of honor or profit.

Part IV –
NOT IMPEACHABLE

$\mathcal{C}$HAPTER XIII:

ARROGANCE

Samuel Chase

Supreme Court Justice. Charge: Conduct Unbecoming a Judge (prior office). On Feb. 9, 1805, the U.S. House of Representatives voted for eight articles of impeachment against Chase, by a vote of 73 to 32. On March 1, 1805, the Senate acquitted Chase. The largest vote in favor of conviction was 19 to 15 (less than 2/3).

Samuel Chase
Samuel Chase was a U.S. Supreme Court Justice with a very sharp tongue. For instance, to his politically wayward son-in-law, he once said, "Yes, you

are young and may be a Democrat, but for an old man to be a Democrat, he must first be a fool." He was no different as a judge; when Chief Justice John Marshall testified at Chase's impeachment trial *in Chase's defense,* Marshall conceded that Chase was "tyrannical, oppressive and overbearing."[dxxix] And that was on a good day.

Chase was impeached by the U.S. House of Representatives for several similarly tart and injudicious remarks and actions in court. In the case of John Fries, Fries had fomented a rebellion over a federal property tax, and he was convicted of treason. A new trial was ordered, and Chase was supposed to preside over it.[dxxx] At the new trial (it was charged at Chase's impeachment), Chase treated the defendant unfairly, for instance by deciding a question of law against Fries in front of the jury, "tending to prejudice the minds of the jury against the case," but then refusing to allow Fries's lawyer to argue the law (not just the facts) to the jury.[dxxxi] This alleged injudiciousness on Chase's part led to Fries being pardoned after the trial. [dxxxii] Senate vote on this impeachment charge against Chase regarding the Fries trial: 16 to 18. Less than 2/3, no conviction.

Another Chase case was a prosecution under the Sedition Act against a publisher, for criticizing the government by libeling President Adams. Chase, the judge in the case, said outside the courtroom that he would punish the defendant as long as he could find an honest jury in Virginia (an open question in Chase's mind), and that the publisher should be hanged — but that's *not* why Chase was later impeached. Chase was impeached for personally urging the grand jury to indict the defendant, arresting rather than summoning the defendant, refusing to excuse a juror who said that he could not be impartial, excluding the testimony of a defense witness, refusing a continuance, interrupting defense counsel, and expressing "unusual, rude, and contemptuous expressions towards the prisoner's counsel, and [] falsely insinuating that the [defendant] wished to excite the public fears and indignation." This resulted in Chase Impeachment Articles II through VII.[dxxxiii] (Despite all the Chase theatrics before and during trial, after the jury rendered its verdict, Chase actually fined the defendant all of $100.) Senate vote on the impeachment charge against Chase regarding the Sedition Act trial: 18 to 16. Less than 2/3, no conviction.

In another case, Chase was accused of giving a political speech from the bench to a grand jury, an "intemperate and inflammatory political harangue [which was] highly indecent, extrajudicial, and tending to prostitute the high judicial character with which he was invested to the low purpose of an electioneering partisan [sic]."[dxxxiv] Chase spoke out against equal rights and against one-man, one-vote, saying that they would institute "mobocracy."[dxxxv] In his defense, Chase explained that the bench was in a bar (yes, Chase held court in a bar), his speech was to a public audience, and there was no other business before the grand jury at the time (other than "the next round is on me," I guess). Senate vote on this barroom impeachment charge: 19 to 15. Less than 2/3, no conviction.

Chase's Federalist supporters alleged that his impeachment was politically motivated, while his Democratic-Republican opponents said that Chase simply shouldn't be a judge. Vice President Aaron Burr presided over the Senate trial, despite the fact that Burr had just killed Alexander Hamilton in a duel, and was under indictment himself for murder. (And you thought Dick Cheney had issues....) As noted, the Senate failed to reach a two-thirds majority on any charge against Chase; the highest vote against Chase was 19 to 15.[dxxxvi] The specific question put to each Senator was: "Is Samuel Chase, the respondent, guilty of a high crime or misdemeanor?"[dxxxvii] (This was important, because it applied the "high crime or misdemeanor" standard of Article II, Section 4 of the Constitution to removal of a federal judge, rather than the "good behaviour" standard of Article III, Section 1.) For something more than one-third of the Senate in 1805, arrogance alone was neither a high crime nor a misdemeanor.

What is most interesting about the Chase Senate impeachment trial, just sixteen years after the U.S. Constitution was written, is the utter absence of any consensus as to what qualified as a high crime or misdemeanor. It was a time of, as one observer called it, an "epidemic of impeachments," for all sorts of reasons.[dxxxviii] From his ringside seat, in his memoirs, John Quincy Adams gave us this view of the vehement debate (even then) over the meaning of the term "high Crimes and Misdemeanors" — including the opinion of the Senate Door-Keeper:

"*[According to Senator Giles of Virginia, t]he power of impeachment was given without limitation to the House of Representatives; the power of trying impeachments was given equally without limitation to the Senate; and if the Judges of the Supreme Court should dare, as they had done, to declare an act of Congress unconstitutional, or to send a mandamus to the Secretary of State, as they had done, it was the undoubted right of the House of Representatives to impeach them, and of the Senate to remove them, for giving such opinions, however honest or sincere they may have been in entertaining them. Impeachment was not a criminal prosecution; it was no prosecution at all. The Senate sitting for the trial of impeachments was not a court, and ought to discard and reject all process of analogy to a court of justice. A trial and removal of a judge upon impeachment need not imply any criminality or corruption in him. Congress had no power over the person, but only over the office. And a removal by impeachment was nothing more than a declaration by Congress to this effect: You hold dangerous opinions, and if you are suffered to carry them into effect you will work the destruction of the nation. We want your offices, for the purpose of giving them to men who will fill them better. In answer to all this, Mr. Smith only contended that honest error of opinion could not, as he conceived, be a subject of impeachment. And in pursuit of this principle he proved clearly enough the persecution and tyranny to which those of Giles and Randolph inevitably lead. It would, he said, establish a tyranny over opinions, and he traced all the arguments of Giles to their only possible issue of rank absurdity. In all this conversation I opened my lips but once, in which I told Giles that I could not assent to his definition of the term impeachment. It was easy to see that Giles was anxious about Smith's vote on the impeachment of Judge Chase. His manner was dogmatical and peremptory. Smith's was not merely mild and hesitating, but continually conceding too much, and, to use an expression of Burke, 'above all things afraid of being too much in the right.' Mr. Smith has so often expressed these opinions that the friends of Judge Chase flatter themselves he will vote for an acquittal on the trial. His opinions were correct on the impeachment of Judge Pickering, but his vote abandoned them. Indeed, Giles's doctrines are very natural inferences from those upon which that case was decided, and I never can have any confidence in the resolute integrity of those who shrunk from the convictions of their own consciences at that time. It is obvious that on Smith's principles Chase must be acquitted, for the articles of impeachment contain no charge which indicates corruption or turpitude. So that Smith and Giles were really trying the judge over the fireside. Old Mathers, the door-keeper, saw this so plainly that after they were gone he said to me, 'If all were of Mr. Giles's opinion, they never need trouble themselves to bring Judge Chase here.' I perceive, also, that the impeachment system is to be pursued, and the whole bench of the Supreme Court to be swept away, because their offices are wanted. And in the present state of things I am convinced it is as easy for Mr. John Randolph and Mr. Giles to do this as to say it.*"[dxxxix]

In 1805, the U.S. Senate couldn't agree on what was an impeachable offense, but the Senate then didn't have the benefit of 230 years of precedent. We are more fortunate.

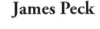

James Peck

Federal Judge. Charge: Abuse of Power. On Apr. 24, 1830, the U.S. House of Representatives voted 123 to 49 in favor of one article of impeachment against Peck. On Jan. 31, 1831, the Senate voted 21 to 22 against conviction.

James Peck

After Justice Chase, the next federal judge to be impeached was James Peck, a judge in Missouri. After Peck issued a decision rejecting land grants by the Spanish king preceding the Louisiana Purchase,[dxl] the attorney for one of the parties wrote a rather tempered anonymous critique of the decision in a

St. Louis newspaper. Peck's response was less tempered: he jailed the attorney for one day for contempt of court, and suspended the attorney's law license for 18 months.

The U.S. House of Representatives voted to impeach Peck for abuse of power. The U.S. Senate voted 21 to 22 against dismissal.[dxli]

Only five weeks after Peck's acquittal, however, the Senate and House passed a law, and the President signed that law, limiting contempt only to acts "in the presence of the said courts, or so near thereto as to obstruct the administration of justice . . . ."[dxlii]

The U.S. Supreme Court also reversed Peck's decision on the land grants.[dxliii] Thus in Peck's case, Congress, the President and the U.S. Supreme Court all punished the sin, not the sinner.

In general, to use the terms that John Quincy Adams used regarding the Chase impeachment, it has been common to see judges threatened with impeachment for corruption and turpitude, not for their decisions in court. The general sense has been that 'The System' provides other outlets for the genuinely aggrieved, like appeals.

Donald Trump

Donald Trump may not be the best President. In fact, as noted above, after only a year of Trump in office, a survey of the American Political Science Association, a nonpartisan organization of political scientists, named him the worst. The Worst of All Time.[dxliv]

However, Trump cannot be impeached for his sustained effort to pack the federal courts with right-wing nut jobs, his unsuccessful attempt to deny health coverage to 25+ million Americans, his budget-busting tax breaks for himself (and other needy billionaires), his hate-thy-neighbor foreign policy, his perpetrating three government shutdowns (including the longest one in history), his aid and comfort to racists and bigots, or his Edifice Complex (wallwallwallwallwallwall). As in the case of Justice Chase and Judge Peck, simply doing the job badly is not an impeachable offense, even if one is setting the all-time record for "badly."

*C*HAPTER XIV:

SMALL POTATOES

Charles Swayne

Federal Judge. Charge: Gratuities, "Ignorance and Incompetency." On Jan. 18, 1905, the U.S. House of Representatives voted in favor of 13 articles of impeachment against Swayne. On Feb. 27, 1905, the Senate voted against conviction on each article.

Charles Swayne – Petty Theft/Poor Performance

Charles Swayne, a Florida federal judge, was impeached in 1905. The House Judiciary Committee reported out 13 articles of impeachment, alleging that Swayne:

- was not a resident of Florida;
- improperly appointed a U.S. Commissioner;
- appointed another Commissioner who lived all of 16 miles away from his office, resulting in "expense and inconvenience";
- exhibited "partiality and favoritism" toward an attorney;
- improperly held three people in contempt of court;
- "squandered and dissipated" the assets of bankrupt companies through high fees;
- held one person in contempt who then committed suicide;
- purchased a house while it was in litigation before him;
- exhibited "ignorance and incompetency," of which "many illustrations could be given";
- had been absent from court for two months;
- had had attorneys and litigants in his court co-sign notes by which he borrowed money; and
- had freed defendants convicted of a crime (meaning, evidently, that he had not sentenced them to prison).[dxlv]

Swayne also was charged with claiming the maximum allowed $10.00 in *per diem* expenses whether or not he had spent that much, and accepting a free round-trip for himself and three family members to California from a railroad whose bankruptcy was pending before him.

If some of these charges sound petty, it's because they are. Swayne's defenders conceded that he had been somewhat generous to himself from time to time, denied that his rulings had been improper, and maintained staunchly that these were not impeachable "high crimes" or "misdemeanors." Swayne's defenders also could argue that if Swayne had made some poor decisions, the appeals court was always there to correct them.

On the three votes on articles of impeachment on which a roll call vote was taken, the House was badly split, voting 165 to 160, 162 to 138 and 159 to 136 in favor of impeachment.[dxlvi] When the Senate voted, on Feb. 27, 1905, none of the charges drew even a majority, much less the required 2/3 majority. The closest vote was 35 (guilty) to 47 (not guilty); the least close was 13 to 69 (regarding the free round-trip tickets, probably a let-he-who-is-without-sin-cast-the-first-stone vote).[dxlvii]

The Senate was divided among 56 Republicans and 33 Democrats;[dxlviii] Senate Republicans reportedly voted strongly against impeachment. Swayne had been appointed by President Harrison, a Republican, to protect voting rights of Republicans in Florida, and he had never been criticized on that count. This may have brought many Republicans to his defense, regardless of the specifics of the charges.[dxlix] But regardless of that, these charges must have seemed like small potatoes to the U.S. Senate.

William O. Douglas

U.S. Supreme Court Justice. Charges: Gratuities, Leftist Politics, Proximity to Salacious Material. In April 1970, a subcommittee of the House Judiciary Committee voted against impeachment proceedings.

Justice William O. Douglas – $350 Isn't Much of a Bribe

"What, then is an impeachable offense? The only honest answer is that an impeachable offense is whatever a majority of the House of Representatives considers [it] to be at a given moment in history."

Thus spake Gerald R. Ford, Republican leader of the U.S. House of Representatives. On July 29, 1974, seven Republican Congressman joined with 21 Democrats on the House Judiciary Committee to vote to impeach President Richard Nixon for abuse of power (10 Republicans voted no). If Ford had said these words on that date, he might have been hailed as a true bipartisan leader, doing his best to heal divisions in America.

But timing is everything. Those words tripped off Ford's lips (what was it about Ford and tripping?) four years earlier, on April 15, 1970. That was when Ford led a partisan assault against Justice William O. Douglas, in the wake of the U.S. Senate's rejection of Nixon Supreme Court nominees Clement Haynsworth and G. Harrold Carswell, the latter only a week earlier.[dl]

Ford's case against Douglas was thin gruel. Here is what Ford nailed to the door, so to speak:

- Ford complained that Douglas's *Points of Rebellion,* all 97 pages of it, advocated an overthrow of The Establishment and was "intended to give historic legitimacy to the militant hippie-yippie movement." Magazine excerpts from the book appeared in the same issue as nude photographs. (Ford somehow overlooked the fact that Douglas's book could be found in some of the same libraries as *Das Kapital.*)
- In 1966, Douglas dissented in the Supreme Court's decision regarding the obscenity conviction of *Eros* magazine. The same publisher published *Avant Garde* magazine. In 1969, three years later, *Avant Garde* published Douglas's article "The Appeal of Folk Singing" (which actually was about folk singing) and paid Douglas $350 for it. A year after that, a defamation judgment against *Fact* magazine, also published by the same publisher, reached the Supreme Court. Douglas dissented again. The case had not been pending before the Supreme Court when Douglas's article was published.
- While on the Supreme Court, from 1961 until he resigned in 1969, Douglas had earned $12,000 a year serving as President of the Parvin Foundation. The founder had gambling interests in Las Vegas.
- Douglas was a member of the board of directors of the Center for the Study of Democratic Institutions, which had sponsored a conference five years earlier on leftist politics.[dli]

This sort of six-degrees-of-separation, headbone-connected-to-the-neck-bone approach to impeachment did not go over well. (That's what happens when you try to nail thin gruel to the door.)

The House Judiciary Committee reluctantly appointed a subcommittee to investigate. The subcommittee disgorged a 1000-page report. Based on that report, the three Democrats on the subcommittee voted against impeachment. One Republican voted in favor of referring the matter to the full House – not because the charges against Douglas had any merit, but because he thought that the subcommittee should have called Justice Douglas to testify, but didn't. A second Republican abstained. And there the matter ended.[dlii]

As Congressman Thompson wrote in defense of Douglas:

"Never in our impeachment history, until Congressman Ford leveled his charges against Mr. Justice Douglas, has it ever been suggested that a judge could be impeached because, while off the bench, he exercised his First Amendment rights to speak and write on issues of the day and to associate with others in educational enterprises."[dliii]

Unwittingly, or perhaps witlessly, Gerald Ford provided a lesson in how not to impeach a public official. It was painfully obvious that Ford was acting/reacting to an incident that had nothing to do with Douglas's competence to serve in office, *i.e.,* the Senate's rejection of the Carswell nomination to the Supreme Court a week earlier. Ford, loyal Republican centurion that he was, visibly was trying to replicate the Republicans' recent success in forcing Justice Abe Fortas to resign. Ford hoped to create yet another Supreme Court vacancy for President Nixon to fill (even though Nixon had four, more than any other President in the past 50 years). In other words, Ford had "unclean hands."

Moreover, Ford's allegations simply failed to undermine Douglas's legitimacy in office, much less prove high crimes or misdemeanors. Although most Members of Congress would have welcomed the opportunity to examine nude photographs in a hearing or Floor speech (with a pointer! On C-SPAN! In prime time!), the fact that these Botticelli knock-offs shared the same glued binding as an article by Douglas didn't strike anyone but Gerald Ford as a sound basis for impeachment. (And unless reports of Ford's low IQ were substantially understated, they probably didn't strike Ford himself as a sound basis for impeachment, either.) These weren't just small potatoes, they were microscopic ones.

Douglas survived Ford's attack, and went on to be the longest-serving Justice in the history of the U.S. Supreme Court, serving for 36 years. He retired in 1975, allowing none other than Gerald Ford (since elevated to Vice President, and then President) to name his successor.[dliv]

Donald Trump

Here are some numbers[dlv]:

$413 million – the fake loans that Trump took from his father to evade the inheritance tax (adjusted for inflation).

$56 million – Trump's personal profit on a single transaction with a Russian oligarch.

$50 million – the value of the penthouse of Trump Tower Moscow that the Trump Organization offered to Vladimir Putin.

$40 million – Trump's self-reported personal profit in his first year in office from leased federal property (the Trump International Hotel in D.C.), in contravention of the Emoluments Clauses.

$26 million – the amount that the Trump Inauguration Committee paid to a friend of Melania Trump.

$10 million – the amount that a Russian oligarch lent to Trump's campaign chairman.

These are not small potatoes, or any other legume. Trump, a master builder, has erected a Trump Tower of impeachable offenses, taller than the Empire State Building and the Sears Tower combined.

$\mathcal{C}$ONCLUSION – ARTICLES
OF IMPEACHMENT

Based on the Constitution's standard of "Treason, Bribery, or other high Crimes and Misdemeanors," as construed by more than two centuries of precedent, here are "fitting and proper"[dlvi] Articles of Impeachment against Donald Trump:

Article I – Divided Loyalty

WHEREAS Donald Trump and members of his immediate family have sought and accepted billions of dollars in business financing from foreign and foreign-influenced sources; for more than 30 years; Donald Trump has curried favor with officials at the highest levels of the Soviet and Russian Governments for permission and assistance to develop Trump properties in Moscow; Trump personally profited by more than $50 million in a transaction with a Russian oligarch in 2008; according to Trump's son, "Russians make up a pretty disproportionate cross-section of a lot of our assets"; efforts to build Trump Tower Moscow continued through Trump's Presidential campaign; Trump signed a letter of intent for Trump Tower Moscow during the campaign; such efforts included a plan to offer a $50 million gratuity to the Russian President; such efforts can be revived at any time, giving Trump an incentive to curry favor with the Russian Government; and Trump has frequently lied about his business interests in Russia;

WHEREAS Russian Government agents hacked into Democratic National Committee e-mails illegally, and disseminated that confidential information through WikiLeaks and by other means; Russian agents conducted an illegal and deceptive social media campaign, for the purpose of supporting the election of Donald Trump as President of the United States; Donald Trump's son, son-in-law and campaign manager met with Russian lobbyists on June 9, 2016 whom they expected would provide "dirt" on Trump opponent Hillary Clinton; and Donald Trump on July 27, 2016 publicly encouraged Russia to hack into Hillary Clinton's e-mails illegally;

WHEREAS Trump named unregistered foreign agent Paul Manafort as his Presidential Campaign Chair from June 2016 to August 2016; unregistered foreign agent Michael Flynn (who had been paid $45,000 to sit next to Russian President Vladimir Putin at a dinner in Moscow) as his National Security Advisor; Rex Tillerson (whom Putin had awarded the "Russian Order of Friendship" and whose company, Exxon-Mobil, had multi-billion-dollar interests in Russia) as Secretary of State; Wilbur Ross (who owns a shipping company with contracts with a Russian company under U.S. sanctions) as Secretary of Commerce; and Steven Mnuchin (who has been a business partner in an entertainment company with a Ukrainian-born businessman whose primary asset is a Russian aluminum company, which Mnuchin released from U.S. sanctions) as Secretary of the Treasury;

WHEREAS on Dec. 1, 2016, Flynn and Trump son-in-law Jared Kushner met with the Russian Ambassador in Trump Tower, and attempted to set up a "back channel" to the Kremlin concealed from U.S. authorities; Kushner failed to disclose multiple meetings with foreigners in his security clearance application; after taking office, Trump ordered security clearance for Kushner and others contrary to the decisions of the national security staff; Trump met in the Oval Office on May 10, 2017 with the Russian Foreign Minister and Russian Ambassador, and disclosed classified information to them; and at international meetings, Trump met privately with Putin and, following one meeting, he confiscated the notes of his translator and ordered her not to discuss the meeting with anyone else;

WHEREAS Trump has, for the benefit of Russia, eased sanctions on Russian individuals and entities; delayed and refused to implement new sanctions against Russia and Russians; threatened to withdraw from the North Atlantic Treaty Organization (NATO); declared NATO "obsolete"; rationalized the Russian invasion of Afghanistan and occupation of Crimea;

attempted to cast doubt on Russian interference in Trump's favor in the Presidential election; and ordered the withdrawal of American troops from Russia's ally Syria: Now, therefore, be it

RESOLVED, That the House of Representatives—

<u>impeaches</u> President Donald Trump, because divided loyalty makes him unable to fulfill his oath of office and for such high crimes and misdemeanors, and asks the U.S. Senate to try him on his removal from office and barring him for any office of honor or profit.

Article II – Corruption

WHEREAS Donald Trump has solicited and received business and financial benefits from foreign leaders since his election as President of the United States; and such benefits violate the Foreign Emoluments clause of the U.S. Constitution and have not been authorized by Congress; Donald Trump has received tens of millions of dollars in income during his Presidency from the Trump International Hotel lease of federal property, in violation of the Domestic Emoluments clause; Trump has accepted revenue and income from the Trump International Hotel in Washington, D.C., Mar-a-Lago in Florida, and other Trump locations from persons and entities seeking access to and Presidential favors from Trump; Trump has proposed to conduct the G-7 international summit at a Trump property in Florida; Trump's inaugural committees accepted millions of dollars in contributions from persons and entities, including foreign persons and entities, who sought access to and Presidential favors from Trump; such inauguration funds were paid in part to Trump through the Trump International Hotel and to a friend of the First Lady, Melania Trump; Trump has allowed his son-in-law and his son-in-law's father to seek a billion dollars in funding from foreign persons and entities who are heavily reliant on U.S. foreign and military policy; and Trump has publicly castigated Nordstrom's for dropping his daughter's branded clothing line: Now, therefore, be it

RESOLVED, That the House of Representatives—

impeaches President Donald Trump, because of bribery, corruption, violation of the Emoluments Clauses and his oath of office, and for such high crimes and misdemeanors, and asks the U.S. Senate to try him on his removal from office and barring him for any office of honor or profit.

Article III – Obstruction of Justice

WHEREAS during the 2016 Presidential campaign, Trump called on Russia to hack Hillary Clinton's e-mails; Russian Government agents illegally hacked and then released thousands of Democratic National Committee e-mails for the benefit of the Trump campaign; Trump falsely claimed that he had no reason to think that Russia was responsible for the hacking; and Trump falsely claimed that he "HA[S] NOTHING TO DO WITH RUSSIA" not long after he signed a letter of intent to build Trump Tower Moscow;

WHEREAS after taking office, Trump asked the FBI Director to end the investigation of Trump's National Security Advisor, an unregistered foreign agent, and then suggested afterward that he had a recording of that meeting disproving this, when he did not;

WHEREAS Trump fired the FBI Director after the Director refused to release a statement exonerating Trump in the Trump-Russia investigation, and then Trump admitted that he had done so because of "this Russia thing"; and Trump ordered the CIA Director to issue a statement exonerating Trump, which the CIA Director refused to do;

WHEREAS after the Attorney General recused himself from that investigation because he himself had met with the Russian Ambassador during the Trump Presidential campaign, Trump publicly and bitterly attacked the Attorney General for that recusal, and ordered the White House Counsel and Trump's former campaign manager to undo that decision, for the sake of Trump's personal protection (and they refused to do so);

WHEREAS Trump ordered the White House Counsel to have the Special Counsel conducting the Trump-Russia investigation dismissed, which the White House Counsel refused to do; and then Trump asked the White House Counsel to make a false statement that Trump had *not* told him to dismiss the Special Counsel;

WHEREAS Trump personally dictated and disseminated a false statement regarding the June 9, 2016 meeting at Trump Tower between Russian lobbyists offering "dirt" on Trump opponent Hillary Clinton, and Trump's son, son-in-law and campaign manager;

WHEREAS during the Trump-Russia investigation, Trump and his attorneys engaged in wholesale witness tampering, both with "carrots" and "sticks," such as personally and public attacking and disparaging witnesses perceived to be hostile, complimenting witnesses deemed friendly, dangling pardons or the possibility of pardons, trying to instigate an investigation of Michael Cohen's father, and exchanging information with Paul Manafort as Manafort feigned cooperation with prosecutors: Now, therefore, be it

RESOLVED, That the House of Representatives—

<u>impeaches</u> President Donald Trump, because of obstruction of justice and violation of his oath of office, and for such high crimes and misdemeanors, and asks the U.S. Senate to try him on his removal from office and barring him for any office of honor or profit.

Article IV – Abuse of Power

WHEREAS Donald Trump tried to prevent the entry of persons from predominantly Muslim countries into the United States, in effect seeking to impose a religious test on entry in violation of the First Amendment; threatened to close the border with Mexico, thus denying entry to those who otherwise would have the legal right to entry (as well as Americans exercising their right to travel); declared a baseless "state of emergency" to try to rationalize the misappropriation of military funds for construction of a wall on the Mexican border; repeatedly has sought to prevent foreign persons from exercising their right under U.S. and international law to seek asylum in the United States; offered to pardon a federal official if he were imprisoned for unlawfully denying entry; separated hundreds of immigrant children from their parents in violation of law, in some cases locking them up in cages and fenced areas, in inhumane conditions and without education, health or privacy; and encouraged the conditions that led to the avoidable deaths, in federal custody, of Felipe Gomez Alonzo, age 8, and Jakelin Caal Maquin, age 7;

WHEREAS Donald Trump repeatedly demanded the investigation and prosecution of his Presidential opponent, Hillary Clinton, thus abusing prosecutorial authority for a political purpose;

WHEREAS Donald Trump overturned the decisions of national security staff and ordered security clearances for security risks Jared Kushner, his son-in-law, and Ivanka Trump, his daughter, even though Kushner had met with the Russian Ambassador to set up a "back channel" to the Kremlin, sought foreign sources to bail him out of a billion-dollar bad investment, and lied repeatedly on his clearance application; Trump directed the Security Director to refuse to testify about this; and Trump revoked the security clearance of the former FBI Director and others to punish them for criticizing Trump;

WHEREAS Donald Trump disclosed classified information to the Russian Foreign Minister and Russian Ambassador in the Oval Office; thwarted efforts to determine whether he had done the same in private meetings with the Russian President; and selectively declassified the FBI's warrant application on Carter Page to seek a political advantage;

WHEREAS Donald Trump pardoned Joe Arpaio and Dinesh D'Souza for political reasons, and improperly dangled pardons, directly or indirectly, in front of Trump-Russia witnesses and the Commissioner for Border Security;

WHEREAS Donald Trump and officials whom he has appointed have pervasively suppressed and distorted information collected by the Executive Branch regarding climate change;

WHEREAS Donald Trump has conducted a broad campaign to employ Presidential authority to attack, intimidate and punish the independent media, for instance ordering his Postmaster General to double shipping rates for Amazon because its largest shareholder also owns the Washington Post; threatening to take away NBC broadcast licenses; authorizing a media merger by Trump-friendly Sinclair while trying to thwart the AT&T-Time Warner merger; seeking an FBI investigation of the New York Times op-ed entitled "I Am Part of the Resistance Inside the Trump Administration"; threating a *Time* reporter with imprisonment; denying White House press credentials to CNN reporter Jim Acosta; and manipulating tariff law to raise the price of newsprint and newspaper production: Now, therefore, be it

RESOLVED, That the House of Representatives—

impeaches President Donald Trump, because of official misconduct, abuse of power, violation of Constitutional rights and violation of his oath of office, and for such high crimes and misdemeanors, and asks the U.S. Senate to try him on his removal from office and barring him for any office of honor or profit.

Article V – Election Fraud
WHEREAS Donald Trump authorized and directed the payment of hundreds of thousands of dollars of "hush money" to Stormy Daniels and Karen MacDonald during the Presidential campaign, women with whom he allegedly had had extramarital affairs; and such payments were illegal corporate campaign contributions and illegal contributions in excess of individual limits, as admitted in the plea agreement of Michael Cohen, Donald Trump's personal attorney: Now, therefore, be it

RESOLVED, That the House of Representatives—

impeaches President Donald Trump, because of violation of campaign finance laws and fraudulent inducement of his election to office, and for such high crimes and misdemeanors, and asks the U.S. Senate to try him on his removal from office and barring him for any office of honor or profit.

Article VI – Personal Misconduct
WHEREAS at least 24 women have accused Donald Trump of physical and sexual improprieties over three decades before his term in office, including sexual harassment, sexual assault and rape, to wit: Jessica Leeds, Ivana Trump, Kristin Anderson, Jill Harth, E. Jean Carroll, Lisa Boyne, Mariah Billado, Victoria Hughes, Temple Taggert, Cathy Heller, Karena Virginia, Tasha Dixon, Bridget Sullivan, Melinda McGillivray, Natasha Stoynoff, Jennifer Murphy, Rachel Crooks, Samantha Holvey, Ninni Laaksonen, Jessica Drake, Summer Zervos, Cassandra Searles and Alva Johnson;

WHEREAS the existence of so many cases of sexual misconduct, over such a long period, imply the existence of many others that have remained unreported;

WHEREAS in 2005, Trump was recorded as saying that he would "grab" women "by the p*ssy": Now, therefore, be it

RESOLVED, That the House of Representatives—

impeaches President Donald Trump, because of the commission of such serious repeated sexual misconduct, constituting crimes and torts, and for such misdemeanors, and asks the U.S. Senate to try him on his removal from office and barring him for any office of honor or profit.

Article VII – Tax Evasion

WHEREAS there is clear and convincing evidence that Donald Trump engaged in inheritance tax fraud in connection with his acquisition of assets and income from his father and mother's property and estate;

WHEREAS there is clear and convincing evidence that Donald Trump engaged in property tax fraud by misrepresenting the value of properties subject to property tax, and by reporting lower values to property tax authorities while reporting higher and inconsistent values for the same properties to the Federal Election Commission, other governmental authorities, financial institutions and others;

WHEREAS there is clear and convincing evidence that Donald Trump engaged in bank fraud, for the same reasons;

WHEREAS there is clear and convincing evidence that Donald Trump engaged in income tax fraud, having lost two civil cases for income tax fraud and falsely claiming the STAR tax credit on his residence;

WHEREAS Donald Trump claimed in Presidential debate that his paying no taxes was "smart," and he has unlawfully refused to produce his tax returns and tax records, in order to cover up these schemes: Now, therefore, be it

RESOLVED, That the House of Representatives—

impeaches President Donald Trump, because of the commission of such tax and banking fraud, and for such misdemeanors, and asks the U.S. Senate to try him on his removal from office and barring him for any office of honor or profit.

We've never had any public official who was <u>*this*</u> *guilty before. Congress, do your job! Impeach Donald Trump, and remove him from office!*

$\mathscr{A}$PPENDIX I –
THE ENGLISH OPENING

The first moves of a game of chess commonly involve the pawns in front of the king and queen, at the center of the board. The English Opening, however, 1. c4, moves the pawn in front of the queen-bishop two squares forward. Howard Staunton, an Englishman and world chess champion, introduced the move in 1843 in recorded champion play.[dlvii] Hence the name "the English Opening."

No one polled grandmasters after Staunton introduced the English Opening. In fact, polling had not been invented yet. But if there had been a poll on the English Opening, the results would have looked something like this:

Off-Kilter	13%
Off the Wall	24%
Off the Chain	15%
Off Your Rocker	48%

Impeachment had an off-the-wall English Opening of its own, between 1376, the first case of impeachment in England, and 1806, the most recent one.

One of the most common approaches to trying to illuminate any provision in the U.S. Constitution is to turn to English legal sources like Blackstone, *et al.,* and ask what Mother England understood the provision to mean. After all, as Oscar Wilde noted in 1887, the United States and England have really everything in common except, of course, language.[dlviii]

(Or perhaps except language and the common law.) This approach does not work well with impeachment, however, because the English impeachment experience was off the chain.

Impeachment in England was rooted in a centuries-long power struggle between the King and Parliament that is foreign to the American experience, both literally and figuratively. A quarter of all impeachments in 700-year English history of impeachment took place in a two-year period, 1640-42, in the run-up to the English Civil War and the execution of Charles I in 1649.[dlix] "It was a medieval means of removing the protection given to a royal servant whom the Commons found objectionable but could not otherwise persuade the Crown to dismiss."[dlx] Some victims, like Lord Lovat, were not only removed from office, but also hung, drawn and quartered[dlxi] — a very effective way of ensuring that they would not return to power. After Lord Lovat's conviction for treason in 1746, at the age of 79, as Lovat left the Tower of London on his way to the wooden gallows to meet his maker, he saw the gallows collapse and kill nine spectators. The spectators wrongly had assumed that they would see Lovat die, not *vice versa*. Lovat is reported to have celebrated their demise with the same joy that they had reserved for him.[dlxii] (Episodes like this could possibly explain why Article I, Section 3 of the U.S. Constitution provides that "Judgment in Cases of Impeachment shall not extend further than to removal from Office, and disqualification to hold and enjoy any Office of honor, Trust or Profit under the United States." No drawing and quartering for us.)

Leaving aside the quaint antics of colonial times, the question remains whether we can we can draw meaningful lessons about impeachment from the parallel English experience on impeachment since the American War of Independence. The answer to that question is: "fuhgeddaboudit." Although English impeachments began in 1376, the last successful impeachments were those of Lord Lovat and his Jacobite colleagues in the 1740s. Then there was an unsuccessful impeachment of Warren Hastings in 1787 (charged with corruption and found innocent), and an unsuccessful impeachment of Lord Melville in 1806 (charged with misappropriating official funds, and found innocent).[dlxiii] That's it.

The reason for the dissipation of interest in impeachment in England is that the Great Britain and the colonies reacted in entirely different manners to the Madness of King George. The United States reacted by detaching itself; Great Britain reacted with detachment, watering down monarchical power. Over time, the House of Commons drew so much power from the monarch to itself that for any other part of English Government, including wayward officials, resistance was futile. A recent House of Commons briefing paper flatly states that "impeachment is considered obsolete."[dlxiv] The near-omnipotent House of Commons hardly has to go through some elaborate quasi-judicial proceeding like impeachment/conviction simply in order to get rid of someone in English government. It's a lot easier than that – a transient note from the Prime Minister does the trick.

There was a brier eruption of interest in impeachment in Great Britain recently during the War in Iraq, after no weapons of mass destruction were found. (In order to justify the U.K.'s entry into the war, Blair had told Parliament that Iraqi WMD could reach England in 45 minutes.) Several Members of Parliament offered a motion to ascertain: "whether there exist sufficient grounds to impeach the Prime Minister on charges of gross misconduct in his advocacy of the case for war against Iraq and his conduct of policy in connection with that war."[dlxv] The motion did not make it to the Floor of the House of Commons for debate. If a majority of Members of Parliament had wanted Blair out, there were much simpler ways to accomplish that.

When it comes to impeachment, a closer foreign analog is Ireland, even though George Bernard Shaw observed in 1906 that Britain, Ireland and America are "three of the most distinctly marked nationalities under the sun."[dlxvi] Article 35(4) of the Constitution of Ireland provides that judges in Ireland can be removed by vote of both houses of the Irish Legislature, the Dail Eireann and the Seanad Eireann, upon "stated misbehavior or incapacity."[dlxvii] This machinery has been started up twice, but in both cases, the judge in question resigned before the vote.[dlxviii]

$\mathcal{A}$PPENDIX II – SHOULD JUDGES BE IMPEACHED?

Can a federal judge be impeached? One can seek the answer to that question in the Constitution. Looking to the U.S. Constitution for the answer, however, is rather like looking at a chicken's skeleton to try to determine whether a chicken can fly, instead of the simple test of tossing a pebble at one. (That's just a simile, PETA. Not a call to action.) Federal judges *can* be impeached, because they *have* been impeached. But it's interesting, nevertheless, to stroll through the garden of the U.S. Constitution, and see what it has to say.

John Pickering's impeachment, barely a decade after the U.S. Constitution was adopted, presented the "case of first impression" regarding how one *can* get rid of a federal judge. Article III is the section of the U.S. Constitution addressing the judiciary. Article III, Section 1 of the U.S. Constitution requires "good behaviour" of federal judges: "The judges, both of the supreme and inferior courts, shall hold their offices during good behaviour." But the Constitution provides no *express* means for enforcing that rule against judges.

The Constitution establishes complex and starkly different rules for the selection and removal of various federal officeholders. There are two commonalities: any officeholder may end his term upon: (1) resignation or (2) death. Beyond these, it gets complicated.

Federal judges like Pickering are appointed by the President with the advice and consent of the U.S. Senate. The Constitutional term "good behaviour" has been *interpreted* to mean that federal judges serve (aside from cases of resignation or death) until impeachment and removal by Congress (or their jobs can be eliminated, as the Judiciary Act of 1802 demonstrated).

Senators are elected, with vacancies are filled by "writs" of the "executive authority" (governor) of the state, under the 17th Amendment. Senators are removed by death, resignation, completion of one's term, or expulsion by two-thirds vote of the Senate. (The case of William Blount seems to have established a firm principle that impeachment does not apply to Senators).

Members of the U.S. House of Representatives are elected only; there is no other way to join the club. They are removed only by death, resignation, completion of one's term, or expulsion by two-thirds vote of the House.

Executive officials are appointed by the President with the advice and consent of the Senate. They serve at the President's pleasure,[dlxix] or until removed by death, resignation, completion of the President's term or impeachment and removal.

The Vice President is elected, or ascends through the Presidential line of succession, with vacancies filled under the 25th Amendment by appointment by the President and approval of both the House and the Senate. The Vice President is removed only by resignation, death, completion of his term, or impeachment and conviction.

The President is elected or ascends through the Presidential line of succession. The President is removed only by resignation, death, completion of his term or impeachment and conviction, subject to suspension under the 25th Amendment when he or she is unable to perform his or her duties.

We leave it to others to determine whether there is any reason to these rules, but there certainly is no rhyme. Here is a summary:

Grounds for Removal:

OFFICE	Death	Resignation	End of Term	Impeachment	Expulsion	Dismissal
President	√	√	√	√		
Vice President	√	√	√	√		
Civil Officers	√	√	(President's)	√		√(implied)
U.S. Senators	√	√	√		√	
House Members	√	√	√		√	
Federal Judges	√	√		√ (implied)		

Article I governs Congress, and under Article I, Section 5, "Each House may ... with the concurrence of two thirds, expel a member." Article II governs the Executive Branch, and under Article II, Section 4, "The President, Vice President and all civil officers of the United States, shall be removed from office on impeachment for, and conviction of, treason, bribery, or other high crimes and misdemeanors." But Article III says nothing at all about the expulsion or removal of judges.[dlxx] Senator Augustus Octavius Bacon (D-GA) introduced a constitutional amendment to bridge this gap by providing for removal of federal judges by two-thirds vote of the U.S. House and the Senate, on grounds of "immorality, imbecility, maladministration, misfeasance or malfeasance in office."[dlxxi] The Bacon Amendment has not been adopted. Until it is, for federal judges, imbecility may not be required, but it is allowed.

The term "during good behaviour" in Article III has been *interpreted* as establishing a lifetime appointment for every federal judge, subject to impeachment and removal from office by Congress. But Article III provides no procedure and no other standard for removal of judges, other than in a casket.

The Impeachments Clause in Article II, Section 4 does provide such a standard: treason, bribery and other high crimes and misdemeanors. Does this impeachment standard apply to judges? On the *yes* side of the double-entry ledger, the Impeachment Clause explicitly extends to "all civil officers of the United States." If "civil" means non-military, and "officers" means everyone who exercises the sovereign authority of the United States Government, then judges are civil officers under the Constitution, the Impeachment Clause applies to them, and they may be impeached.

Also on the *yes* side of the ledger is the Appointments Clause in Article II, Section 2 of the Constitution, which sheds a little more light on the tenure of judges. It says that the President "shall nominate, and by and with the Advice and Consent of the Senate, shall appoint Ambassadors, other public Ministers and Consuls, Judges of the supreme Court, and all other Officers of the United States, whose Appointments are not herein otherwise provided for, and which shall be established by Law ...." *If* the term "other Officers" includes "Judges of the supreme Court" and other federal judges, and *if* the term "Officers" in this clause and "officers" in the Impeachment Clause of

Article II, Section 4 are equivalent (or at least overlap), then federal judges are "civil officers" under the Constitution, and therefore they are subject to impeachment. [dlxxii]

There was precedent for *yes* at the time that the U.S. Constitution was written. "Throughout the period of English history when impeachment was in vogue and frequently exercised, many judges, among them Lord Chancellors and Lord Chief Justices, were impeached in Parliament."[dlxxiii] As noted above, the Massachusetts House of Representatives sought to impeach an anti-revolutionary judge on Massachusetts's highest court for taking money from the British Government during American Revolution. And in England, impeachment had been used by Parliament against the highest judge, Francis Bacon, who (as noted above) famously asserted that the numerous bribes he had taken had had no effect whatsoever on his decisions.

On the *no* side of the ledger, suggesting that federal judges are not subject to impeachment, is the fact that Article III doesn't say that they are. The Founding Parents may not have been infallible in capitalization, spelling or punctuation, but they were scrupulous about organization – everything went in the right place. For instance, the general oath of office, applying to Members of Congress, Executive Branch officers, judges and even state legislators, is not found in Articles I, II or III, but rather in Article VI, because Article I governs the legislature, Article II governs the Executive Branch, Article III governs the judiciary, and the oath extends to all of them. The fact that the Impeachment Clause appears in Article II, not Article III (the judiciary Article) suggests that maybe the Founders did not intend that Article III judges be subject to impeachment.

Also arguing for *no* is the fact that dating from colonial times, there was a separate and widely known procedure for removing judges lacking "good behaviour," called addressing. Addressing is a vote by both houses of the legislature to remove a judge. Ten of the oldest thirty states use it today: Arkansas (on good cause, by two-thirds votes), Connecticut (two-thirds votes), Maine, Maryland (two-thirds votes), Massachusetts (with the consent of the governor's council), Mississippi (two-thirds votes), New Hampshire (for reasonable cause), South Carolina (two-thirds), Texas (two-thirds), Wisconsin (two-thirds). Seven of the original thirteen states had addressing at the time of the Constitution. It was proposed that addressing be included in the Constitution, but it was voted down by a vote of 1 for to 12 against. This was out of concern that removal of judges by legislative majority vote, without legal standards, would compromise federal judicial independence.[dlxxiv] After the Senate failed to muster a two-thirds majority to remove Justice Samuel Chase during his impeachment, one of the House impeachment managers introduced a Constitutional amendment to allow "addressing" by majority vote, but it was never adopted by the States.[dlxxv]

On the other other hand, 47 states (including all ten of the states employing addressing), *also* provide for impeachment of judges by the State House, and removal by the State Senate – and impeachment under state constitutions has, from time to time, been applied to judges. (What about the other three states? Hawaii and Oregon rely on non-legislative commissions instead, and Washington State requires a joint resolution supported by a three-quarters vote. Furthermore, in Missouri and Nebraska, impeachments are tried by the State Supreme Court rather than the Senate, and in New York, the Senate and the Supreme Court join together to vote.)[dlxxvi]

In any event, federal judges *have* been impeached – 15 so far. Eight of them have been convicted, and removed from office, starting with Judge Pickering. So although the Constitution may leave room for doubt about whether federal judges can be impeached, history seemingly does not.

$\mathscr{A}$PPENDIX III –

THE BLUE EXPEL THE GREY

There were a large number of federal impeachments and expulsions resulting from the attempt by the Confederacy to exit the Union.

Regarding Congressmen and federal judges, in 1861, Congressmen John Bullock Clark (MO), John William Reid (MO) and Henry Cornelius Burnett (KY) were expelled from the House, by two-thirds vote, for disloyalty to the Union.[dlxxvii] All of them were from border states occupied by Union forces.[dlxxviii] In 1862, Federal judge West Humphreys of Tennessee was impeached and convicted by the Senate for aiding the Confederacy. He was the only federal judge who was impeached and convicted during the Civil War.

There were 11 states that formally seceded from the Union during the Civil War, and factions from two border slave states (Kentucky and Missouri) attempted to do so, although Union soldiers occupied them militarily from the start of the war. Those 13 rebellious states had 26 U.S. Senators. Twenty-four of the 26 U.S. Senators who represented those states left the U.S. Senate – by various means.

Fourteen U.S. Senators, all Democrats, were expelled for supporting the Confederacy. They were Sens. James Mason (VA), Robert Hunter (VA), Thomas Clingman (NC), Thomas Bragg (NC), James Chesnut Jr. (SC), Alfred Nicholson (TN), William Sebastian (AR), Charles Mitchel (AR), John Hemphill (TX), Louis Wigfall (TX), John Breckinridge (KY), Trusten Polk (MO), and Waldo Johnson (MO).[dlxxix] Sen. Breckinridge of Kentucky had swept the Southern States in the 1860 Presidential election, coming in second to Lincoln in the electoral vote (while not winning a single vote in

New York, New Jersey, Pennsylvania or Rhode Island).[dlxxx] Breckinridge was expelled from the Senate nevertheless. His border state colleague, Lazarus Powell (KY), was formally accused of supporting the Confederacy, but he was not expelled, and he remained in the U.S. Senate.

Six other Senators had their resignations formally acknowledged by Senate resolution, declaring their seats vacant: Albert Brown (MS), Jefferson Davis (MS), Stephen Mallory (FL), Clement Clay (AL), Robert Toombs (GA) and Judah Benjamin (LA).[dlxxxi] Davis became President of the Confederate States of America.

As for five other Senators from the Confederacy, their terms simply expired, on March 3, 1861. These were Benjamin Fitzpatrick (AL), David Yulee (FL), Alfred Iverson, Sr. (GA), John Slidell (LA), James Hammond (SC).[dlxxxii]

Outside the Confederacy, Jesse Bright (IN) was expelled for helping a friend sell guns to the Confederacy. (He wrote a letter of introduction addressed to "His Excellency Jefferson Davis.")[dlxxxiii]

Aside from Lazarus Powell, who managed to hang onto his Senate seat despite accusations of supporting the Confederacy, the *only* other Senator of those 26 from rebel states who avoided expulsion, resignation or the end of his term was Andrew Johnson (TN). Johnson, a pro-Union slave-owner, never faced a charge of supporting the Confederacy. He became the Union's Military Governor of Tennessee, then 16th Vice President of the United States, and then (after Lincoln's assassination) 17th President of the United States. As noted above, Johnson was impeached by the U.S. House of Representatives, and escaped conviction in the U.S. Senate by one vote.

$\mathscr{A}$PPENDIX IV –
THE GOVERNORS VS.
THE KLAN

Several governors were impeached for standing up to the Ku Klux Klan, and Confederate resistance during Reconstruction. This has nothing to do with Donald Trump, but it's an interesting sidelight regarding a traumatic time in American history. (If you think that the country is divided now ... .)

William Holden. The Klan started asserting itself immediately after the Civil War. In North Carolina, President Andrew Johnson appointed William Holden as Governor in 1865. Holden, a newspaper publisher, originally had been a supporter of slavery and secession, but before North Carolina left the Union, he changed his positions. Holden was sent as a delegate to a North Carolina state convention to vote *against* secession. After Lincoln asked North Carolina to provide troops against the Confederacy, however, Holden voted *for* secession. Nevertheless, he criticized the Confederacy editorially, and ran for North Carolina Governor as a peace candidate in 1864.

After his appointment as Governor, courtesy of President Andrew Johnson, Holden returned to the ballot in a special election in 1865, a year after his defeat as a peace candidate. Jonathan Worth and his Confederate supporters defeated Holden in that special election, 56% to 44%. Worth was reelected in 1866, but declined to run for reelection in 1868. Holden won that election. Worth, reflecting the bitterness over Union troops remaining in Southern states years after the Civil War was over, told Holden, "I surrender the office to you under what I deem Military duress."

Klan-directed violence flared in many parts of North Carolina during Holden's new term of office. In February 1870, an African-American local commissioner was lynched by the Klan. In May 1870, a Republican, white State Senator was murdered by the Klan.

Holden tried to end the violence. He hired two dozen detectives to investigate and put down the violence. In July 1870, Holden hired George Kirk, a colonel in the Union Army who nevertheless was a Southerner from Tennessee, to put down what Holden called an insurrection. Holden declared martial law in two counties. Kirk gathered 300 volunteers, and arrested 100 people whom Kirk deemed responsible for the Klan-directed violence. None of them was prosecuted, however. Kirk's forces and the Klan fought each other, with a total of 28 casualties. This led to a populist backlash against Holden. In September 1870, Holden lifted martial law, and disbanded Kirk's forces.

In the meantime, however, Holden's Democratic opponents swept to power in the North Carolina legislature. They blamed Holden for the violence. In short order, the North Carolina House impeached Holden on Dec. 14, 1870, and the North Carolina Senate convicted him and removed him from office on March 22, 1871. Six impeachment counts against Holden passed. All of them related to Holden's efforts to stop the Klan. All of them passed on a party-line vote.

In 2011, 140 years later, a very different North Carolina Senate voted unanimously to pardon Holden.[dlxxxiv]

Henry Warmoth. Henry Warmoth was a "carpetbagger" who became Governor of Louisiana. He was born in Illinois. During the Civil War, Warmoth was dishonorably discharged, but President Lincoln reinstated his status as a soldier. Warmoth moved to Louisiana in 1865, ran for Governor as a Republican in 1868, and won. He was 26 years old. Warmoth tried to find some kind of middle ground on Reconstruction, which actually alienated both Republicans and Democrats. By 1871, he was forced to secure the statehouse with state militia forces. He did not run for reelection in 1872, and that election descended into violence. The results of that election, as recognized today, had the Republican candidate winning by 57% to 43%, but Warmoth nevertheless declared the Democrat the winner. President Grant deployed federal troops to ensure that the Republican took office.

In the meantime, Warmoth, with barely a month left before the end of his term, was impeached and convicted for trying to steal the election from the Republicans and hand it to the Democrats.

Warmoth's post-impeachment temporary replacement was American's first African-American Governor. The Republican candidate then was sworn into office. The fight was not over, though; in September 1874, 5000 supporters of the defeated Democratic candidate, mostly former Confederate soldiers, overthrew the Republican Governor for three days, until federal troops restored the Republican to power.[dlxxxv]

Adelbert Ames. Adelbert Ames, born in Maine, rose to be a two-star General in the Union Army. Congress appointed Ames to be provisional Governor of Mississippi during Reconstruction, in 1868. In 1870, the Reconstructionist Mississippi Legislature appointed Ames to the U.S. Senate. In 1873, Ames ran for Governor of Mississippi against a former Confederate General, a "carpetbagger" (Ames) against a "scalawag." Ames won, 58% to 42%.

Shortly thereafter, there was massive Klan-organized violence against African-Americans throughout the state, for the purpose of taking it over. (This was the Klan's infamous "Mississippi Plan"). Ames was unable to restore order. Violence and threats of violence suppressed the Republican vote almost entirely, giving Democrats a five-to-one majority in the state legislature. In the 1875 election, thanks to overwhelming voter suppression, five counties with large black majorities polled only 12, 7, 4, 2, and 0 total Republican votes. The Democrats removed the African-American Lieutenant Governor and then impeached Ames, planning to replace him with the Democrat next in line in the legislature. Ames, seeing defeat in the Senate as inevitable, resigned in early 1876.

Ames himself recovered well from the experience. After his service as Governor of Mississippi, he lived another 57 years, passing away in 1933 in Ormond Beach, Florida at the age of 97. He was the last surviving full-rank General who had served in the Civil War.[dlxxxvi]

Jack Walton. The ugliest confrontation between the Klan and a Governor came in Oklahoma, in 1923. In 1921, the Klan wiped out a black community in Tulsa that was reputed to be the richest black community in the country. They did it by adopting a new invention called the airplane, then

16 years old. The Klan employed airplanes to drop firebombs (nitroglycerin and turpentine, mostly) on the black neighborhood, and strafe the neighborhood with rifles from above. 100-300 people died, the neighborhood was burned to the ground, and everyone left.[dlxxxvii]

Watching this at a distance were the good people of Oklahoma City. They had elected Jack Walton, an anti-Klan, anti-Prohibition, early New Deal Democrat, as mayor. He ran as an anti-Klan candidate for Governor in 1922, and won.

After Walton was sworn in, seeing that things were not getting better in Tulsa, he declared martial law there, and brought in the National Guard. Walton also suspended *habeas corpus*, an action which is expressly forbidden by the Oklahoma State Constitution. He tried to get the Legislature to outlaw the Klan, but failed. He then declared martial law throughout the entire state.[dlxxxviii]

The Legislature, which was largely pro-Klan and pro-Prohibition, quickly decided that they had had enough of this. They impeached Walton and removed him from office in less than a year.

As explained above, Henry Johnston, another Democrat and also something of a liberal, was elected in the next election. When the Legislature tried to impeach Johnston, he called out the National Guard to occupy the Capitol and prevent the Legislature from meeting at all. They waited until the next regular session, when Johnston couldn't prevent them from meeting, and then they impeached and removed him as well.

Walton, understandably bitter about this, ran for US Senate and lost the general election. He then ran for Corporation Commissioner, and won. He also ran twice again for Governor, losing the primary both times.[dlxxxix]

ENDNOTES

i   https://twitter.com/ewarren/status/1119331296470237185

ii   https://www.realclearpolitics.com/video/2019/04/16/ocasio-cortez_so_
         many_reasons_to_impeach_trump_number_one_is_emoluments.html

iii   https://www.realclearpolitics.com/video/2019/01/04/new_democratic_
         congresswoman_rashida_tlaib_on_trump_were_going_to_impeach_the_
         motherfcker.html

iv   https://theweek.com/speedreads/728623/trump-tells-puerto-ricans-have-
         good-time-throws-paper-towel-rolls

v   https://www.washingtonpost.com/news/the-fix/wp/2017/10/18/trumps-
         alleged-knew-what-he-signed-up-for-remark-to-military-widow-is-worth-
         caution-but-fits-a-clear-pattern/

vi   https://allthatsinteresting.com/donald-trump-quotes#8

vii   https://www.amazon.com/Guilty-Doonesbury-book/dp/0030125111

viii   https://www.nytimes.com/interactive/2018/02/19/opinion/how-does-
         trump-stack-up-against-the-best-and-worst-presidents.html

ix   U.S. Constitution, Article II, Section 4.

x   https://catalog.hathitrust.org/Record/000405801

xi   *See* A. Beveridge, <u>Life of John Marshall</u> 157 & 173 (1919).

xii   www.jstor.org/stable/1098896

xiii   Expulsion from the House or Senate is governed by a different clause in the
         U.S. Constitution. U.S. Constitution, Art. I, Section 5.

xiv   H.R. Rep. No. 101-36, Impeachment of Walter L. Nixon, Jr., Report of the
         Committee on the Judiciary to Accompany H. Res. 87, 101st Cong., 1st
         Sess. (1989) at 5 (1989).

xv   Humphrey, *op. cit.* at 294.

xvi   http://watergate.info/1974/07/25/barbara-jordan-speech-on-impeachment.
         html

xvii   On Feb. 8, 1999, in closing arguments: en.wikipedia.org/wiki/Impeachment_
         of_Bill_Clinton

xviii   Ball, "The Democrats Will Likely Impeach," TIME magazine (Mar.
         25, 2019)

xix Translator Harry Reeve, www.gutenberg.org/files/815/815-h/815-h.htm

xx Cortez A. M. Ewing, "The Impeachment of James E. Ferguson," *Political Science Quarterly* Vol. 48, No. 2 (Jun., 1933), pp. 184-210 at 205, https://www.jstor.org/stable/2143345.

xxi https://www.britannica.com/topic/impeachment

xxii http://memory.loc.gov/service/mss/mtj/mtj1/038/038_0303_0306.pdf

xxiii https://www.chicagotribune.com/news/ct-xpm-2004-12-19-0412190440-story.html

xxiv www.law.cornell.edu/wex/stare_decisis

xxv www.aqr.org.uk/glossary/commitment-bias

xxvi U.S. Const., art. III, Section 3.

xxvii U.S. House Judiciary Committee, <u>Constitutional Grounds for Presidential Impeachment</u> 11 (Feb. 1974).

xxviii *United States v. Cramer,* 325 U.S. 1, 40 (1945).

xxix *United States v. Burr,* No. 14,693, 25 Fed. Cas. 55 (Cir. Ct. D. Va. 1807), http://press-pubs.uchicago.edu/founders/documents/a3_3_1-2s22.html

xxx https://www.history.com/news/aaron-burrs-notorious-treason-case

xxxi en.wikipedia.org/wiki/Third_Treaty_of_San_Ildefonso

xxxii en.wikipedia.org/wiki/War_of_the_Pyrenees

xxxiii See Frederick J. Turner, "Documents on the Blount Conspiracy, 1795-1797," *The American Historical Review* Vol. 10, No. 3 (Apr., 1905), pp. 574-606, www.jstor. org/stable/1832281, penelope.uchicago.edu/Thayer/E/Journals/AHR/10/3/Documents_on_the_Blount_Conspiracy*.html

xxxiv en.wikipedia.org/wiki/George_Washington%27s_Farewell_Address

xxxv Annals of the Congress of the United States (5th Cong.) 3152-54 (1851), play.google.com/books/reader?id=9BhLAQAAMAAJ&hl=en

xxxvi Bernard C. Steiner and James McHenry, *The life and correspondence of James McHenry* (1907), cited in en.wikipedia.org/wiki/William_Blount#cite_note-9

xxxvii founders.archives.gov/documents/Jefferson/01-29-02-0371

xxxviii <u>Extracts</u>, pp. 5-8.

xxxix Rep. Benjamin Butler, quoted in George H. Hayes, II, *The Senate of the United States* 858 (1938).

xl https://founders.archives.gov/documents/Jefferson/01-30-02-0427#TSJN-01-30-0430-fn-0001

xli *See* The U.S. Constitution, www.law.cornell.edu/constitution

xlii "[T]he Senate failed to make clear whether its decision stemmed from a belief that no senator could be impeached or from the belief that someone who ceased to hold a 'civil office' [because he already had been 'sequestered'] also ceased to be impeachable." www.senate.gov/artandhistory/history/common/expulsion_cases/Blount_expulsion.htm

xliii   en.wikipedia.org/wiki/William_Blount

xliv   https://www.gq.com/story/treasonsplainer

xlv   https://en.wikipedia.org/wiki/Business_projects_of_Donald_Trump_in_Russia

xlvi   https://en.wikipedia.org/wiki/Felix_Sater

xlvii   1 Mueller Report 66-76.

xlviii   https://www.washingtonpost.com/politics/2018/11/30/is-floating-million-trump-tower-penthouse-vladimir-putin-illegal/?utm_term=.b7052298d8d6

xlix   https://www.nytimes.com/2019/03/18/business/deutsche-bank-donald-trump.html

l   https://money.cnn.com/2017/01/31/investing/deutsche-bank-us-fine-russia-money-laundering/index.html

li   https://www.newsweek.com/trump-sold-40-million-estate-russian-oligarch-100-million-and-democratic-802613

lii   Jonathan Chait, "Will Trump Be Meeting His Counterpart – or His Handler?," *New York Magazine* (May 2018), http://nymag.com/intelligencer/2018/07/trump-putin-russia-collusion.html

liii   https://www.businessinsider.com/donald-trump-jr-said-money-pouring-in-from-russia-2018-2

liv   https://en.wikipedia.org/wiki/Paul_Manafort

lv   https://www.justsecurity.org/63838/guide-to-the-mueller-reports-findings-on-collusion/

lvi   Max Boot, "Here are 18 Reasons Trump Could Be a Russian Asset," *Washington Post* (Jan. 13, 2019), https://www.washingtonpost.com/opinions/here-are-18-reasons-why-trump-could-be-a-russian-asset/2019/01/13/45b1b250-174f-11e9-88fe-f9f77a3bcb6c_story.html?utm_term=.9ca887b57f68

lvii   https://en.wikipedia.org/wiki/Trump_Tower_meeting#Participants

lviii   https://themoscowproject.org/explainers/trumps-russia-cover-up-by-the-numbers-70-contacts-with-russia-linked-operatives/

lix   David Graham, "The Coincidence at the Heart of the Russia Hacking Scandal," *The Atlantic* (July 2018), https://www.theatlantic.com/politics/archive/2018/07/russia-hacking-trump-mueller/565157/

lx   https://www.justsecurity.org/63838/guide-to-the-mueller-reports-findings-on-collusion/

lxi   https://themoscowproject.org/collusion/first-presidential-debate-somebody-sitting-bed-weighs-400-pounds/

lxii https://www.nytimes.com/2018/07/16/us/politics/trump-putin-summit.html

lxiii 1 Mueller Report 14-36.

lxiv Max Bergmann *et al.,* "Conspiracy Against the United States: The Story of Trump and Russia," https://www.americanprogressaction.org/issues/democracy/reports/2018/11/27/172558/conspiracy-united-states-story-trump-russia/

lxv 1 Mueller Report 123-127.

lxvi https://www.justsecurity.org/63838/guide-to-the-mueller-reports-findings-on-collusion/

lxvii https://www.nytimes.com/2017/12/06/us/politics/michael-flynn-russia-sanctions-ripped-up-whistleblower.html

lxviii https://en.wikipedia.org/wiki/Links_between_Trump_associates_and_Russian_officials#Trump_administration_members

lxix https://www.cnbc.com/2018/03/13/rex-tillersons-tax-deal-may-have-made-year-in-trumps-orbit-worth-it.html

lxx https://en.wikipedia.org/wiki/Links_between_Trump_associates_and_Russian_officials#Trump_administration_members

lxxi https://www.nytimes.com/2019/02/28/us/politics/jared-kushner-security-clearance.html

lxxii 2 Mueller Report, pp. 65-76.

lxxiii https://en.wikipedia.org/wiki/Donald_Trump%27s_disclosures_of_classified_information

lxxiv https://en.wikipedia.org/wiki/Nixon_interviews

lxxv https://www.washingtonpost.com/opinions/here-are-18-reasons-why-trump-could-be-a-russian-asset/2019/01/13/45b1b250-174f-11e9-88fe-f9f77a3bcb6c_story.html?utm_term=.1d1556a98384

lxxvi https://www.nytimes.com/2018/12/19/us/politics/sanctions-oleg-deripaska-russia-trump.html

lxxvii https://www.businessinsider.com/court-document-shows-oleg-deripaska-loaned-paul-manafort-10-million-2018-6

lxxviii https://www.nytimes.com/2019/01/29/us/politics/steven-mnuchin-russia-sanctions.html

lxxix https://www.nbcnews.com/politics/national-security/trump-admin-has-not-imposed-new-sanctions-russia-required-law-n962216

lxxx https://www.nytimes.com/2019/01/14/us/politics/nato-president-trump.html

lxxxi https://www.nytimes.com/2018/07/10/world/europe/trump-nato-summit-latvia-baltics.html

lxxxii   Max Boot, "Here are 18 Reasons Trump Could Be a Russian Asset," *Washington Post* (Jan. 13, 2019), https://www.washingtonpost.com/opinions/here-are-18-reasons-why-trump-could-be-a-russian-asset/2019/01/13/45b1b250-174f-11e9-88fe-f9f77a3bcb6c_story.html?utm_term=.9ca887b57f68

lxxxiii https://www.nytimes.com/2019/02/14/world/middleeast/us-syria-troop-withdrawal.html

lxxxiv   https://thehill.com/homenews/administration/425034-trump-i-have-been-tougher-on-russia-that-any-other-president

lxxxv   1 Mueller Report 110-122, 185-187.

lxxxvi   https://www.washingtonpost.com/opinions/here-are-18-reasons-why-trump-could-be-a-russian-asset/2019/01/13/45b1b250-174f-11e9-88fe-f9f77a3bcb6c_story.html?utm_term=.1d1556a98384

lxxxvii Condon, The Manchurian Candidate (1959).

lxxxviii *In re Chapman,* 166 U.S. 661, 669-70 (1897) (the U.S. Supreme Court, per Fuller, C.J.),

lxxxix   119 Cong. Rec. 31368, 93d Cong. 1st Sess.

xc   Journal of the House of Representatives of the United States, Volume 19, Issue 2, at p. 110.

xci   119 Cong. Rec. 31368, 93d Cong. 1st Sess.

xcii   George Clinton preceded him, serving uncomfortably under both Thomas Jefferson and James Madison. en.wikipedia.org/wiki/List_of_Vice_Presidents_of_the_United_States

xciii   www.politifact.com/truth-o-meter/statements/2010/may/24/chris-matthews/chris-matthews-says-cheney-got-34-million-payday-h/

xciv   Grant Administration scandals were so numerous that they have their own Wikipedia page, with a "Scandal Summary Table" for anyone having trouble keeping track: en.wikipedia.org/wiki/Grant_administration_scandals#Scandal_summary_table

Scandal	Description	Date
Black Friday	Speculators tied to Grant corner the gold market and ruin the economy for several years.	1869
New York custom house ring	Alleged corruption ring at the New York Custom House under two of Grant's appointees.	1872

Star Route postal ring	Corrupt system of postal contractors, clerks, and brokers to obtain lucrative Star Route postal contracts.	1872
Salary grab	Congressmen receive a retroactive $5,000 bonus for previous term served.	1872
Breach of Treaty of Fort Laramie (1868)	Organized a White House cabal to plan a war against the Lakotas to allow mining of gold found in Black Hills.	1874
Sanborn moiety extortion	John Sanborn charged exorbitant commissions to collect taxes and split the profits among associates.	1874
Secretary Delano's Department of Interior	Interior Secretary Columbus Delano allegedly took bribes in exchange for fraudulent land grants.	1875
U.S. Attorney General Williams' DOJ	Attorney General George H. Williams allegedly received a bribe not to prosecute the Pratt & Boyd company.	1875
Whiskey Ring	Corrupt government officials and whiskey makers steal millions of dollars in national tax evasion scam.	1876
Secretary Belknap's Department of War	War Secretary William Belknap allegedly takes extortion money from trading contractor at Fort Sill.	1876
Secretary Robeson's Department of Navy	Secretary of Navy George Robeson allegedly receives bribes from Cattell & Company for lucrative Navy contracts.	1876
Safe Burglary Conspiracy	Private Secretary Orville Babcock indicted over framing a private citizen for uncovering corrupt Washington contractors.	1876

xcv en.wikipedia.org/wiki/Crédit_Mobilier_of_America_scandal
xcvi en.wikipedia.org/wiki/1872_Republican_National_Convention
xcvii Hinds' Precedents ch. LXXIX, § 2510 at 1019, www.govinfo.gov/content/pkg/GPO-HPREC-HINDS-V3/pdf/GPO-HPREC-HINDS-V3-28.pdf at pp. 39.
xcviii Hinds' Precedents op. cit., ch. LXXIX, § 2510 at 1018, GPO Reprint at pp. 38.

xcix   Definition of "dictum," Black's Law Dictionary (2d ed.), thelawdictionary.org/dictum/

c   U.S. Constitution, Article I, Section 5.

ci   en.wikipedia.org/wiki/Michael_Myers_(politician)

cii   "In the Matter of Representative Michael J. Myers," H. Rep. No. 96-1387, 96th Cong., 2d Sess., ethics.house.gov/sites/ethics.house.gov/files/Hrpt96-1387pt1.pdf

ciii   www.congress.gov/bill/96th-congress/house-resolution/794

civ   en.wikipedia.org/wiki/Michael_Myers_(politician)

cv   en.wikipedia.org/wiki/Abscam

cvi   https://en.wikipedia.org/wiki/Abscam

cvii   en.wikipedia.org/wiki/James_Traficant

cviii   https://www.bartleby.com/73/275.html

cix   en.wikipedia.org/wiki/James_Traficant

cx   *United States v. Traficant*, 368 F.3d 646 (6th Cir. 2004).

cxi   www.congress.gov/bill/107th-congress/house-resolution/495

cxii   en.wikipedia.org/wiki/James_Traficant

cxiii   en.wikipedia.org/wiki/War_Is_a_Racket

cxiv   en.wikipedia.org/wiki/Trader_post_scandal

cxv   en.wikipedia.org/wiki/William_W._Belknap

cxvi   This may not have been as odd as it sounds; this was a biblical "levirate marriage," with the genders switched. https://en.wikipedia.org/wiki/Levirate_marriage

cxvii   en.wikipedia.org/wiki/Trader_post_scandal

cxviii   en.wikipedia.org/wiki/George_Armstrong_Custer

cxix   en.wikipedia.org/wiki/Trader_post_scandal

cxx   3 Hinds, *op. cit.,* § 2449 at pp. 911-14.

cxxi   3 Hinds, *op. cit.,* § 2453 at pp. 919-20.

cxxii   3 Hinds, *op. cit.* § 2455 at p. 922.

cxxiii   3 Hinds, *op. cit.,* § 2459 at p. 934.

cxxiv   3 Hinds, *op. cit.* § 2467 at pp. 945-46.

cxxv   en.wikipedia.org/wiki/Impeachment_in_the_United_States

cxxvi   en.wikipedia.org/wiki/Alcee_Hastings

cxxvii   www.senate.gov/artandhistory/history/common/briefing/Impeachment_Hastings.htm

cxxviii   www.senate.gov/artandhistory/history/common/briefing/Impeachment_Hastings.htm . The Senate elected not to vote on disqualifying Hastings from future office, which may not have seemed important at the time, but turned out to be. Hastings was elected to Congress in 1992, and has served in Congress since then.

cxxix   https://www.upi.com/Archives/1991/06/29/Jury-convicts-federal-judge-of-bribery/3180678168000/

cxxx   https://en.wikipedia.org/wiki/Robert_Frederick_Collins

cxxxi   J. Campbell & J. Murray, The Lives of the Lord Chancellors and Keepers of the Great Seal of England (1818).

cxxxii   Rep. Frank Thompson Jr. & Daniel Pollitt, "Impeachment of Federal Judges: An Historical Overview," N.C. Law Rev., Vol. 49, No. 1, p. 87.

cxxxiii Trump's nomination of Eminem for President is reported here: https://www.motherjones.com/politics/2016/08/trump-files-watch-donald-nominate-eminem-for-president/

cxxxiv   See Amended Complaint, Blumenthal v. Trump, No. 1:17-CV-01154 (D.D.C. 2017).

cxxxv   https://www.usnews.com/news/best-countries/slideshows/philippine-president-rodrigo-dutertes-9-most-controversial-quotes?slide=5

cxxxvi   Amended Complaint 66, Blumenthal v. Trump, No. 1:17-CV-01154 (D.D.C. 2017).

cxxxvii 1 Mueller Report 180-190.

cxxxviii https://en.wikipedia.org/wiki/Robert_Wodrow_Archbald

cxxxix   Id.

cxl   Thompson, op. cit., pp. 104-05.

cxli   Robert W. Archbald, Judge of the United States Commerce Court, H. Rept. No. 946, 62d Cong., 2d sess. (1912), 48 Cong Rec. (House) July 8, 1912 (8697) (hereinafter "Archbald Impeachment Report"), at p. 175.

cxlii   3 Deschler's Precedents, ch. 14 § 18, at 2244, www.govinfo.gov/content/pkg/GPO-HPREC-DESCHLERS-V3/pdf/GPO-HPREC-DESCHLERS-V3-5-5-5.pdf

cxliii   history.house.gov/Historical-Highlights/1901-1950/The-impeachment-of-Judge-Harold-Louderback/

cxliv   Thompson, op. cit., p. 105.

cxlv   Cannon's Precedents of the House of Representatives ch. CCI § 513, at p. 710, www.govinfo.gov/content/pkg/GPO-HPREC-CANNONS-V6/pdf/GPO-HPREC-CANNONS-V6.pdf

cxlvi   Cannon's Precedents of the House of Representatives ch. CCI § 514, at p. 711, www.govinfo.gov/content/pkg/GPO-HPREC-CANNONS-V6/pdf/GPO-HPREC-CANNONS-V6.pdf

cxlvii   history.house.gov/Historical-Highlights/1901-1950/The-impeachment-of-Judge-Harold-Louderback/

cxlviii 3 Deschler's Precedents, ch. 14 § 17, at 2200, www.govinfo.gov/content/pkg/GPO-HPREC-DESCHLERS-V3/pdf/GPO-HPREC-DESCHLERS-V3-5-5-4.pdf. Garner had been elected Vice President the year before, but he hadn't taken office yet. After he assumed the office of Vice President, eight days after the impeachment vote, he presided over Louderback's trial in the Senate. Garner seemed to have been nonplussed by his new responsibilities; he said that the Vice Presidency wasn't "worth a bucket of warm piss." *See* en.wikipedia.org/wiki/John_Nance_Garner

cxlix   6 Cannon's Precedents of the House of Representatives ch. CCI § 520, at p. 728, www.govinfo.gov/content/pkg/GPO-HPREC-CANNONS-V6/pdf/GPO-HPREC-CANNONS-V6.pdf

cl   6 Cannon's Precedents of the House of Representatives ch. CCI § 515, at p. 713-16, www.govinfo.gov/content/pkg/GPO-HPREC-CANNONS-V6/pdf/GPO-HPREC-CANNONS-V6.pdf

cli   3 Deschler's Precedents, ch. 14 § 18, at 2212, www.govinfo.gov/content/pkg/GPO-HPREC-DESCHLERS-V3/pdf/GPO-HPREC-DESCHLERS-V3-5-5-5.pdf . More than forty Senators asked the Senate to change its rules after the Louderback impeachment trial so that 12 Senators could take impeachment testimony, rather than inflicting this on the body as a whole. The Senate did so, in 1935. But during the Ritter trial, the Senate remained *en banc* for testimony. The result, according to Ritter, is that as few as three Senators heard what he had to say. http://palni.contentdm.oclc.org/cdm/ref/collection/archives/id/101576

clii   en.wikipedia.org/wiki/Harold_Louderback#Impeachment_and_acquittal; 6 Cannon's Precedents of the House of Representatives ch. CCI § 524, at p. 742, www.govinfo.gov/content/pkg/GPO-HPREC-CANNONS-V6/pdf/GPO-HPREC-CANNONS-V6.pdf

cliii   www.fjc.gov/node/1384026

cliv   Although there had been massive turnover in the meantime. The U.S. House of Representatives went from 216 Democrats in the 72nd Congress to 322 Democrats in the 74th Congress. *See* history.house.gov/Institution/Party-Divisions/Party-Divisions.

clv   en.wikipedia.org/wiki/Whitehall_(Henry_M._Flagler_House)

clvi   It's a crime to do so, under what was then 28 USC § 373, and is now 28 USC § 454.

clvii   en.wikipedia.org/wiki/Al_Capone#Tax_evasion

clviii   3 Deschler's Precedents, ch. 14 § 18, at 2214-32, www.govinfo.gov/content/pkg/GPO-HPREC-DESCHLERS-V3/pdf/GPO-HPREC-DESCHLERS-V3-5-5-5.pdf

clix   Deschler, *op. cit.* at p. 2237.

clx   80 Cong. Rec. 5370–86, 74th Cong. 2d Sess., Apr. 11 & 13, 1936.

clxi   80 Cong. Rec. 5373, 74th Cong. 2d Sess., Apr. 11, 1936.

clxii   80 Cong. Rec. 5374, 74th Cong. 2d Sess., Apr. 11, 1936.

clxiii   80 Cong. Rec. 5375, 74th Cong. 2d Sess., Apr. 11, 1936.

clxiv   80 Cong. Rec. 5379, 74th Cong. 2d Sess., Apr. 11, 1936.

clxv   80 Cong. Rec. 5377, 74th Cong. 2d Sess., Apr. 11, 1936.

clxvi   Deschler, *op. cit.* at p. 2244-45.

clxvii   Dylan Thomas, "Do Not Go Gentle Into That Good Night" (1951), www.poets.org/poetsorg/poem/do-not-go-gentle-good-night

clxviii   http://palni.contentdm.oclc.org/cdm/ref/collection/archives/id/101576

clxix   en.wikipedia.org/wiki/Halsted_L._Ritter

clxx   https://en.wikipedia.org/wiki/Seven_deadly_sins

clxxi   Trump's comments on Indians are found at: https://www.motherjones.com/politics/2016/09/trump-files-donald-indian-blood/

clxxii   https://www.transparency.org/news/pressrelease/dirty_money_hub_dubai_must_clean_up_its_real_estate_sector

clxxiii   https://www.americanprogress.org/issues/security/news/2017/06/14/433966/trumps-conflicts-interest-united-arab-emirates/

clxxiv   15 U.S.C. § 78dd-1, *et seq.*

clxxv   https://www.blankrome.com/publications/fcpa-enforcement-under-trump-administration-no-piling-otherwise-business-usual

clxxvi   https://www.washingtonpost.com/politics/2018/11/30/is-floating-million-trump-tower-penthouse-vladimir-putin-illegal/?utm_term=.c4355282570d

clxxvii   https://www.washingtonpost.com/politics/2018/11/30/is-floating-million-trump-tower-penthouse-vladimir-putin-illegal/?utm_term=.c4355282570d

clxxviii   https://www.theatlantic.com/politics/archive/2016/09/trump-buying-politicians/498749/

clxxix   Amended Complaint 66, *Blumenthal v. Trump,* No. 1:17-CV-01154 (D.D.C. 2017).

clxxx   https://www.nytimes.com/2019/08/28/us/politics/barr-trump-hotel-party.html

clxxxi   https://www.nbcnews.com/politics/donald-trump/how-much-time-trump-spending-trump-properties-n753366

clxxxii   https://www.cnbc.com/2017/01/25/mar-a-lago-membership-fee-doubles-to-200000.html

clxxxiii   https://www.washingtonpost.com/politics/you-pay-and-you-get-in-at-trumps-beach-retreat-hundreds-of-customers—and-growing-security-concerns/2019/04/03/7205bf28-5646-11e9-8ef3-fbd41a2ce4d5_story.html?utm_term=.1acb2a54f9c5&wpisrc=nl_most&wpmm=1

clxxxiv   https://amp.usatoday.com/amp/2748260002

clxxxv   https://sunlightfoundation.com/2019/04/12/this-week-in-conflicts-wait-continues-for-trumps-taxes-and-department-of-defense-is-spending-hundreds-of-thousands-of-dollars-at-trump-branded-properties/

clxxxvi   https://www.huffpost.com/entry/trump-mar-a-lago-party-tents-government-shutdown_n_5c26e042e4b0407e9082b572

clxxxvii https://www.cnbc.com/2018/02/15/trump-inaugural-committee-paid-26-million-to-friend-of-melania-trump.html

clxxxviii http://www.bostonmassacre.net/trial/trial-summary1.htm

clxxxix   https://www.measuringworth.com/calculators/ukcompare/

cxc   https://www.encyclopedia.com/history/news-wires-white-papers-and-books/oliver-peter-1713-1791

cxci   *See* 2 The Records of the Federal Convention of 1787, at 389 (Charles Pinckney).

cxcii   www.ourdocuments.gov/print_friendly.php?flash=true&page=transcript&doc=3&title=Transcript+of+Articles+of+Confederation+%281777%29

cxciii   This is the only place in the U.S. Constitution where the phrase "of any kind whatever" appears. It's as though they were saying, as a certainly later President would, "let me make this perfectly clear."

cxciv   5 Annals of Cong. 1583 (1798) (Joseph Gales ed., 1834) (James Bayard).

cxcv   5 Opinions of the Office of Legal Counsel 187, 188 (1981).

cxcvi   Plaintiffs' Memorandum in Opposition to Defendant's Motion to Dismiss at 46, *Blumenthal v. Trump,* No. 1:17-CV-01154 (D.D.C. filed Oct. 26, 2017).

cxcvii   www.archives.gov/founding-docs/constitution-transcript

cxcviii   https://www.washingtonpost.com/graphics/2017/politics/trump-hotel-business/?tid=a_inl_auto&utm_term=.dec2ebabaac5

cxcix   https://www.washingtonpost.com/politics/at-president-trumps-hotel-in-new-york-revenue-went-up-this-spring—thanks-to-a-visit-from-big-spending-saudis/2018/08/03/58755392-9112-11e8-bcd5-9d911c784c38_story.html?utm_term=.f1dd0617c2e9

cc   *Id.*

cci   *Id.*

ccii   https://thehill.com/business-a-lobbying/431436-trump-organization-says-it-donated-nearly-200k-in-foreign-profits-in-2018

cciii   Amended Complaint 52-56, *Blumenthal v. Trump,* No. 1:17-CV-01154 (D.D.C. 2017).

cciv   https://www.usatoday.com/story/news/2018/05/16/trumps-dc-hotel-earns-his-company-40-m-during-first-year-office/616833002/

ccv   Amended Complaint, 58-61 &70, *Blumenthal v. Trump*, No. 1:17-CV-01154 (D.D.C. 2017).

ccvi   en.wikipedia.org/wiki/The_Trump_Organization#International

ccvii   *Id.*

ccviii   Amended Complaint 66, *Blumenthal v. Trump*, No. 1:17-CV-01154 (D.D.C. 2017).

ccix   Amended Complaint 44-49, *Blumenthal v. Trump*, No. 1:17-CV-01154 (D.D.C. 2017).

ccx   Amended Complaint 74 & 71, *Blumenthal v. Trump*, No. 1:17-CV-01154 (D.D.C. 2017).

ccxi   https://www.nytimes.com/2019/08/26/world/europe/trump-doral-g7.html

ccxii   Congressional Research Service, "Impeachment Grounds: Part 2: Selected Constitutional Convention Materials," Rpt. No. 98-894A (1998), https://www.senate.gov/CRSpubs/27014603-8d4e-4ee2-b5cc-19b81e252abd.pdf

ccxiii   The Richard Nixon illustration is by way of *Futurama*, in which Richard Nixon's severed head was a recurring character. *See* https://twitter.com/robonixon. Everything that my children needed to know about Richard Nixon, they learned from Futurama. "Aruuuuuu."

ccxiv   http://watergate.info/1972/06/23/the-smoking-gun-tape.html

ccxv   www.upi.com/Archives/1984/08/08/Recalling-the-Watergate-break-in/6804460785600/

ccxvi   Deschler, ch. 14 § 15, at pp. 2167-68. https://www.govinfo.gov/content/pkg/GPO-HPREC-DESCHLERS-V3/pdf/GPO-HPREC-DESCHLERS-V3-5-5-2.pdf

ccxvii   en.wikipedia.org/wiki/Impeachment_process_against_Richard_Nixon

ccxviii   http://watergate.info/impeachment/articles-of-impeachment

ccxix   http://watergate.info/impeachment/articles-of-impeachment

ccxx   http://watergate.info/impeachment/articles-of-impeachment

ccxxi   http://watergate.info/impeachment/analysis-judiciary-committee-impeachment-votes

ccxxii   Alexander Hamilton, The Federalist Papers: No. 65 (1788).

ccxxiii   "I am the government," as French King Louis XIV allegedly said: en.wikiquote.org/wiki/Louis_XIV_of_France

ccxxiv   en.wikipedia.org/wiki/Nixon_interviews

ccxxv   https://www.brainyquote.com/quotes/theodore_roosevelt_118459

ccxxvi   *United States v. Nixon*, 418 U.S. 683 (1974).

ccxxvii   John & Marcia Labovitz, Presidential Impeachment pp. 123-24 (1978).

ccxxviii	www.nytimes.com/1974/06/21/archives/panel-hears-irs-weighed-fraud-charge-for-nixon-reports-confirmed.html
ccxxix	John & Marcia Labovitz, <u>Presidential Impeachment</u> p. 124 (1978).
ccxxx	en.wikipedia.org/wiki/Impeachment_process_against_Richard_Nixon
ccxxxi	John & Marcia Labovitz, <u>Presidential Impeachment</u> p. 125 (1978).
ccxxxii	John & Marcia Labovitz, <u>Presidential Impeachment</u> p. 125 (1978).
ccxxxiii	en.wikipedia.org/wiki/Impeachment_process_against_Richard_Nixon
ccxxxiv	en.wikipedia.org/wiki/Whitewater_controversy
ccxxxv	https://en.wikipedia.org/wiki/Impeachment_of_Bill_Clinton
ccxxxvi	http://academic.brooklyn.cuny.edu/history/johnson/clinton_impeachment_articles.htm
ccxxxvii	www.cnn.com/ALLPOLITICS/stories/1998/12/11/impeachment.01/;www.cnn.com/US/9812/12/impeachment.01/index.html
ccxxxviii	Gingrich and Livingston both had extramarital affaris. *See* https://www.washingtonpost.com/wp-srv/politics/special/clinton/stories/livingston122098.htm
ccxxxix	Office of the Clerk of the U.S. House of Representatives, "Final vote results for roll calls 543-546" (Dec. 19, 1998).
ccxl	https://www.theguardian.com/us-news/2019/mar/31/trump-golf-cheats-new-book
ccxli	*United States v. Nixon,* 816 F.2d 1022 (5th Cir. 1987).
ccxlii	*United States v. Nixon,* 816 F.2d 1022 (5th Cir. 1987).
ccxliii	*United States v. Nixon,* 816 F.2d 1022 (5th Cir. 1987).
ccxliv	www.upi.com/Archives/1985/08/29/US-District-Judge-Walter-Nixon-of-Mississippi-accepted-a/3131494136000/
ccxlv	*United States v. Nixon,* 816 F.2d 1022 (5th Cir. 1987).
ccxlvi	en.wikipedia.org/wiki/Walter_Nixon
ccxlvii	The proceedings were broadcast on C-SPAN. https://www.c-span.org/video/?9812-1/consideration-judge-nixon-impeachment
ccxlviii	https://www.nytimes.com/1989/11/04/us/senate-convicts-us-judge-removing-him-from-bench.html
ccxlix	www.nytimes.com/1989/11/04/us/senate-convicts-us-judge-removing-him-from-bench.html
ccl	*Proceedings of the Court for the Trial of Impeachments, The People v. Sulzer* at 46-51, babel.hathitrust.org/cgi/pt?id=mdp.39015030827037. (Thank you, Google, for digitizing these proceedings.)

ccli   https://twitter.com/realdonaldtrump/status/819159806489591809?
            lang=en

cclii   https://en.wikipedia.org/wiki/Business_projects_of_Donald_
            Trump_in_Russia

ccliii   https://www.businessinsider.com/donald-trump-jr-said-
            money-pouring-in-from-russia-2018-2

ccliv   https://www.nytimes.com/2019/04/18/us/politics/trump-obstruc-
            tion-of-justice.html

cclv   2 Mueller Report, pp. 24-47.

cclvi   2 Mueller Report, pp. 43-51, 93-97 & 107-112.

cclvii   https://www.nytimes.com/interactive/2016/01/28/upshot/don-
            ald-trump-twitter-insults.html?mtrref=www.google.com

cclviii   2 Mueller Report, pp. 55-57.

cclix   2 Mueller Report, pp. 57-61.

cclx   2 Mueller Report, pp. 65-76.

cclxi   2 Mueller Report, pp. 84-93.

cclxii   2 Mueller Report, pp. 98-106.

cclxiii   2 Mueller Report, pp. 120-155.

cclxiv   Those were:

1. making false or misleading statements to lawfully authorized investigative officers and employees of the United States;

2. withholding relevant and material evidence or information from lawfully authorized investigative officers and employees of the United
   States;

3. approving, condoning, acquiescing in, and counselling witnesses
   with respect to the giving of false or misleading statements to lawfully authorized investigative officers and employees of the United
   States and false or misleading testimony in duly instituted judicial
   and congressional proceedings;

4. interfering or endeavouring to interfere with the conduct of investi-
   gations by the Department of Justice of the United States, the Federal
   Bureau of Investigation, the office of Watergate Special Prosecution
   Force, and Congressional Committees;

5. approving, condoning, and acquiescing in, the surreptitious payment of substantial sums of money for the purpose of obtaining the
   silence or influencing the testimony of witnesses, potential witnesses

or individuals who participated in such unlawful entry and other illegal activities;

6. endeavouring to misuse the Central Intelligence Agency, an agency of the United States;

7. disseminating information received from officers of the Department of Justice of the United States to subjects of investigations conducted by lawfully authorized investigative officers and employees of the United States, for the purpose of aiding and assisting such subjects in their attempts to avoid criminal liability;

8. making or causing to be made false or misleading public statements for the purpose of deceiving the people of the United States into believing that a thorough and complete investigation had been conducted with respect to allegations of misconduct on the part of personnel of the executive branch of the United States and personnel of the Committee for the Re-election of the President, and that there was no involvement of such personnel in such misconduct: or

9. endeavouring to cause prospective defendants, and individuals duly tried and convicted, to expect favoured treatment and consideration in return for their silence or false testimony, or rewarding individuals for their silence or false testimony. http://watergate.info/impeachment/articles-of-impeachment

cclxv   http://watergate.info/impeachment/articles-of-impeachment
cclxvi   https://taxprof.typepad.com/files/154tn1013-yin.pdf
cclxvii https://www.washingtonpost.com/business/economy/confidential-draft-irs-memo-says-tax-returns-must-be-given-to-congress-unless-president-invokes-executive-privilege/2019/05/21/8ed41834-7b1c-11e9-8bb7-0fc796cf2ec0_story.html?utm_term=.50c37bcdfcab&wpisrc=nl_most&wpmm=1
cclxviii https://www.huffpost.com/entry/trump-subpoena-congress_n_5cc34150e4b08e4e3481df9c
cclxix   https://www.washingtonpost.com/politics/2019/03/04/president-trump-has-made-false-or-misleading-claims-over-days/?utm_term=.5387bd33bb0f
cclxx   https://www.washingtonpost.com/politics/2019/03/04/president-trump-has-made-false-or-misleading-claims-over-days/?utm_term=.5387bd33bb0f

cclxxi   https://www.usatoday.com/story/news/politics/2019/04/02/president-trump-false-claims-father-born-germany/3346343002/

cclxxii   http://watergate.info/impeachment/articles-of-impeachment

cclxxiii   https://www.theatlantic.com/ideas/archive/2019/04/mueller-report-impeachment-referral/587509/

cclxxiv   U.S. Dep't of Justice Manual § 1721.

cclxxv   *Id.* § 1723.

cclxxvi   *Washington Post,* "Trump and his allies are blocking more than 20 separate Democratic probes in an all-out war with Congress" (May 11, 2019), https://www.washingtonpost.com/politics/trump-and-his-allies-are-blocking-more-than-20-separate-democratic-probes-in-an-all-out-war-with-congress/2019/05/11/4d972274-733a-11e9-9eb4-0828f5389013_story.html?utm_term=.641976d8b99c&wpisrc=nl_most&wpmm=1

cclxxvii   https://edition.cnn.com/2019/05/01/politics/pelosi-document-trump-administration-unprecedented-stonewalling/index.html

cclxxviii   U.S. House Judiciary Committee, <u>Constitutional Grounds for Presidential Impeachment</u> 1516 (Feb. 1974).

cclxxix   https://en.wikipedia.org/wiki/Third_degree_(interrogation)

cclxxx   en.wikipedia.org/wiki/John_Wilkes_Booth

cclxxxi   https://en.wikipedia.org/wiki/Lafayette_S._Foster

cclxxxii   en.wikipedia.org/wiki/List_of_United_States_presidential_vetoes

cclxxxiii   en.wikipedia.org/wiki/Swing_Around_the_Circle

cclxxxiv   www.senate.gov/artandhistory/history/resources/pdf/Johnson_TenureofOfficeAct.pdf

cclxxxv   https://westegg.com/inflation/infl.cgi

cclxxxvi   en.wikipedia.org/wiki/Impeachment_of_Andrew_Johnson

cclxxxvii   en.wikipedia.org/wiki/1868_United_States_presidential_election

cclxxxviii   en.wikipedia.org/wiki/Impeachment_of_Andrew_Johnson

cclxxxix   ww.nps.gov/anjo/learn/historyculture/the-articles-of-impeachment.htm

ccxc   www.nps.gov/anjo/learn/historyculture/article-x.htm

ccxci   en.wikipedia.org/wiki/Impeachment_of_Andrew_Johnson

ccxcii   https://en.wikipedia.org/wiki/Benjamin_Wade

ccxciii   en.wikipedia.org/wiki/Impeachment_of_Andrew_Johnson

ccxciv   https://en.wikipedia.org/wiki/1868_Democratic_National_Convention

ccxcv   By john mintier – Photo by John Mintier via https://www.flickr.com/photos/miklo68/399072616/, CC BY-SA 3.0, https://commons.wikimedia.org/w/index.php?curid=5528898

ccxcvi   *United States v. Blagojevich,* 794 F.3d 729 (7th Cir. 2015), *cert. denied,* 136 S. Ct. 1491 (2016), *rehearing denied,* 136 S. Ct. 2386 (2016), http://images.politico.com/global/2015/07/21/blagoopn.pdf

ccxcvii   https://www.chicagotribune.com/politics/ct-president-trump-considering-rod-blagojevich-commutation-20190808-y3ixmutnfnd5havbgdgtxcvyd4-story.html

ccxcviii   Cortez A. M. Ewing, "The Impeachment of James E. Ferguson," *Political Science Quarterly* Vol. 48, No. 2 (Jun., 1933), pp. 184-210, https://www.jstor.org/stable/2143345 (a beautifully written piece).

ccxcix   Ewing, *op. cit.* at 185.

ccc   *Id.* at 186.

ccci   *Id.* at 191 n.1.

cccii   *Id.* at 189.

ccciii   *Id.* at 193.

ccciv   *Id.* at 194.

cccv   *Id.* at 199.

cccvi   *Id.* at 201.

cccvii   *Id.* at 202-03.

cccviii   *Id.* at 205.

cccix   Texas State Historical Association, "Salaries of State Executive Officers," tshaonline.org/handbook/online/articles/msb03

cccx   Actually, $3,071,013. US Inflation Calculator, usinflationcalculator.com

cccxi   Ewing, *op. cit.* at 187.

cccxii   The terms "despotic will" and "imperious will" seem like colorful, hyperbolic terms that threaten the solemn nature of impeachment proceedings. Of course, that depends on the nature of the charges. If the terms were applied to the imaginary impeachment of Genghis Khan, who erected pyramids from the skulls of his enemies, they would be neither colorful nor hyperbolic.

cccxiii   *Id.* at 201.

cccxiv   *Id.* at 206.

cccxv   *Id.* at 206.

cccxvi   The source of the Trump-Hitler anecdote is https://www.motherjones.com/politics/2016/09/trump-files-donalds-big-book-hitler-speeches/

cccxvii   Most recently, https://www.politico.com/story/2019/03/22/trump-barr-clinton-investigation-1232147 . Earlier, for instance, by tweeting "Attorney General Jeff Sessions has taken a VERY weak position on Hillary Clinton crimes (where are E-mails & DNC server) & Intel leakers!" https://twitter.com/realDonaldTrump/status/889790429398528000

cccxviii	https://www.washingtonpost.com/politics/2019/04/23/white-house-instructs-official-ignore-democratic-subpoena-over-security-clearances/?utm_term=.89016bba026f&wpisrc=nl_most&wpmm=1
cccxix	https://www.reuters.com/article/us-iran-space-launch-usa/trump-iran-photo-tweet-raises-worries-about-disclosure-of-us-surveillance-secrets-idUSKCN1VK280
cccxx	https://www.nytimes.com/2017/08/25/us/politics/joe-arpaio-trump-pardon-sheriff-arizona.html
cccxxi	https://www.nytimes.com/2018/05/31/us/politics/dinesh-dsouza-facts-history.html
cccxxii	https://www.justice.gov/pardon/clemency-statistics
cccxxiii	https://www.cnn.com/2019/04/12/politics/trump-cbp-commissioner-pardon/index.html
cccxxiv	https://www.justsecurity.org/63838/guide-to-the-mueller-reports-findings-on-collusion/
cccxxv	https://www.desmogblog.com/2018/09/12/buried-altered-silenced-4-ways-government-climate-information-has-changed-trump-took-office
cccxxvi	United Nations, *Universal Declaration of Human Rights* Art. 14(1) (1948).
cccxxvii	https://www.washingtonpost.com/business/economy/trump-personally-pushed-postmaster-general-to-double-rates-on-amazon-other-firms/2018/05/18/2b6438d2-5931-11e8-858f-12becb4d6067_story.html?utm_term=.d2b0bcee8271
cccxxviii	https://www.businessinsider.com/jeff-bezos-national-enquirer-investigation-timeline-2019-2
cccxxix	https://thehill.com/policy/technology/404923-trump-renews-attacks-on-nbc-license
cccxxx	https://www.washingtonpost.com/politics/trump-threatens-reporter-with-prison-time-during-interview/2019/06/21/b622b84c-9420-11e9-b58a-a6a9afaa0e3e_story.html?wpisrc=nl_most&wpmm=1
cccxxxi	https://en.wikipedia.org/wiki/Deaths_of_Jakelin_Caal_and_Felipe_G%C3%B3mez_Alonzo#Felipe_G%C3%B3mez_Alonzo
cccxxxii	https://www.latimes.com/nation/la-na-migrant-child-border-deaths-20190524-story.html
cccxxxiii	https://www.businessinsider.com/aclu-lawsuits-vs-trump-administration-2017-10
cccxxxiv	U.S. Const., Art. II, Section 1.
cccxxxv	https://en.wikiquote.org/wiki/Louis_XIV_of_France
cccxxxvi	en.wikipedia.org/wiki/William_Sulzer.

cccxxxvii   Jacob Alexis Fredman, *The Impeachment of Governor William Sulzer* 21 (1939).

cccxxxviii en.wikipedia.org/wiki/1912_New_York_state_election

cccxxxix   en.wikipedia.org/wiki/1912_New_York_state_election

cccxl   en.wikipedia.org/wiki/1912_United_States_presidential_election

cccxli   Matthew L. Lifflander, *The Impeachment of Governor William Sulzer: A Story of American Politics* 132 (2012).

cccxlii   newspaperarchive.com/philadelphia-inquirer-jul-13-1913-p-1/

cccxliii *Proceedings of the Court for the Trial of Impeachments, The People v. Sulzer* at 46-51, babel.hathitrust.org/cgi/pt?id=mdp.39015030827037. (Thank you, Google, for digitizing these proceedings.)

cccxliv Stuart G. Gibboney, "Some Legal Aspects of the Impeachment of William Sulzer," Virginia L. Rev., Vol. 1, No. 2 (Nov. 1913), pp. 102-107, https://www.jstor.org/stable/1064180

cccxlv   en.wikipedia.org/wiki/1912_New_York_state_election

cccxlvi Fredman, op. cit., at 266.

cccxlvii en.wikipedia.org/wiki/1914_New_York_state_election

cccxlviii https://hallofgovernors.ny.gov/WilliamSulzer

cccxlix en.wikipedia.org/wiki/American_Party_(1914)

cccl   "Impeachment of G. Thomas Porteous, Jr.," H. Rep. No. 111-427 ("Porteous Report"), at pp. 5-7.

cccli   en.wikisource.org/wiki/Articles_of_Impeachment_Against_United_States_District_Court_Judge_G._Thomas_Porteous,_Jr.

ccclii   Porteous Report, at pp. 15-16.

cccliii   en.wikisource.org/wiki/Articles_of_Impeachment_Against_United_States_District_Court_Judge_G._Thomas_Porteous,_Jr.

cccliv   Porteous Report, at pp. 17 & 20.

ccclv   Porteous Report, at p. 21.

ccclvi   www.nytimes.com/2002/02/20/business/2001-bankruptcy-filings-set-a-record.html

ccclvii Porteous Report, at p. 22.

ccclviii Porteous Report, at pp. 23-137.

ccclix   Porteous Report, at pp. 8-11.

ccclx   Porteous Report, at pp. 19-20.

ccclxi   Your humble scribe voted in favor of each count.

ccclxii   The Trump 13-cent-check incident is recounted here: https://www.motherjones.com/politics/2016/08/trump-files-spy-magazine-prank/

ccclxiii https://en.wikipedia.org/wiki/Karen_McDougal#Alleged_affair_with_Donald_Trump

ccclxiv   https://en.wikipedia.org/wiki/Stormy_Daniels%E2%80%93 Donald_Trump_scandal

ccclxv   ww.vox.com/2019/2/27/18243038/individual-1-cohen-trump-mueller

ccclxvi   http://fm.cnbc.com/applications/cnbc.com/resources/editorialfiles/2018/08/21/U.S.%20v.%20Michael%20Cohen%20Information.pdf

ccclxvii   https://www.nytimes.com/2019/02/27/us/politics/michael-cohen-trump-hush-money.html

ccclxviii   Sentencing Memorandum on Behalf of Michael Cohen at 23, *United States v. Cohen,* No. 1:18-CR-850 (S.D.N.Y. Nov. 30, 2018), https://www.lawfareblog.com/document-michael-cohen-files-sentencing-memorandum

ccclxix   https://thehill.com/homenews/administration/421175-dem-rep-calls-trump-unindicted-co-conspirator-in-cohen-case

ccclxx   U.S. House Judiciary Committee, <u>Constitutional Grounds for Presidential Impeachment</u> 5 (Feb. 1974).

ccclxxi   *Id.* at 14.

ccclxxii   *Id.* at 15.

ccclxxiii   *See, e.g.,* Fla. Stat. 856.011.

ccclxxiv   U.S. House Judiciary Committee, <u>Constitutional Grounds for Presidential Impeachment</u> 7 (Feb. 1974).

ccclxxv   Actually, it's always been a "he." No adherent to the female gender has ever been impeached under Federal law. Missouri Secretary of State Judith Moriarity was the first woman ever impeached under state law. In 1991, she was impeached for motherly love. She backdated a qualifying document to allow her son to run for office.

ccclxxvi   <u>Uniform Code of Military Justice</u> Art. 133, 10 U.S.C. § 933 (2012).

ccclxxvii   Lynn W. Turner, "The Impeachment of John Pickering," *The American Historical Review*, Vol. 54, No. 3 (Apr., 1949), pp. 485, 487, https://www.jstor.org/stable/1843004

ccclxxviii   Turner, *op. cit.* at 488, 496 & 495.

ccclxxix   en.wikipedia.org/wiki/John_Pickering_(judge)

ccclxxx   Turner, *op. cit.* at 489-90.

ccclxxxi   *Annals of Congress,* 7 Cong., 2 sess., pp. 460, 544, 642, cited in Turner, *op. cit.* at 491 n.19.

ccclxxxii   When the Federalists were in charge of government, they passed the Sedition Act. Under that Act, they imprisoned a Congressman for criticizing the Federalist President. They arrested a State Senator for calling for repeal of the Act. They fined a spectator $100 for suggesting that he would like to see the insertion of an unpleasant object into the

President's buttocks. Jefferson later pardoned them all, and repealed the Sedition Act. Thompson, *op. cit.,* at 92-94.

ccclxxxiii Extracts from the Journal of the United States Senate in All Cases of Impeachment 17981904 (1912) pp. 20-22.

ccclxxxiv Humphrey, *op. cit.* at 294.

ccclxxxv Turner, *op. cit.* at 502.

ccclxxxvi Plumer's Memorandum, p. 163, cited in Turner, *op. cit.* at 500.

ccclxxxvii archive.org/stream/memoirsofjohnqui01badam/memoirsofjohn-qui01badam_djvu.txt . Adams refers to impeachment 120 times in his memoirs.

ccclxxxviii Turner, *op. cit.* at 492-93.

ccclxxxix Extracts, pp. 33-34.

cccxc Turner, *op. cit.* at 493.

cccxci Journal, 42nd Cong., 3d sess., p. 512; Globe, pp. 1899, 1900.

cccxcii https://constitutionallawreporter.com/2017/04/25/historical-mark-w-delahay/

cccxciii Hinds' Precedents ch. LXXIX, §§ 2504-05, www.govinfo.gov/content/pkg/GPO-HPREC-HINDS-V3/pdf/GPO-HPREC-HINDS-V3-28.pdf at pp. 29-31. Asher Hinds was the Clerk of the U.S. House of Representatives. His multivolume collection of House precedents was published in 1907. It contains 700+ pages on the subject of impeachment, §§ 2001-2515.

cccxciv https://en.wikipedia.org/wiki/Jack_Tarpley_Camp_Jr.

cccxcv https://www.bbc.com/news/magazine-31741615

cccxcvi The report on Donald Trump's casino-chip bailout is derived from this report: https://www.motherjones.com/politics/2016/09/trump-files-fred-trump-funneled-cash-donald-using-casino-chips/

cccxcvii https://www.thefix.com/apprentice-crew-member-claims-trump-snorted-adderall-set

cccxcviii https://davidfeldmanshow.com/howie-kleins-update-on-trumps-ad-derall-addiction-december-18-2018/

cccxcix https://en.wikipedia.org/wiki/Adderall#Psychological

cd https://www.recoveryfirst.org/prescription-abuse/adderall/dangers-of-snorting/

cdi https://www.deadiversion.usdoj.gov/faq/prescriptions.htm

cdii Neb. Dep't of Health and Human Services, Alcohol and Substance Abuse Disorders 4-7 (2016), http://dhhs.ne.gov/licensure/Documents/ResourceGuideForHCProfessionals.pdf

cdiii	The photo of Greitens with the semi-automatic weapon is from Greitens' gubernatorial campaign. www.economist.com/ united-states/2018/05/17/missouris-governor-is-likely-to-be-impeached
cdiv	Report of the Missouri House Special Investigative Committee on Oversight 9 35 (Apr. 11, 2018).
cdv	*Id.* at 16 52(m).
cdvi	*Id.* at 21 70(a).
cdvii	*Id.* at 23 78.
cdviii	en.wikipedia.org/wiki/Eric_Greitens
cdix	See the campaign photo above. www.economist.com/united-states/ 2018/05/17/missouris-governor-is-likely-to-be-impeached
cdx	www.realclearpolitics.com/epolls/approval_rating/governor/mo/gover-nor_greitens_job_approval-6281.html
cdxi	"The Garden of Allah," <u>Actual Miles: Henley's Greatest Hits</u> (1995).
cdxii	<u>Order Granting Defendant's Motion For Summary Judgment,</u> *Bradshaw v. Unity Marine Corp.,* No. G-00-558 (S.D. Tex. June 27, 2001), web.archive.org/web/20160304032847/http:/www.lsnc.net/ special/crayon.pdf .
cdxiii	http://www.ca5.uscourts.gov/docs/default-source/judicial-council-or-ders/fifth-circuit-judicial-council-order-07-05-351-0086-third-order.pdf
cdxiv	en.wikipedia.org/wiki/Samuel_B._Kent
cdxv	en.wikipedia.org/wiki/Samuel_B._Kent
cdxvi	Your humble scribe voted in favor of the Kent Articles of Impeachment.
cdxvii	en.wikisource.org/wiki/Articles_of_Impeachment_Against_United_ States_District_Court_Judge_Samuel_B._Kent
cdxviii	en.wikipedia.org/wiki/Samuel_B._Kent
cdxix	https://www.businessinsider.com/women-accused-trump-sexual-misconduct-list-2017-12
cdxx	https://en.wikipedia.org/wiki/E._Jean_Carroll#Sexual_assault_alle-gations
cdxxi	https://en.wikipedia.org/wiki/Pseudonyms_of_Donald_Trump
cdxxii	https://www.nytimes.com/2016/10/08/us/donald-trump-tape-tran-script.html
cdxxiii	Trump Press Secretary Sarah Huckabee Sanders, https:// www.bostonglobe.com/news/nation/2017/12/11/here-how-sar-ah-sanders-defended-trump-against-accusations-misconduct/ FRGMNLOS6oe0pUCx8VspgK/story.html
cdxxiv	https://poll.qu.edu/national/release-detail?ReleaseID=2509
cdxxv	https://www.rainn.org/statistics/criminal-justice-system

cdxxvi   https://en.wikipedia.org/wiki/Karen_McDougal#Alleged_affair_with_Donald_Trump;https://en.wikipedia.org/wiki/Stormy_Daniels%E2%80%93Donald_Trump_scandal

cdxxvii   *United States v. Claiborne*, 727 F.2d 842, 845 (9th Cir.), *cert. denied*, 469 U.S. 829 (1984); *United States v. Hastings*, 681 F.2d 706, 710-11 (11th Cir.1982), *cert. denied*, 459 U.S. 1203 (1983); *United States v. Isaacs*, 493 F.2d 1124, 1144 (7th Cir.) (per curiam), *cert. denied*, 417 U.S. 976 (1974).

cdxxviii   www.nytimes.com/1983/12/09/us/us-judge-accused-of-taking-a-bribe.html

cdxxix   *See State Bar of Nevada v. Claiborne*, 756 P.2d 464, 499 (Nev. 1988).

cdxxx   www.fjc.gov/history/judges/claiborne-harry-e

cdxxxi   https://www.motherjones.com/politics/2016/09/trump-files-fred-trump-funneled-cash-donald-using-casino-chips/

cdxxxii   *United States v. Claiborne*, 765 F.2d 784, 796-99 (9th Cir. 1985).

cdxxxiii   en.wikipedia.org/wiki/Harry_E._Claiborne#Impeachment_and_removal

cdxxxiv   *Nixon v. United States*, 506 U.S. 224 (1993).

cdxxxv   en.wikipedia.org/wiki/Harry_E._Claiborne

cdxxxvi   The references to Trump and the New England Patriots are based on: https://www.bostonmagazine.com/news/2016/03/08/donald-trump-patriots/ and https://www.inc.com/jeff-haden/how-robert-kraft-bought-new-england-patriots-built-franchise-worth-38-billion.html

cdxxxvii   https://www.nytimes.com/interactive/2018/10/02/us/politics/donald-trump-tax-schemes-fred-trump.html

cdxxxviii   https://www.ais-cpa.com/tax-fraud-by-the-numbers-the-trump-timeline/

cdxxxix   https://www.washingtonpost.com/blogs/plum-line/wp/2018/10/04/trump-may-be-guilty-of-massive-tax-fraud-dont-let-it-fall-down-the-memory-hole/?utm_term=.12b50ebf86db

cdxl   https://www.ais-cpa.com/tax-fraud-by-the-numbers-the-trump-timeline/

cdxli   https://www.washingtonpost.com/blogs/plum-line/wp/2018/10/04/trump-may-be-guilty-of-massive-tax-fraud-dont-let-it-fall-down-the-memory-hole/?utm_term=.12b50ebf86db;https://twitter.com/realDonaldTrump/status/1047469711938736128

cdxlii   https://www.vox.com/2019/4/11/18306167/maryanne-trump-barry-tax-returns-trump

cdxliii   https://www.cnbc.com/2019/02/28/watch-alexandria-ocasio-cortez-question-michael-cohen-about-trump-tax-returns.html

cdxliv   https://www.washingtonpost.com/politics/how-much-does-trump-claim-his-golf-courses-are-worth-it-depends-who-needs-to-know/2016/08/21/71828f3a-5f3c-11e6-9d2f-b1a3564181a1_story.html?utm_term=.d99efdf8c7e4; *see also* https://www.washingtonpost.com/graphics/2019/politics/trump-statements-of-financial-condition/?utm_term=.73c5c792fc4c

cdxlv   https://www.realclearpolitics.com/video/2019/03/12/david_cay_johnston_we_will_see_trumps_tax_returns_and_find_out_how_much_money_he_got_from_kremlin.html

cdxlvi   https://www.youtube.com/watch?v=-qXjsMK_MnU

cdxlvii   https://www.cnn.com/2019/04/04/politics/trump-audit-fact-check/index.html

cdxlviii   https://www.cnn.com/2019/04/07/politics/mick-mulvaney-trump-tax-returns/index.html

cdxlix   en.wikipedia.org/wiki/Kenesaw_Mountain_Landis

cdl   en.wikipedia.org/wiki/Kenesaw_Mountain_Landis

cdli   *Id.*

cdlii   Thompson, *op. cit.*, at pp. 117-18.

cdliii   For the story on Trump and the USFL, see https://www.washingtonpost.com/news/early-lead/wp/2016/03/03/donald-trump-was-such-a-usfl-bully-that-a-fellow-owner-threatened-to-punch-him/?utm_term=.7828cb3af272

cdliv   Amended Complaint 66(a), *Blumenthal v. Trump,* No. 1:17-CV-01154 (D.D.C. 2017).

cdlv   https://explorer.usaid.gov/cd/ARG

cdlvi   Amended Complaint 52-56, *Blumenthal v. Trump,* No. 1:17-CV-01154 (D.D.C. 2017).

cdlvii   https://www.politifact.com/truth-o-meter/statements/2019/apr/08/donald-trump/republicans-dismiss-trumps-windmill-and-cancer-cla/

cdlviii   For the record of Trump posing as his own publicist, *see* https://en.wikipedia.org/wiki/Pseudonyms_of_Donald_Trump. The *Washington Post's* "John Miller" transcript is here: https://www.washingtonpost.com/news/the-fix/wp/2016/05/16/donald-trufraudps-john-miller-interview-is-even-crazier-than-you-think/?utm_term=.e92ba106cb06

cdlix   https://en.wikipedia.org/wiki/Party_divisions_of_United_States_Congresses

cdlx   https://en.wikipedia.org/wiki/1868_Democratic_National_Convention

cdlxi   http://www.pewresearch.org/fact-tank/2014/08/08/how-the-watergate-crisis-eroded-public-support-for-richard-nixon/

cdlxii   https://en.wikipedia.org/wiki/Mueller_Report

cdlxiii   https://en.wikipedia.org/wiki/Nixon_interviews

cdlxiv   https://www.nytimes.com/2019/05/30/us/politics/trump-russia-help-elected.html

cdlxv   https://idioms.thefreedictionary.com/Apres+moi+le+deluge

cdlxvi   https://www.washingtonpost.com/politics/2019/03/14/if-trump-shot-someone-dead-fifth-avenue-many-supporters-would-call-his-murder-trial-biased/

cdlxvii   **Alien Newscaster Morbo**: Morbo will now introduce tonight's candidates… Puny Human No. 1, Puny Human No. 2, and Morbo's good friend, Richard Nixon.
    Richard Nixon's Head: Hello, Morbo, how's the family?
    Morbo: Belligerent and numerous.
    https://en.wikiquote.org/wiki/Futurama/Season_2

cdlxviii   https://www.theguardian.com/us-news/2019/oct/23/donald-trump-immune-shoot-fifth-avenue-murder

cdlxix   https://www.vox.com/world/2019/10/16/20908262/turkey-syria-kurds-trump-invasion-questions

cdlxx   https://www.huffpost.com/entry/conflict-of-interest-donald-trump-syria-kurds-turkey_n_5d9bb7bfe4b0fc935edf5be0

cdlxxi   https://www.bloomberg.com/news/articles/2019-10-27/kurdish-led-syria-forces-accept-russian-brokered-pullback-deal

cdlxxii   https://www.axios.com/trump-nuclear-bombs-hurricanes-97231f38-2394-4120-a3fa-8c9cf0e3f51c.html

cdlxxiii   Nickname by Martin O'Malley.

cdlxxiv   https://www.politico.com/story/2019/09/04/donald-trump-sharpie-hurricane-map-1481733

cdlxxv   https://en.wikipedia.org/wiki/Atlantic_hurricane

cdlxxvi   https://en.wikipedia.org/wiki/Hurricane_Dorian

cdlxxvii   https://twitter.com/realdonaldtrump/status/1168174613827899393?lang=en

cdlxxviii   https://www.washingtonpost.com/opinions/trumps-dorian-response-par-for-the-course/2019/09/03/e0148242-ce8c-11e9-8c1c-7c8ee785b855_story.html

cdlxxix   https://www.politico.com/story/2019/09/04/donald-trump-sharpie-hurricane-map-1481733

cdlxxx   https://www.politico.com/story/2019/09/04/donald-trump-sharpie-hurricane-map-1481733

cdlxxxi   https://www.theguardian.com/us-news/2019/jul/07/donald-trump-
          inept-and-dysfunctional-uk-ambassador-to-us-says
cdlxxxii https://www.nytimes.com/2019/05/08/us/politics/trump-execu-
          tive-privilege-mueller-report.html
cdlxxxiii https://www.nbcnews.com/politics/white-house/white-house-or-
          ders-mcgahn-not-comply-congressional-subpoena-n1002846
cdlxxxiv https://www.foxnews.com/politics/criminal-contempt-resolution-on-
          barr-ross-brings-another-no-holds-barred-showdown-to-the-house
cdlxxxv   https://www.bloomberg.com/news/articles/2019-10-09/trump-urged-
          top-aide-to-help-giuliani-client-facing-doj-charges?srnd=premium
cdlxxxvi https://taskandpurpose.com/snodgrass-mattis-book
cdlxxxvii https://www.propublica.org/article/trump-inc-podcast-never-before-
          seen-trump-tax-documents-show-major-inconsistencies
cdlxxxviii https://www.bloomberg.com/news/articles/2019-09-27/
          democrat-weighs-releasing-complaint-about-irs-trump-tax-audit
cdlxxxix https://www.vanityfair.com/news/2019/10/the-mystery-of-the-
          trump-chaos-trades
cdxc   https://www.cbsnews.com/news/trump-doral-g7-summit-next-year-
          trump-national-miami-white-house-says-today-dismissing-concerns-
          over-ethics-optics/
cdxci   https://news.yahoo.com/trump-drops-plan-host-g-021324406.html
cdxcii   https://www.nytimes.com/2019/10/21/us/politics/trump-doral-emolu-
          ments-clause.html
cdxciii   https://www.nytimes.com/2019/06/20/world/middleeast/iran-us-
          drone.html
cdxciv   https://www.independent.co.uk/news/world/americas/us-politics/
          trump-airports-revolutionary-war-4th-of-july-speech-gaffe-a8990021.
          html
cdxcv   https://twitter.com/GovofCO?ref_src=twsrc%5Egoogle%7
          Ctwcamp%5Eserp%7Ctwgr%5Eauthor
cdxcvi   https://www.politico.com/story/2019/09/25/
          senate-vote-national-emergency-border-wall-1510795?cid=apn
cdxcvii   https://www.washingtonpost.com/politics/trump-tries-to-distance-us-
          from-chaos-in-syria-says-kurdish-allies-are-no-angels/2019/10/16/7b-
          6c5ac8-f037-11e9-b2da-606ba1ef30e3_story.html
cdxcviii https://www.nbcnews.com/news/latino/ocasio-cortez-detained-mi-
          grants-being-told-drink-out-toilets-n1025431
cdxcix   https://www.theguardian.com/us-news/video/2019/aug/22/
          trump-says-he-is-the-chosen-one-to-take-on-china-video

d   https://www.vanityfair.com/news/2019/08/donald-trump-king-of-israel

di   https://www.vanityfair.com/hollywood/2019/10/trump-turkey-kurds-syria-great-and-unmatched-wisdom-colbert

dii   http://www.msnbc.com/rachel-maddow-show/trump-insists-there-was-attempted-overthrow-us-government

diii   https://www.washingtonpost.com/politics/trump-compares-impeachment-probe-to-lynching-draws-widespread-condemnation/2019/10/22/2fa24af2-f4d4-11e9-ad8b-85e2aa00b5ce_story.html

div   https://www.vox.com/2019/7/15/20694616/donald-trump-racist-tweets-omar-aoc-tlaib-pressley The House then voted to condemn Trump for "legitimiz[ing] fear and hatred of new Americans and people of color." https://www.msnbc.com/hardball/watch/house-passes-resolution-condemning-trump-s-racist-comments-63973445642

dv   https://www.usatoday.com/story/news/politics/2019/10/23/donald-trump-describes-republican-critics-human-scum/4076555002/

dvi   https://www.nytimes.com/2019/05/09/us/politics/giuliani-ukraine-trump.html

dvii   https://www.washingtonpost.com/politics/2019/09/24/full-trump-ukraine-timeline-now/

dviii   https://twitter.com/RudyGiuliani/status/1142085975230898176

dix   https://www.washingtonpost.com/politics/2019/09/20/giuliani-admits-asking-ukraine-about-joe-biden-after-denying-it-seconds-earlier/

dx   https://www.nbcnews.com/politics/politics-news/rudy-giuliani-butt-dials-nbc-reporter-heard-discussing-need-cash-n1071901

dxi   https://www.washingtonpost.com/politics/2019/09/24/full-trump-ukraine-timeline-now/

dxii   https://www.washingtonpost.com/national-security/trump-ordered-hold-on-military-aid-days-before-calling-ukrainian-president-officials-say/2019/09/23/df93a6ca-de38-11e9-8dc8-498eabc129a0_story.html

dxiii   https://slate.com/news-and-politics/2019/10/mick-mulvaney-ukraine-confession.html

dxiv   https://www.washingtonpost.com/politics/2019/09/24/full-trump-ukraine-timeline-now/

dxv   https://www.washingtonpost.com/politics/2019/09/24/full-trump-ukraine-timeline-now/

dxvi   https://www.washingtonpost.com/world/national-security/trump-involved-pence-in-efforts-to-pressure-ukraines-leader-though-aides-say-vice-president-was-unaware-of-pursuit-of-dirt-on-bidens/2019/10/02/2-63aa9e2-e4a7-11e9-b403-f738899982d2_story.html dxvii   https://www.cnn.com/2019/10/25/politics/white-house-decision-ukraine-funds-major-gaps-omb/index.html

dxviii   https://www.nytimes.com/2019/10/03/us/politics/trump-china-bidens.html

dxix   https://www.washingtonpost.com/politics/trump-publicly-calls-on-china-to-investigate-bidens/2019/10/03/2ae94f6a-e5f2-11e9-b403-f738899982d2_story.html

dxx   https://www.china-briefing.com/news/the-us-china-trade-war-a-timeline/

dxxi   https://www.foxnews.com/politics/fox-news-poll-record-support-for-trump-impeachment

dxxii   https://www.nytimes.com/2019/10/10/us/politics/fox-news-poll-trump-impeachment.html

dxxiii   https://news.gallup.com/poll/267491/congress-approval-support-impeaching-trump.aspx

dxxiv   https://theweek.com/speedreads/870524/trump-cannot-participate-impeachment-inquiry-white-house-lawyer-tells-house-democrats

dxxv   Congressional Research Service, "The Impeachment Process in the U.S. House of Representatives (Oct. 10, 2019) at p. 4, https://fas.org/sgp/crs/misc/R45769.pdf

dxxvi   https://www.politico.com/news/2019/10/22/trump-vengeance-john-brennan-russia-053970

dxxvii   https://www.washingtonpost.com/national-security/state-dept-intensifies-email-probe-of-hillary-clintons-former-aides/2019/09/28/9f15497e-e1f2-11e9-8dc8-498eabc129a0_story.html

dxxviii https://www.cnn.com/2019/05/09/politics/pelosi-congress-impeachment-trump/index.html

dxxix   A. Beveridge, Life of John Marshall 195 (1919)

dxxx   Humphrey, *op. cit.* at 288.

dxxxi   Annals, *op. cit.* at 55.

dxxxii   Alexander Pope Humphrey, "The Impeachment of Samuel Chase," The Virginia Law Register, Vol. 5, No. 5 (Sept., 1899), pp. 281, 285, www.jstor.org/stable/1098896

dxxxiii Annals, *op. cit.* at 56-59.

dxxxiv   Annals, *op. cit.* at 59.

dxxxv   A. Beveridge, Life of John Marshall 169 (1919).

dxxxvi   Humphrey, *op. cit.* at 288.

dxxxvii Humphrey, *op. cit.* at 294.

dxxxviii Humphrey, *op. cit.* at 290.

dxxxix   John Quincy Adams, *op. cit.* at pp. 322-23.

dxl	Thompson, *op. cit.* at p. 101.
dxli	<u>Annals</u>, *op. cit.* 141-144; Hinds, *op. cit.,* § 2383 at 804.
dxlii	Today 32. U.S.C. 7265(a)(1) (2012).
dxliii	*Soulard v. United States*, 36 U.S. (10 Pet.) 100 (1836).
dxliv	https://www.nytimes.com/interactive/2018/02/19/opinion/how-does-trump-stack-up-against-the-best-and-worst-presidents.html
dxlv	3 Hinds, *op. cit.,* § 2470 at pp. 950-51, www.govinfo.gov/content/pkg/GPO-HPREC-HINDS-V3/pdf/GPO-HPREC-HINDS-V3-27.pdf
dxlvi	3 Hinds, *op. cit.,* § 2475 at p. 958.
dxlvii	3 Hinds, *op. cit.,* § 2485 at p. 979.
dxlviii	en.wikipedia.org/wiki/58th_United_States_Congress
dxlix	Thompson, *op. cit.,* pp. 103-04.
dl	en.wikipedia.org/wiki/William_O._Douglas#Impeachment_attempts
dli	Thompson, *op. cit.,* pp. 89-91.
dlii	CQ Almanac, "Justice Douglas Impeachment" (1970), library.cqpress.com/cqalmanac/document.php?id=cqal70-1292316;www.nytimes.com/1970/12/17/archives/douglas-announces-intention-to-remain-on-court.html
dliii	Thompson, *op. cit.* at p. 118.
dliv	Ford named Justice John Paul Stevens to replace him. Stevens would have become the longest-serving Justice, displacing Douglas, if Stevens had not decided to retire in 2010, when he was merely the third-longest-serving Justice. Stevens, who has lived just under a century, was in the stands at Wrigley Field when Babe Ruth "called his shot" in the 1932 World Series, pointing to the bleachers and then hitting a home run to the same spot. Stevens also was fortunate enough to meet both Charles Lindbergh and Amelia Earhart. en.wikipedia.org/wiki/John_Paul_Stevens . Stevens has never met Zelig or Forrest Gump, however.
dlv	All of these figures are sources elsewhere herein.
dlvi	Lincoln, "The Gettysburg Address" (Nov. 19, 1863), http://www.abrahamlincolnonline.org/lincoln/speeches/gettysburg.htm
dlvii	en.wikipedia.org/wiki/English_Opening
dlviii	Oscar Wilde, "The Canterville Ghost," <u>Lord Arthur Savile's Crime & Other Stories</u> 90, 94 (1891).
dlix	U.K. Parliament Website, www.parliament.uk/site-information/foi/foi-and-eir/commons-foi-disclosures/other-house-matters/impeachment-2015/
dlx	W. McKay and C.W. Johnson, <u>Parliament & Congress</u> 511 (2010).
dlxi	House of Commons Briefing Paper No. CBP7612, *op. cit.* at 11.
dlxii	en.wikipedia.org/wiki/Simon_Fraser,11th_Lord_Lovat

dlxiii   U.K. Parliament Website, www.parliament.uk/site-information/foi/foi-and-eir/commons-foi-disclosures/other-house-matters/impeachment-2015/

dlxiv   House of Commons Briefing Paper No. CBP7612, *op. cit.* at 3.

dlxv   The Guardian, "MPs plan to impeach Blair over Iraq war record" (Aug. 26, 2004).

dlxvi   George Bernard Shaw, "Caesar and Cleopatra" Section: Notes, p. 120 (1906).

dlxvii   Constitution of Ireland at p. 140, www.taoiseach.gov.ie/eng/Historical_Information/The_Constitution/Constitution_of_Ireland_Aug_2012_.pdf

dlxviii   House of Commons Briefing Paper No. CBP7612, "Impeachment" p. 14 (2016).

dlxix   The U.S. Constitution doesn't say this. It became a matter of great debate during the impeachment of President Andrew Johnson, as discussed separately, and the issue later was resolved by a holding of the U.S. Supreme Court.

dlxx   The U.S. Constitution, www.law.cornell.edu/constitution

dlxxi   Turner, *op. cit.* at 507.

dlxxii   *See Buckley v. Valeo*, 424 U.S. 1 (1976) (per curiam).

dlxxiii   Shimon Shetreet & Sophie Turenne, Judges on Trial: The Independence and Accountability of the English Judiciary 7:27 at 310 (2d ed. 2014). Prof. Shetreet was a clerk to a judge of the Israel Supreme Court, and later an Israeli Minister.

dlxxiv   Turner, "The Impeachment of John Pickering," 54 Am. Hist. Rev. 485, 492 (1949).

dlxxv   A. Beveridge, Life of John Marshall 221 (1919).

dlxxvi   http://www.judicialselection.com/judicial_selection/methods/removal_of_judges.cfm?state

dlxxvii   Congressional Research Service, "Expulsion, Censure, Reprimand, and Fine: Legislative Discipline in the House of Representatives" at 24 (2016) https://fas.org/sgp/crs/misc/RL31382.pdf.

dlxxviii   Congressional Research Service Report No. RL31382, "Expulsion, Censure, Reprimand, and Fine: Legislative Discipline in the House of Representatives" (2016). The Confederacy formed its own Congress, in 1861. Congress_of_the_Confederate_States#First_general_elections

dlxxix   en.wikipedia.org/wiki/List_of_United_States_senators_expelled_or_censured#Expelled_senators

dlxxx   en.wikipedia.org/wiki/1860_United_States_presidential_election

dlxxxi   www.senate.gov/artandhistory/history/common/expulsion_cases/pdf/
            CW150_14Mar1861_VacancyResolution.pdf

dlxxxii   www.senate.gov/artandhistory/history/common/expulsion_cases/
            CivilWar_Expulsion.htm

dlxxxiii   en.wikipedia.org/wiki/Jesse_D._Bright

dlxxxiv   www.carolana.com/NC/Governors/wwholden.html;en.wikipedia.
            org/wiki/William_Woods_Holden;en.wikipedia.org/wiki/Jonathan_
            Worth_(governor); en.wikipedia.org/wiki/Kirk–Holden_war.

dlxxxv   en.wikipedia.org/wiki/Henry_C._Warmoth;   en.wikipedia.org/wiki/
            William_Pitt_Kellogg;en.wikipedia.org/wiki/1872_Louisiana_guber-
            natorial_election;en.wikipedia.org/wiki/Battle_of_Liberty_Place

dlxxxvi   en.wikipedia.org/wiki/Adelbert_Ames;   en.wikipedia.org/wiki/
            Mississippi_Plan

dlxxxvii   en.wikipedia.org/wiki/Tulsa_race_riot

dlxxxviii   ww.okhistory.org/publications/enc/entry.php?entry=WA014

dlxxxix   en.wikipedia.org/wiki/Jack_C._Walton

Made in the USA
Monee, IL
24 February 2020